WAKE-UP CALL

How I Changed my Life and Business—and You Can Too

*by the Creator of
Therapeutic Accounting®*

Harvey A. Bookstein, CPA

ACKNOWLEDGEMENTS

I have many people to thank for helping me achieve one of the items on my bucket list – to write a book. The book started out in one direction and changed dramatically due to the comments made by my family, friends, and business associates. I am grateful for their help with the book, and for all they've contributed to my life.

All of my children – Marc Bookstein, Michelle Lewis, Joel Miller and Roni Kritzberg – supported my desire to write this book and spent time helping me understand myself better. They were also generous in being interviewed about our relationship and about who I used to be and what I became after my wake-up call from the 1994 Northridge earthquake.

I also appreciate the time my aunt and uncle, Goldie and Marv Bookstein, spent in remembering and sharing facts from a long time ago that I could not remember.

Some of my partners – Ted Roth, Dave Zaslow, Tom Schulte and Dave Roberts – were kind enough to be interviewed for the book. I'm grateful for their honest assessment of who I am and how I've changed in the time we've been working together.

I certainly cannot forget about my friends, who had to dig deep to express their thoughts about my transformation and our shared histories. They were: Len and Stella Kleinrock, Dan and Linda Rosenson, Michael Rosenfeld, Steve Berlinger, Joe Ruvolo, and my oldest friend, Bob Karp.

Toward the end of the time it took to write this book, I asked my rabbi of over 25 years, Rabbi Donald Goor, if he would offer some observations about me. I was surprised and touched by his words.

This book could never have been completed if my assistant, Lisa

Rom, had not spent endless hours transcribing the recordings of my notes and the comments of those who were interviewed.

I'd like to also thank my writer and editor, Philip Goldberg. Without his guidance and wordsmith skills, this book would never have been completed.

I need to give a special acknowledgement to Dr. Sylvia Jones, who helped me find a better way to live my life, and who was kind enough to speak about our seventeen years of therapy sessions. The process of working with her was much more time consuming and difficult than I initially imagined, but the effort has made me a much happier man.

Finally, I can never thank my wife, Harriet, enough, not only for her help writing, editing, and fact-checking this book, but for giving me a chance to be as happy as I am. She helped me prioritize my thinking and rise to the top with family values, religious customs, friendships, and charity. And she's a great lover to boot!

Contents

Introduction

*I*have been in the accounting business most of my life. I mean that literally. My father was an accountant, and I started working for him at the age of seven. I was an accounting major at San Fernando Valley State College (now California State University, Northridge). I started my first job in an accounting firm in 1970, at Kenneth Leventhal & Company. I became a Certified Public Accountant in 1972. I opened my own firm on the first day of January, 1975, but I am not a typical accountant. This is my business card:

I have never been a "green eyeshade accountant," meaning one who only crunches numbers and prepares financial statements, tax returns, and the like. I've performed all the traditional functions of the profession in my career, and I still do many of them. I have tremendous respect for my fellow accountants who do their jobs with competence and integrity. In our society CPAs serve an important function, and I'm proud to call myself one of them, but I was never personally fulfilled within the usual boundaries of the trade, and I naturally found myself doing things differently. In 1999, I gave it a name: *Therapeutic Accounting*®

Like all accountants, I work in the domain of money, and the primary language I speak is numbers. But financial issues are also personal, and sometimes profoundly emotional. As a therapeutic accountant, I often work with clients on both emotional and financial levels. I speak with them about their marriages, children, health concerns, thoughts about retirement and death, and their strongly held values. Often, feelings come up that are usually expressed only to therapists, clergy, or best friends. I see it as my responsibility to understand my clients as complete persons. By taking a holistic approach, I can guide them toward financial decisions that serve their most important personal needs. As I once wrote, "All accountants have been trained to use their brains, but our schoolbook learning does not include training our hearts." As a therapeutic accountant, I use both of those vital organs.

One reason for writing this book was to explain what being a therapeutic accountant means to me. I hope other accountants will move in a similar direction, to the best of their ability and in accord with their talents and personalities. I believe that by expanding what we do in this more holistic way we will better serve our clients, just as physicians have learned to treat patients as complete individuals, not as machines with broken parts in need of repair. There is no question that I do a far better job for my clients with this approach than I possibly could if I limited myself to conventional accounting. And by the way, I think this basic principle is true for any profession; whether you're an architect, engineer, attorney, doctor, or schoolteacher, you should strive to go beyond what you were trained to do and what is normally expected of you. By expanding your vision, you can give more and derive greater fulfillment in the process. This book isn't just about Therapeutic Accounting®; it's about living a therapeutic life.

The other reason for writing this book is to tell my own story. My personal journey parallels the evolution of my professional life; I grew from an unhappy workaholic with a narrow perspective and a dysfunctional family to a more complete, better balanced human being who is more self-aware, more capable of giving and receiving love, and more fulfilled than I ever knew was possible. I think others can benefit from the lessons I've learned, and that's why I decided to go ahead with this project after many years of contemplating it.

I hesitated for a long time because I didn't want to come across like a prima donna. I was concerned that telling my personal story would seem like an exercise in narcissism; that talking about what I've learned about business, accounting, and life in general would be viewed as preaching from a soapbox. Authors of advice and self-help books sometimes seem arrogant to me, and I didn't want to look that way to others. I didn't want to say, "I know how to make you happy," or, "This is how you should practice accounting." I just wanted to say, "I've learned certain things you might benefit from, and here is my humble attempt at telling my story."

When I expressed these concerns to people I trust, they all encouraged me to write the book. One of them, Doug Kruschke, a consultant to my CPA firm, said, "You have a different set of tools in your tool chest than most people, and others will benefit from what you've discovered." A fellow accountant told me, "You have something that can help other accountants help their clients. It would almost be malpractice not to share it." The kicker was when my therapist, Dr. Sylvia Jones, said, "This has always been your problem: you don't fully appreciate how much you have to offer."

So here it is: a book about my life, the principles that have guided me, and all I've learned. Part One is autobiographical; it describes the arc of my career and the personal transformation I have undergone. Part Two focuses on the values and principles I have come to see as essential for achieving success and living a fulfilling life. As in real life, the personal and the professional are intimately related, so themes in each part may overlap.

One of my hopes is that people who know me will know me better after they've read the book. I also believe every professional, especially those who serve clients directly—not just accountants, but lawyers, doctors, financial advisers, and others—will derive benefit from the lessons I've learned about conducting business successfully and honorably. My biggest hope is that the book encourages readers to make positive changes in their lives that lead to greater happiness and fulfillment. I want people to know they can do so in a balanced way, without sacrificing their financial aspirations or personal goals.

I would love readers to come away saying, "I can be tough and in control, and also have a heart. I can be a lion at work and let my soft side come out at home and in my concern for the well-being of others." I want them to know that personal growth and self-knowledge will not only make them happier, but make them better and stronger in *business* too.

One more thing I hope comes through in these pages: you don't have to wait for a cataclysmic event to start making positive changes in your life. That's what I did, and I was lucky my wake-up call came when I could still hear the message and act on it. Unfortunately, I've known many people who waited too long.

As you'll see in the coming chapters, I have lived two distinct lives. They were separated by that wake-up call. In my case, it wasn't a heart attack, a death in the family, or a financial disaster; it was what is commonly called an act of God. The literally earthshaking experience of January 1994 turned out to be a true blessing. It was a catalyst for changes that brought me joy and happiness I never knew was possible.

We all have wake-up calls—those moments in life when the universe screams, "Something is missing from your life, and there's still time to change!" Some of us are lucky enough to take the message seriously and then find help and support so we can follow through. I count myself tremendously lucky. I had no idea how to handle the changes I needed to make. I wasn't even sure what those changes were. Others stepped up with the knowledge and skills I needed. If I get any credit at all, it's for being open enough to seek advice, listen to it, and tenaciously follow through.

Not everyone needs to change as dramatically as I did, but we all stand to gain from being open to learning and growth. I can't think of anything more exhilarating, or more important. I hope my story is a catalyst for you to do whatever it takes to build a more fulfilling life for yourself and everyone you care about, at home and at work. Thank you for reading this book.

PART ONE

CHAPTER 1
All Shook Up

January 17, 1994, began like every other weekday morning. I woke at 4:00 a.m., brushed my teeth, threw on my sweats, and walked to my garage. That was my routine. I would drive down the hill to Balboa Park, a peaceful stretch of green in the sprawling suburbs of the San Fernando Valley, to jog with a group of friends. After the run, I would go to my gym to shower, change into work clothes, and drive to my office in Santa Monica. Why did I run early in the morning? Because I'd been persuaded that I needed exercise, and my attitude at the time was this: if you have to add a non-work task to your schedule, stretch the day earlier or later, but never interrupt your working hours. And my working hours were long. Breakfast? I'd either eat at a meeting with a client, gobble down some quick junk food, or skip eating altogether. What mattered most was work.

That morning, in the garage, I realized I'd left my keys in the house, something I'd never done before. In my stocking feet, carrying my running shoes, I went back into the house for the keys. I spotted them on the kitchen counter. As I walked over to get them, I checked the clock. I saw it turn from 4:30 to 4:31. That's the precise moment my world shook. Literally shook. In the months to come, my whole life would get all shook up, changing my personality, values, approach to work, and family circumstances. But at 4:31 that morning the shakeup was physical and powerful—a mighty 6.7 on the Richter scale, to be exact. It would later be called the Northridge Earthquake, and the epicenter was only a few miles from my home.

The noise was terrifying and deafening. Dishes and glasses flew from the cabinets and smashed onto the floor and appliances. In the adjacent room, the wall supporting the fireplace crumbled like a bird's nest. Upstairs, a bureau and other large pieces of furniture toppled over and landed like bombs. Most horrifying of all, I heard screams from my daughter and son, then 14 and 10, and my then-wife, Kathy. I have no memory of how I got upstairs, but I know I stepped on many shards of glass as I ran to the staircase and then to the bedrooms, without stopping to put on shoes. All I could think of was protecting my family—and the miracle that I was able to do so because I'd forgotten my keys. Somehow, amid the panic, the fallen furniture, and the floors littered with glass and debris, I managed to project an air of calm and competence, even though I was petrified inside. We all made it out of the house without injury, except for glass cuts and emotional trauma.

After the Shock

Outside, we joined our neighbors in the street. The world around us seemed oddly quiet, perhaps because everyone was too stunned to speak and everything that was going to fall had already fallen. We heard sirens in the distance, no doubt from Ventura Boulevard, the main thoroughfare running east-west across the Valley. We lived in a fairly new development on a hillside in Tarzana, and only about a quarter of the houses were occupied. The homes were basically intact, although chunks of wall were missing from some, and the street itself had cracks. My neighbors looked shocked, confused, and frightened. Most of us were barefoot or wearing socks or slippers, and our pajamas and bathrobes weren't heavy enough to ward off the early morning chill. We shivered and contemplated our futures, as the sun rose on Martin Luther King Day.

We spent the next night in the driveway of our shattered home, in a van I borrowed from a friend. It was simply too dangerous to stay in the house, not knowing how bad the structural damage was or how bad the aftershocks would be. My kids slept in the back, and my wife and I slept in the front seat. I kept a gun at my side, knowing that looters might take advantage of the abandoned houses. Sure enough, looters came. We could hear their trucks moving up the hill. When they got close enough to hear a gunshot, I fired a bullet into the air. They turned around and drove back down the hill.

The official toll from the Northridge quake was fifty-seven dead and more than eight thousand injured. About sixteen hundred people required hospitalization. Damage estimates were as high as $25 billion. And we were lucky. It would have been far worse if the earthquake had hit just a few hours later, and even worse had it occurred on a workday instead of a national holiday. Many of the buildings that collapsed were empty at the time, and few cars were on the road. The Los Angeles freeway system, parts of which are as busy as any road network in the world, incurred major damage that took months to repair, clogging the surface streets and disrupting millions of lives. Schools and colleges were closed; public events were cancelled; theme parks shut their doors; the Postal Service suspended mail delivery.

Because of the closed roads and disruption of municipal services, the local economy took months to recover. Film and television production halted for a long time, for example, causing a chain reaction that hit all auxiliary businesses that service the entertainment industry. My alma mater, California State College, Northridge, situated close to the epicenter, sustained extremely heavy damage. But in the long run that turned out to be a blessing. The rebuilt parts of campus were so modern that CSUN was able to enroll another ten to twenty thousand students. And in the long run the quake turned out to be a blessing for me as well.

Assessing the Damages

Once the house was examined and we knew it was safe, we returned home and set about rebuilding damaged areas and replacing our broken belongings. Our family spent a few months getting back to some reasonable semblance of normalcy. Rebuilding my life would take much longer, because first I had to examine myself, figure out what was broken, tear down what wasn't working, and then decide what to replace it with and how. You see, something happened in the first horrifying moments of the earthquake; something so powerful I couldn't dismiss it or turn away from it, and so mysterious that to this day I can't explain it. I prayed.

I was not religious. I feel I am a spiritual person, but I would have to say I'm still an agnostic. However, when my house came tumbling down around me and I thought I was going to die, I found myself saying internally, to who or what might be God: "If I live, I will do everything in my power to be half as happy in my personal life as I am in my business life." I don't know what to call it—prayer, cosmic bargaining, or whatever—and I have no idea where it came from. I certainly don't know how I came up with "half."

Later on, when things returned to normal, I was haunted by that deal I'd made with God, or whoever, or whatever. It made me realize how *unhappy* my personal life was. I'd obviously come to expect very little of life if the most I could promise was trying to be half as happy as I was in business. In any event, I lived, and to me a deal is a deal. Now I had to fulfill my end of it. I had no idea where to begin, but I was determined to bring to the task all the persistence, energy, integrity, inventiveness, and dogged determination I always brought to my business dealings.

Keeping My Bargain

The earthquake was a game-changer, a wake-up call, a turning point, and every other cliché you can think of. This dramatic reminder of the life's fragility triggered in me a long, intense period of introspection.

I could not get the bargain I made out of my mind: "If I live, I will do everything in my power to be half as happy in my personal life as I am in my business life." I'm a natural born deal-maker, and I take pride in living up to my end of every deal I make. Only in business, I never make a deal without thinking it through from top to bottom and doing my due diligence about every possible implication and nuance of a contract. I want to know exactly what I'm agreeing to and exactly what I must do to fulfill my part of the agreement. Now I was in uncharted territory. Had I made a promise to anyone or anything other than myself? It *felt* like I'd made a commitment, and one of my core beliefs is that you should honor your commitments to the letter. I had to follow through. I didn't really have a choice.

But how? I knew business like I knew my name. I knew what to look for, what to inquire about, what to check on, and what to verify before signing on the dotted line. My personal life? That terrain was as foreign as Mongolia. I had no idea how to go about being happier in that territory. What were the standards? What were the metrics? I didn't even know I was *unhappy* until I heard myself make that promise as my house tumbled down around me. That's how unconscious I was, and how disconnected I was from anything outside of business. It became painfully obvious that before I could understand why I was unhappy, or what I could do about it, I had to exercise the same due diligence I brought to business propositions. The starting point was to look honestly at myself and my life.

Prior to that, I'd been on autopilot. I did what I'd always done, one day after the other. Not that I was an unfeeling robot. I loved my work and derived tremendous satisfaction from it. I was creative at work. I was alive and energetic at work. I felt the ups and downs of my work deeply. Everywhere else I was simply disconnected. I went through the motions, doing what I thought I was supposed to do as a husband, father, neighbor, citizen—all the roles I had taken on as part of living a normal adult life. I wouldn't say it was a treadmill; it was more like following a script I never questioned, with stage directions I'd somehow worked out in previous days, weeks, months, and years. As an accountant, as a business adviser, as the managing partner of a small boutique accounting firm with a top-notch reputation, I knew exactly who I was. Other than that, I didn't have a clue.

Cracks in the Foundation

At the time of the earthquake I had been married for almost twenty-three years. I met my first wife, Kathy, when we were both undergraduates at what was then called San Fernando Valley State College (it is now California State University, Northridge, or CSUN). We lived in the same dorm, a privately owned facility across the street from campus. That year, the school had run out of room on the women's side, so they took one side of the square-shaped men's wing and put women in it. Kathy was one of them. We married in 1971, when I was twenty-four and she was about a year and a half younger.

Kathy and I were different in almost every important way. For one thing, she was an artist, and a damn good one. Art came as naturally to her as accounting did to me. When she was seven or eight years old she was already painting watercolors and *selling* them. Art was her second language, a visual language whose alphabet consisted of colors, shapes, and textures. Mine was the language of numbers. She thought in abstractions; I thought concretely. She was conceptual; I was linear and literal. To her, time was ephemeral; to me time was as tangible as my heartbeat—and almost as important. She couldn't balance a checkbook;

I couldn't *not* balance checkbooks, and I could practically do it with my eyes closed.

For the first few years of our marriage, Kathy worked as a salesperson in the art supplies department at May Company. In her spare time she worked on her own art, and to my annoyance the house was always a mess because she'd be juggling twenty projects at once. At one point I arranged for her to show her portfolio to some clients of mine, who were animators at Disney. They promptly offered her a job. The offer wasn't a favor to me, or any kind of quid pro quo; they simply recognized her talent and hired her. She painted backgrounds for a variety of animation projects, before such work was computerized, and she thrived on it until we had our first child, eight years into our marriage. Then she left Disney to be a full-time mom. In retrospect, that may have been a mistake. The job had been the high point of her life. She was working in an incredibly creative atmosphere in a prestigious company, and then, suddenly, she plunged into a job for which she had hardly any training. To her, motherhood was difficult, and being out of the creative work environment was frustrating.

Years later, I came to realize that the primary reason I had gotten married was to have children. Kathy, it seems, had little interest in that, at least at the time. Nor did she have the skills, the natural inclination, or the background to be a good parent. I don't say this to demean her or to blame her. I believe she would agree with my statement. She simply wasn't prepared for the challenges of being a mom. For one thing, her own parents were not good nurturers. She had grown up feeling her mother hated her. As it turned out, "hate" may have been too strong a word. But the perception that prompted her to feel unloved wasn't far off the mark. Kathy had been adopted. Her parents were older than most first-time parents, and her father wanted her but her mother never truly did. I actually found out Kathy was adopted before she knew, because I had to track down her birth certificate to get a marriage license. It was quite traumatic for her to discover her origins at age twenty-two. Years later, I realized her upbringing explained a great deal about why she had so much difficulty being a parent.

Work-Life Imbalance

As I said, I don't blame our failed marriage on Kathy. God knows, in many ways I was a worse father than she was a mother. I became a worker daddy, the guy who brought home the bacon. In truth, I was a workaholic. I had been one since childhood, when I started helping my father process tax returns. As a professional, I strived mightily to give my clients value—not just ordinary value, but top value, the best value, the highest possible grade of value—and to do right by my partners and colleagues. I worked thirteen- or fourteen-hour days, and I worked every Saturday and, during the tax season, every Sunday too. That left Sundays during the nontax season for being with my family—my dysfunctional, screaming family.

Somehow, I took on the role of authority figure in the household. I turned into the disciplinarian, even though I was never home to know what was going on and was never clear about what my kids had done to deserve punishment. I would walk through the front door, usually around 8:30 or 9:00 p.m., and the first thing I heard was Kathy screaming about how badly our son and daughter had behaved, reciting everything they'd done wrong during the day. The kids—Michelle, who was born in 1978, and Marc, who was four years younger—would be hiding, because their mother had told them, "When Dad gets home, you're going to get it."

So, I would come home, exhausted, not to a sanctuary but to a war zone, and then I had to follow through on Kathy's threats. I didn't do it physically; I never believed in corporal punishment, because it seemed to be a way for parents to blow off steam, not an effective way to teach children valuable lessons. Kathy didn't agree with that philosophy, but she couldn't lift a hand to the kids either. I was an emotional discipliner. I spanked them with my voice. I didn't always want to do it, and I often felt guilty afterward, but if I didn't administer the discipline I'd have an argument with my wife. It was a lose-lose proposition, and I didn't have the awareness or the skill to find a workable alternative that would be better for me, my marriage, and most important, my children. In fact, I've come to believe that one reason the marriage worked well enough to last as long as it did was that it fed both of our needs: my need to feel guilty and Kathy's need to feel like a victim. Not that I was greeted by anger and turmoil every night. It only seemed that way, because that scenario was more the rule than the exception. On nights when I came home to a relatively quiet and pleasant family, I was surprised and relieved. But we always had an undercurrent of negativity. Kathy was a glass-is-half-empty person and would complain about everything that had gone wrong that day, and everything she thought was wrong about me, usually in a loud, angry voice. Later on, when we were divorced, friends told me they'd often been upset by the way she put me down in front them. They said they tried to let me know. But I never noticed, and their hints didn't register.

Even on the peaceful nights, I would be so worn out from my long day of work that I wasn't fully available for what should have been precious moments with my children. I remember occasions when Marc was six or seven, and he would say, "Daddy, will you come up and read me a book?" Somehow, I'd never make it upstairs. In later years, after I snapped out of it and realized the mistakes I'd made, I was haunted by the image of that little boy fighting to stay awake to grab a few minutes of intimacy with his dad, only to fall asleep crushed. But that's how I was.

My office became my home. It was my safety zone. Work was not only my livelihood and my vocation; it was an escape valve, a retreat, and my only source of satisfaction. My lovely house on the hill was where I drove at the end of the workday, because that's where I slept. I loved my children with all my heart, but I neglected them and didn't give them what they really needed from their dad. I thought at the time I was just doing what a husband and father was supposed to do. Later, after a lot of therapy, I realized that at some point I had unconsciously decided to avoid Kathy as much as possible. Unfortunately, to do that I also had to avoid my kids, which meant they were being cheated big-time. I came to see that as a terrible sin. I wish I could delete that history and replace it with a better one. After I finally snapped out of it, I made every effort to make up for my mistakes by learning how to be a genuinely good father, and I succeeded to a large extent. But I know Michelle and Marc were damaged by their parents' ignorance and shortcomings.

The Man in the Mirror

Before the earthquake I was barely conscious that my marriage was unhappy. I knew we weren't exactly living a happily-ever-after fairy tale. It didn't take a genius to know my life was more like a Eugene O'Neill or Tennessee Williams drama than Father Knows Best or Ozzie and Harriet. On the surface our home *looked* like those old TV shows, but reality was a whole lot different. I just assumed most marriages were like mine and the perfect families on TV were make-believe. Not for a nanosecond did I think, "I've got to do something about my life. This isn't working for me." I would have considered that a waste of energy. At most, I thought, "Maybe I should bring home flowers" or "Maybe I should get home earlier and spend time with the family." But it didn't weigh on me. I didn't think there were any alternatives.

In fact, that was the problem. It *should* have weighed on me. I *should* have known how bad things were. I *should* have thought I deserved better, and that Kathy and Michelle and Marc did too. But I was oblivious. I was a workhorse, and my considerable powers of observation, analysis, discernment, and problem-solving were used almost entirely in the service of business.

In the rare moments when I allowed some introspection to sneak past the gatekeepers in my mind, I would tell myself, "I'm going to start doing things differently." So I'd try to come home a little earlier, or I'd buy flowers for Kathy. But it didn't make a dent in the marital tension or the way Kathy ran the house and dealt with the kids, so I would quickly revert to my previous ways. I just didn't know how to change myself in a deep and enduring way, and I certainly couldn't change my wife. I only grew more exhausted from the effort, and I convinced myself I had no alternative: that was just how life was meant to be for husbands and fathers with responsibility. So, day after day, I put one foot ahead of the other and poured my passion and energy into my work.

It literally took an earthshaking event to wake me up. After the earthquake and my strange, unprecedented promise, I started thinking seriously about my life for the very first time.

Chapter 2
Determined to Change

I plunged into the process of repairing the house and helping my family recover from the earthquake. Once that effort was underway, the strange promise I made took hold of my mind. My days of psychological oblivion were over; now it was time for an honest appraisal of my life.

I was never the introspective type. My energy and attention were always directed outward, my focus narrow as a laser beam. I was all business all the time. Psychotherapy? To me that might as well have been astrology, or voodoo. I had no use for navel-gazing. Looking back on my childhood years and analyzing parental upbringing seemed the ultimate waste of time. My sights were set on the future: look ahead, plan ahead, forge ahead. I wasn't the "sharing" type, even informally. When people talked about their fears, or expressed how they felt about their parents or spouses, I felt uncomfortable. I might listen, but I would never reveal my own feelings. I was so out of touch with my feelings, I didn't even know I *had* any. The truth is, I didn't know what feelings were.

During the immediate post-earthquake period, I did a lot of thinking, but I still had no interest in therapy. One of my partners at the time was seeing a psychologist, and I would make wisecracks and stupid jokes about how he was wasting his time and money. In retrospect, I must have sounded like an idiot, maybe even a *cruel* idiot, for mocking what was obviously a sincere effort at self-understanding and personal change. "Who cares how your mother treated you?" I would say. "So what if you didn't get along with your father? It's history. You can't rewrite it. It is what it is, and it's irrelevant to moving forward." I couldn't have been more wrong.

But as I oversaw the process of putting the house back together, clearing up the mess, and replacing all the broken items, I realized I too was broken, and I too was a mess. I needed to put myself back together. Of course, I had no idea what that meant. I just knew something had to change, and I didn't seem able to think it through all by myself and figure out what steps to take. Self-reflection seemed very different from thinking through a business decision. Then I realized it wasn't *completely* different. After all, in business I would constantly bump into situations that were beyond my own knowledge and skills. That's why, like any good business leader, I routinely called upon experts, from lawyers to real estate specialists to fellow accountants. Why not call upon someone with expertise in helping people get their lives together? I had to admit the downside risks weren't high.

My first foray into therapy was highly unorthodox and extreme. It involved marathon sessions, in which the client and the therapist were immersed together for extended periods. A friend who felt he'd gotten a great deal of benefit from it introduced me to the method. He was so enthusiastic about it, and so convinced it was right for me, that he gave me the first session as a gift. To call this therapy intense is an understatement. Once a week I spent twelve or fourteen hours at a stretch in a room with the therapist, and she didn't let me leave until we resolved whatever issue we were dealing with. I did this every Sunday for about two months.

Theoretically, this was supposed to be more efficient than conventional therapy because you could get more done in one day than by spreading the same amount of time over months of weekly sessions.

Well, maybe it works for some people, like the friend who introduced me to it, but this technique wasn't right for me. I didn't know any better at first, even though it didn't feel quite right, but another friend straightened me out. Her name is Stella Kleinrock, and she and her husband Len Kleinrock are among my closest friends. Stella is a therapist herself, and she was thrilled I'd finally given therapy a chance. But she didn't like that format, or any other style that promised a quick fix. "It's none of my business," she said one evening, "but I care about you and I think I need to share something with you. This marathon therapy isn't going to give you value in the long run."

Having time in between sessions isn't just a matter of convenience, she explained. It's an important part of the dynamic, because the intervals give clients a chance to think about what comes up in therapy and to gradually work their way into important decisions and new behaviors. Time also lets the unconscious process new information, which can lead to fresh insight. Plus, as I later learned, marathon therapy can be risky; uncovering long-buried feelings too quickly and intensely can create fresh wounds that are hard to heal. For some people, the rush of feelings can be so overwhelming that it leads to breakdowns.

I trusted Stella's judgment. "OK, I'll stop the marathon sessions," I said. "Who would you recommend I see instead?" I couldn't ask for a better source. As my close friend, Stella felt I deserved a shot at a more meaningful life, and she knew me as well as anyone did. She knew my issues, my background, my wife and kids, and she knew a big part of me was resistant to therapy. She also knew that when I make a commitment to something I'm a bulldog. I give all I have, and I persevere relentlessly until I get done what has to be done. Like a good professional, she said she'd do some homework and come up with a referral.

After doing her due diligence, Stella recommended a colleague named Sylvia Jones. Years later, I asked why she made that recommendation, even though she didn't know Dr. Jones well. "I knew about her work, and I'd heard her give case presentations," she said. "I had a strong hunch she'd be the right person. She has warmth, but also intellectual strictness. I knew she was too bright for you to be able to wrap her around your finger." Stella knew I can be a world-class manipulator when I want to be, and that it wouldn't work with Dr. Jones.

What can I say? Based on the way things worked out, Stella Kleinrock should go down as one of the great matchmakers in history.

Too Broken to Repair

By the time I started seeing Dr. Jones, the thought of temporarily separating from Kathy had entered my mind. Sometime earlier, Linda Rosenson, the wife of my best friend Dan, asked me, "Why do you stay with a wife who's so mean to you?" Her question came as a shock. I hadn't consciously registered that Kathy was always complaining about me and demeaning me in front of others. I was used to her behavior and I figured that kind of thing was normal for some couples. But Linda saw it, and to her this wasn't normal at all. I guess she couldn't keep it to herself any longer, because the signs of my unhappiness were becoming more and more obvious. Her remark planted a seed in my unconscious that slowly germinated. Watered by my new habit of self-reflection, the seed was suddenly sprouting.

At one point I told myself, "If you keep coming home to the same routine, how can the routine ever become different? Maybe if you get away for a while you'll figure out how to make this work. You'll come back with a new game plan the whole family will buy into, and you can all get a fresh start." In retrospect, I know this was a ridiculous thought. Some things are too broken to be repaired. They have to be let go and replaced. But that's how I was thinking at the time.

I didn't act on my thought right away. I couldn't. The idea of moving out of my home horrified me. Such an act was totally opposed to the kind of person I always strived to be: a responsible father and husband. Even a brief separation, like a sabbatical, felt like an act of betrayal.

One of the first and most important things Dr. Jones did was help me find the courage to separate. She knew this would be an important step, and she knew that deep inside I felt I had to do it. I just needed some kind of "permission," and she gave me that. Her compassion—not only for me, but for my family, whom she hadn't met yet—was comforting, and her professional opinion that separating was neither unethical nor unwise was extremely reassuring.

A Space of My Own

I started making plans. I would rent a small, cheap apartment not far from my home, to keep my expenses down and stay close to my kids. Dr. Jones questioned my need to deprive myself of comfort and suggested taking a different tack. She said I needed a comfortable, peaceful place where I could work on myself without a lot of distractions. Furthermore, she didn't think I should skimp on creature comforts. "This is the time to take care of *yourself*," she said. I had always been a caretaker and a provider. I never hesitated to spend money to give my wife and children what they needed and, whenever possible, what they *wanted* as well. My own needs and wants were always minimal. Now, said Dr. Jones, it was time to think about myself a little more. She suggested I surround myself with things that gave me pleasure and would create a serene atmosphere conducive to self-reflection.

When I started working on this book, I asked Dr. Jones why she steered me in that direction. "Because it was clear you'd taken on a great deal of guilt," she said. "Not just about the separation, but going back to your early life as well, and that guilt interfered with your ability to give to yourself instead of always thinking about everyone else." Living well would be a step in the direction of taking better care of myself, she said. "When you're feeling guilty it's natural to feel like you have to deprive or punish yourself. You think, 'I have to suffer because I made my parents suffer and now I'm making my wife and kids suffer.'" She added that I'd been carrying around guilt ever since childhood, because the only way I could get the attention I needed from my parents was through what she called "negative attention." In other words, I was a troublemaker. "It didn't come without a price," said Dr. Jones. "You felt you caused your parents a lot of pain and suffering, and you felt very guilty about it."

I'll come back to that guilt-producing childhood later. The point here is that Dr. Jones gained such quick, accurate insights into her new client that she was able to guide me in exactly the right direction, whether I knew it or not.

Stranger in a Strange Land

About six months after the earthquake, I told Kathy I needed to move out for a while. She did not take the news well. I tried to reassure her. "I'll be back soon," I said, "and we'll start anew." I wasn't lying. I was 99.99 percent certain I needed nothing more than a temporary separation—three months, tops—for the purpose of reflection and renewal. Since I believed the troubles in the marriage were 100 percent my fault, I figured if I could fix myself the marriage would also be fixed. A temporary separation would free my mind to figure out how to get my marriage back on track, just as I'd always figured out how to solve tough business problems. At the time I would have sworn on five thousand Bibles, or five thousand tax returns, that I would find a solution and reunite with my family. I had every intention of doing exactly that.

I settled into a top-floor apartment in an upscale building in Santa Monica. The new place was a five-minute drive to my office and about a half hour to my house in the Valley. I had an ocean view, good air, and a fine stereo system, with music I enjoyed. I even bought candles. On the surface, the apartment couldn't have been more pleasant. But it felt like hell. Being away from my home and my family was hard. On top of feeling lonely and guilty, I was both frustrated and confused, searching for answers to questions I barely knew how to ask. I was a stranger in a strange land, wandering around in a brand-new landscape of the mind and heart. But I was determined to do self-reflection right, just as I always do business right, and I approached this challenge with the same dogged determination. Come hell or high water I would get this deal done, just like I got all my deals done.

I didn't date, I didn't socialize, I didn't have a whole lot of fun. I worked as hard as ever, and for just as many hours. I spent time with my children, mainly on Sundays. I ate out a lot. And I spent more time alone than I ever had in my life, thinking about myself and all the forces that carried me to that place at that time. This was a difficult period for me. I remember going to a movie by myself one night. Being alone was so depressing, I don't think I saw the screen at all. I do remember men and women sitting together, holding hands and laughing. At this Jim Carrey comedy, I was the only one in the theater who didn't laugh once. I had lost my sense of humor. It felt everyone in the world was happy except me.

During that time, Dr. Jones was my life raft. If not for our twice-a-week sessions, I don't know if I could have handled the loneliness, or managed to give the self-discovery process the time it needed.

Realizations and Fears

After about three months, I started to become aware of a powerful and frightening truth bubbling up inside of me: as unhappy and depressed as I felt, the thought of going back to my old routine was even worse. I dreaded it. With Dr. Jones's help, I decided to extend my separation. Now I finally began to loosen up a bit. I added some socializing to my daily life, but for the most part everything on the outside remained more or less the same. Inside, I was frustrated because I still hadn't accomplished my goal of figuring out how to make my marriage work. I wasn't used to being stumped that long by a problem I set out to fix. But this wasn't business. And every time I thought of my former life, a feeling of dread welled up within me. I began to think I'd never find the formula for repairing my marriage. Some things are simply not fixable. If this were a business, I thought, I'd have to consider cutting my losses. I can't tell you how scary such thoughts were to me.

Dr. Jones urged me to write in a journal, as an aide to self-reflection. I religiously followed her advice. She was right; journaling in solitude uncovered thoughts and feelings I'd never have dug up otherwise. At one point I wrote something very revealing: "As miserable as I am being separated, it's better than living in a bad marriage." That may sound obvious to you, but when I read it myself the force of the words hit me like a tornado. For the first time I realized I would not be going back home.

Throughout that period I was haunted by the mysterious vow I made during the earthquake, to do everything in my power to be half as happy in my personal life as I was in my business life. I came to view that pledge in terms of a great quote from Albert Einstein: "Try not to become a person of success, but rather try to become a person of value." I started to think I could never become a person of value if I went back to my former life. I could never get close to being half as happy in that setting as I was at the office. The time had come to turn the page—not just to start a new chapter, but to open a whole new book.

You'd think this discovery would be liberating. Well, eventually it was. But at the time this decision plunged me into an even darker place than I already occupied. Even before I decided to go through with divorce, I was besieged by guilt over betraying my marital vow. To me, that vow was a binding contract, and honoring my commitments meant everything to me. My integrity was built on it. Plus, I couldn't even bear thinking about the damage it might do to my kids. But at least those fears made sense. They were rational. My other terrors were off the charts. I felt that everything I'd achieved in life was in jeopardy. Divorce is expensive, I thought. It will cost me a fortune. I might lose *everything*. I carried that chain of thought to such a crazy extreme that I imagined myself destitute and living with the homeless guys on the streets of Santa Monica, begging my former clients for spare change.

These fears were so irrational that in my calmer moments I knew how absurd they were. After all, if I knew about anything in this life, it was money. I understood money. I knew how to make money. I knew how to keep it and grow it. If ever there was someone who didn't have to worry about being destitute, it was me. But the feeling of terror wouldn't go away. Here's what Dr. Jones said when asked to recall that period of my life: "You were about to become homeless internally. You were going to leave your wife and family. And on top of that you saw yourself as someone who didn't know how to connect with other people. You didn't believe people really loved you, or that they *could* love you. You saw yourself as extremely unlovable. Homelessness became a metaphor for being alone and unloved."

She adds that feeling I had failed to save my marriage led to a related feeling: that I wouldn't be able to stay on top of things in business either. "You were falling apart emotionally," said Dr. Jones, "and when someone is in that state, he questions his ability to do everything, even the things he does extremely well. All his confidence is undermined." She called me "a man in panic." Using the earthquake as a metaphor, she said, "Your foundation was falling apart. Everything you were at the time was crumbling: who you were as a father; who you were as a husband; where you lived; how you saw yourself in the future. All of it was in jeopardy because you had never seen yourself as the kind of man who would abandon *any* responsibility, let alone your family."

No Turning Back

I worked hard with Dr. Jones, wrestling with my pain, my feelings of guilt and my fear of losing everything. We talked a lot about the concept of choice, and we looked realistically at the possible consequences of the choices I had to make. What would it feel like not to live with my children all the time? Would Kathy encourage the kids to turn against me? Would they hate me and resent me forever? Would I lose the respect of my extended family? My friends? My partners, co-workers, and clients? Would any woman want to date me? Would anyone ever want to share the rest of my life with me? What would happen financially?

I knew I would never be penniless. But I also knew the cost of a hotly contested divorce can be enormous. I'd seen many a wealthy man's worth reduced to mediocre assets after a rough breakup. I lost many hours of sleep over that. The pressure got so intense I even broke my silence and mentioned my fear to my friends, Dan and Linda Rosenson. Like Dr. Jones, they reminded me of an obvious fact: I might have to give up some of my assets in a divorce settlement, but I would *not* have to give up my experience, my knowledge, or my brain power. I'd be all right financially.

Of course, they were absolutely right, but fear doesn't listen to logic or look at numbers. To assuage my anxiety, the Rosensons actually offered to lend me a substantial amount of money if I should ever need it. I never would need it, of course, and in truth their gracious offer didn't do much to assuage my fear at the time; I was more afraid of not being able to pay back my friends than of losing my money in the first place. But the gesture itself meant more to me therapeutically than anything I could imagine: someone actually loved me enough, and cared about me enough, to put a major promise like that on the table. Maybe I wasn't completely unlovable after all.

There was no turning back now. Internally, I committed to moving ahead with divorce. When I shared that decision with Dr. Jones, it felt to me like I'd made a sacred vow. I started mapping out a strategy that would minimize the damage to me, to Kathy, and especially to Michelle and Marc.

Chapter 3
Discovering Who I Am

I felt as if the earthquake aftershocks never stopped. The emotional ground beneath my feet kept shaking. And now, even before I announced my decision to get divorced, gone was my security zone—my house, my family, my marriage. Gone too was my self-image as a man of stability, dependability, and responsibility. Who was I really? What was I becoming? To answer those questions, Dr. Jones convinced me to do something I would never have imagined a few short months earlier: examine, clearly and unflinchingly, the forces that had led, step by step, to my becoming who I was. We started to poke around in an area I had always ignored, because I believed it was irrelevant: my childhood, my parents, my entire past. I quickly learned William Faulkner was right when he said, "The past is not dead. In fact, it's not even past."

Roots

I was born in 1947, the second year of the great baby boom. My parents were both Jews of eastern European origin. My mother, Celia, grew up in Maine, and my father, Harold, was from Detroit. Nicknamed "Jimmy" for some reason I never understood, he enlisted in the Navy on December 7, 1942, exactly one year after the Japanese attack on Pearl Harbor. He served on a destroyer called the *Hitchcock*, where he was an editor for the ship's newspaper. He got out of the service in

1945 and spent time in California before returning to Detroit. He soon married his sweetheart, Celia, and whisked her away to Los Angeles to start a new life.

My parents had two reasons for leaving the Midwest. One was that my father was stationed in San Diego during the war and fell in love with Southern California. The other was that his mother—my grandma—did not approve of his choice for a bride. She had two objections. First, Celia, my mother, was twenty-six and my father was twenty-three, a reversal of the usual husband-wife age difference. Second, she had a disability. The word they used at the time was "cripple." She had been delivered by an inebriated doctor, who dislocated her leg while pulling her from the womb. As a result, she walked with a limp her entire life and always used a cane. Incidentally, her disability added another layer to the guilt I carried around in my psyche. For some reason, I thought it happened when *I* was born, and I felt responsible for her limp throughout my childhood.

In any event, my grandmother was so stubborn about her son's marriage that she refused to attend the wedding. My grandfather, by all accounts a gentle and decent man, apparently went along with the boycott to placate his wife. It would be years before my father reconciled with his mother, and that only came about when my Uncle Marvin arranged for them to meet in Los Angeles.

Humble Beginnings

My parents arrived in L.A. with fifty bucks and an old, beat-up car. Following in the footsteps of his own father, who sold furniture back in Michigan, my dad got a job as a salesman in a Santa Monica furniture store. My mother worked as a bookkeeper in the same shop. Like other young couples in the postwar years, they wanted to live the American dream, and that meant finding a way for my father, the primary breadwinner, to make more money. At the time I was born, their economic status was what I call upper lower class. I grew up an only child, watching my parents move up the ladder to the middle class. Dad had a lot of drive, and its horsepower was doubled by a powerful additive: an ambitious Jewish wife.

For some reason, probably because he had a knack for number-crunching, my father set his sights on an accounting career. He'd never gone to college, so he wasn't eligible to become a Certified Public

Accountant (CPA). But there was an alternative at the time that no longer exists: he could take a course and become a Public Accountant (PA). With World War II over, the U.S. government was making it as easy as possible for people to get jobs and build up the economy, and the PA license was a way to qualify people to do tax returns and basic bookkeeping tasks. More sophisticated accounting procedures, like producing financial statements, were reserved for CPAs. So Harold Bookstein, furniture salesman, signed up for a correspondence course and spent his nights and weekends studying. He passed, and when tax season rolled around in 1950, he started spending nights and weekends working on tax returns. He worked at the kitchen table in the 900-square-foot house he'd bought with the help of a government program to help veterans purchase their first homes.

Our two-bedroom, one-bath house was at 4211 Sunnyside Avenue in what is now the 90066 ZIP code, just south of Venice and east of what would become Marina Del Rey. The area had all been farmland before the nation mobilized for World War II. When McDonnell Douglas, Hughes, and other aerospace companies built factories in the area, workers needed housing, and in short order a neighborhood of small homes cropped up. On my way to and from school, I would walk past new cottage-style houses and a few remaining small farms.

The Family Business

My father prepared about ten tax returns the first year and fifteen the next. The third year he was up to about seventy. The moonlighting added extra money to the Bookstein bank account, but it was far from enough to inspire the confidence my father needed to quit selling furniture. Then, at the beginning of the 1953 tax season, he took a big risk. He withdrew his entire savings—about $2,000—and placed ads for his tax preparation services in the Yellow Pages and in the *Los Angeles Times*. Taking a leap of faith that people would respond to the ads, he rented a storefront office on Lincoln Boulevard in Venice. This was before H&R Block had tax specialists in practically every neighborhood in the country. I recently saw a picture of my mother standing in front of the building, next to a sign with the words Bookstein Tax Services. The sign looked bigger than the building itself.

The response far exceeded expectations. In fact, so many people called that my father couldn't handle all the work himself. He hired seven or eight CPAs on a commission basis to help prepare tax returns, making space for them by placing rented trailers in the parking lot behind the building. He did 3,500 manual tax returns that year—an amazing number in the pre-computer era—and he never had to advertise again. Dad was off and running, and a job in the furniture business opened up for someone else. Actually, *two* jobs: my mother quit hers too, becoming the bookkeeper, receptionist, greeter, and office manager for Harold Bookstein, Accountant.

The business thrived. Every tax season, temporary CPAs piled into the trailers and churned out tax returns. Eventually, I would be one of them, and so would my future business partners. In fact, my father became so successful that his younger brother Marvin, back in Detroit, was inspired to cut back on his hours as an insurance salesman and go into the tax return business himself, later even selling his agency.

He ended up doing very well and eventually sold his tax business to a publicly traded company for good money. A few years later that company failed, and Uncle Marvin bought his business back for ten cents on the dollar. He built it back up again and then sold it to his chief competitor, H&R Block, for a small fortune. As for my father, a few years after starting his business he bought a small commercial building on Lincoln Boulevard, a few doors down from the rented space where he'd been working. My dad not only had more room than before, he also added income by leasing space to a barbershop and a retail store. The building even came with a one-bedroom apartment above the office. That he had real estate interests as well as his own accounting business must have made an impression on me, because I would eventually do the same.

Holy Terror

By 1956, when I was nine, my parents were ready to move up in the world—literally. We moved up to Pacific Palisades, to a house on Sunset Boulevard more than twice the size of our previous home. My parents had everything a young couple in that era could ask for, even a swimming pool in the backyard. They had only one disappointment: me. I was a rotten child. I don't remember if I was rotten as a one-year-old, but I was certainly rotten by the time I was three. I wasn't violent or anything. I wasn't cruel to pets. I didn't steal or cheat. I was just difficult. I was disobedient and rebellious, the kind of kid who refuses to do what anyone wants him to do, especially his parents. To this day, if you *ask* me for something I'll give you the shirt off my back. But don't *tell* me what to do, and don't dare talk about what I *have* to do or *should* do. I was never good at taking orders, which is one reason I always knew I would own and operate my own business.

Maybe I became a nasty kid because I was picked on so much by my peers. I never fit in. I didn't like doing the things other kids did, or talking about the things they talked about. I wasn't into sports—not only because I was shorter and heavier than most of the boys, but because I didn't give a damn. I didn't even like games that had nothing to do with running or jumping, like Ping-Pong. When I was forced to play sports at school, I was always the last one picked, and always put in a position where I less likely to screw up and hurt the team. *I* got hurt plenty, though, because other boys liked to push me around. If a gym teacher made us run, I'd be the last to finish. If we were told to climb a rope, I'd never leave the ground. In short, I was a classic nerd. But there are nice nerds and naughty nerds, and I was definitely in the second category. I just wasn't likeable.

This made me the perfect target for kids who wanted to show off. I can't count the number of times I had my books knocked out of my hands or was tripped by an outstretched leg, or called cruel and unusual names. Today, they would say I was a victim of bullying. I'm sure it bothered me at the time, but I developed enough defense mechanisms so it didn't *seem* to bother me. I was smart enough not to fight back physically: I was at such a huge disadvantage with bigger, tougher kids that I knew it would only make things worse. I took the abuse and rationalized it away, until sometime in junior high when I learned how to use my head to get even.

Meanwhile, I took it out on grown-up authority figures. I was disruptive in class and rude to my teachers. I spent a lot of time in the principal's office for one misdeed or another. At home, I was consistently nasty to my parents. I not only didn't do what they told me to do, I let them know exactly what I thought of their rules. If there was a law against contempt for parents, I'd have been jailed for life.

Rebel without a Cause

My parents didn't know what to do with me. They tried everything to straighten me out and get me to respect them, up to and including corporal punishment. As a last straw, they took me out of the fifth grade and put me in the Urban Military Academy, hoping the structure and discipline would fix me. The school was close to home, but a million miles away from anything I'd experienced before. Talk about a bad fit! That school, with its precision marching, martial uniforms, and corporal punishment fit this pudgy, headstrong Jewish nerd like spiked heels on Shaquille O'Neal. The commandants had all kinds of ways to punish disobedience. They smacked me on the knuckles with a ruler. They pushed me around physically. They made me stand in the corner with a big, pointy dunce cap on my head. Nothing worked. I only got angrier and more defiant. Eventually, my parents realized the experiment was a flop. After the sixth grade, they decided I'd had enough and withdrew me from the academy. I believe they were more disappointed in themselves than in the school.

That's how headstrong and willful I was: even the authorities at a military academy couldn't straighten me out. If anything, *I* straightened *them* out. At the very least, I got even. I found out who the brass reported to and wrote letters to their superiors exposing their abuse. On one occasion I even called the press. In my two years at that military school, I got five commandants fired!

That was a dramatic example of a skill I had developed: the fine art of manipulation. Maybe it was a natural talent, or maybe I learned it subconsciously as a defense mechanism, but I became skilled at finding ways to manipulate people to gain advantage. One incident when I was six or seven stands out. My mother lost her temper over something I did, and I made things worse by putting on a show of defiance. She started hitting me with a belt. It wasn't the first time she had done that, but this time I thought, "I've got to put a stop to this." When one of her blows landed on my upper thigh, close to the groin area, I seized my chance. Howling in pain, I shouted, "Now I'll never have children, and you'll never be a grandma!" It worked. She put the belt down and never lifted a finger to me again.

When I was working on this book, my Uncle Marvin and Aunt Goldie verified what a fiendish kid I was. They recalled the time I was sent to visit them when I was thirteen. The trip was a Bar Mitzvah present, and I took a train from L.A. to Michigan, with a stop in Chicago, all by myself. "You got upset about something and just took off," Marvin told me. "We had a devil of a time finding you. You stayed gone for about half a day." All I remember is that I got pissed about something and took off. I walked the streets for so long they had a search party looking for me.

Aunt Goldie recalled another incident. "One day, we piled my three kids and my friend's three kids and you into the car and went to the zoo. You were the oldest of the seven children, and you gave us the most trouble. You were so mischievous you would goad the others into doing things they shouldn't have done." Marvin summed it up: "You were an angler. Even at that age you knew how to work people. So you worked the kids to make mischief. You were a troublemaker, and you knew exactly what you were doing."

The Art of Manipulation

That talent for messing with people's minds was a great discovery for a spiteful kid like me. It was a fantastic way to get even with my tormentors. My attitude became, "Do me wrong and I guarantee you'll never do me wrong again." I got better and better at it with experience, and I used the skill many times over the years in ways I am not proud of now.

The memory of one incident, when I was a teenager, still gives me chills. My father had a nervous cough, which was aggravated by stress. At times it got so bad he couldn't stop coughing, and he'd almost pass out. Once, when I did something that upset him badly—I can't remember what it was, since I upset my father pretty much every day— he got enraged and started scolding me. As his voice got louder and more agitated, I just stood there and laughed. I laughed and laughed, as if he were a circus clown, which naturally made him even angrier. Finally, he lost it. He hit me in the mouth with his fist. The pain was excruciating. But I kept on laughing. He hit me a second time, and then started coughing. I kept laughing. He coughed even worse, and before long he couldn't stop. He coughed so badly I thought he might die right there in front of me. Thankfully, he calmed down enough to stop coughing and walk away.

Believe me, it takes a lot of will power to stand your ground in the face of terrible pain and laugh as if you mean it while your own father is choking. But I was able to do it because I knew it was to my advantage. I ended up using that ability to manipulate people in my adult life too. I confess that at first I used it for mean, spiteful purposes, like getting revenge. Eventually I learned to channel that skill into decent, productive purposes, like getting to the truth, or making win-win business deals, or getting people to stop doing harmful or unethical things.

Therapy with Dr. Jones wised me up about that. She taught me that my vindictiveness was the dark side of my exceptional ability to analyze and strategize. We examined the issues that contributed to my acting out so destructively. I learned that, in most circumstances, I could solve problems without resorting to my old vindictiveness. As a consequence, in all the years since the earthquake I've used my talent in healthy ways that served good purposes while attempting not to hurt anyone.

Young Workenstein

Looking back on my childhood, I often joke that I was the reason my parents never had a second child. After me, who would want another one? But I've come to realize, through therapy, that they largely brought my bad behavior on themselves. Acting out was my way to get their attention. They not only worked long hours at the office, they also had a busy social life, with what seemed like a thousand friends. Plus, my father was the president of a men's service club—I forget which one, but I remember him wearing one of those funny hats with a tassel. The point is, they were always busy, and I don't remember a lot of fun-filled times together as a family. In fact, I always felt like a third wheel in my home. I felt excluded and unwanted. I don't know if I really *was* unwanted, but in therapy I realized I'd always felt that way, and I suspect my mother had a child only because that's what women did at the time. The bottom line was, I learned to get my parents' attention the only way I knew how, by being a bratty child, a rude adolescent, and a nasty teenager.

And here comes a strange paradox. As I said, I was a holy terror, making our home more like a nuclear bomb site than the ideal nuclear family of 1950s suburbia. But there was another place where I spent time with my parents, and things were different there. In modern America, it's considered an unusual place for a child and his parents to be together day after day, but to me it seemed as normal as sharing a box of cornflakes at breakfast. I refer to work.

From the age of seven on, I spent a lot of time at the office of Harold Bookstein, Accountant. I wasn't just hanging around watching TV or playing games. I was working. That's right, I started working at *seven*.

Needless to say, this made my life vastly different from the lives of my peers. My classmates didn't work with their parents. They played. Me? I hardly ever played, and I rarely watched sports or attended social events. In fact, between the classroom and my dad's office, I didn't see much of the real world at all.

I may not have developed the usual social skills, and my parents were not exactly great nurturers or role models for living a complete life in the world, but I got a hell of a business education. For a future accountant and entrepreneur, it was the best apprenticeship anyone could imagine. At first, I did menial things like filing and taking out the trash. But, at age nine I started math-checking tax returns. Then I started theory-checking the returns as well. That means I looked for technical errors in the returns prepared by my father and the CPAs. Had they taken the right credits? Was there support in the file to back up the W-2 form? At the age of twelve I started preparing income tax returns for ordinary working people with no expenses to deduct and no business interests. By the time I was sixteen, I was sitting across a table from my father's clients, interviewing them in order to accurately prepare their returns. They were pretty taken aback the first time they saw a teenager in that seat. Some of them thought it was a practical joke. But they quickly learned I knew what I was doing.

As strange and as narrow as my life was, I never felt deprived. Why? Because I enjoyed what I was doing. I also felt proud of the work I did. Not that my parents praised me much. But I knew they were pleased. That wouldn't have been enough to keep me going if I didn't also like the work itself, but the truth is I *loved* it. I was in my element. The work felt as natural to me as throwing a ball or playing a piano was to other kids. My mother, to her credit, recognized that trait in me when I was very young. Instead of reading me books at bedtime, like most mothers did, she would give me math problems!

The Apprentice

I "apprenticed" with my father all the way through high school and college. Dad was a wise but disciplined teacher. He taught me more about accounting than most aspiring professionals learn in business school. He schooled me in the basics, of course—what numbers to put where, what the numbers mean, what the rules and regulations are, and so forth. He made sure I knew all the ins and outs of what I call the historical side of accounting—the transactions of the past that constitute the raw data of a tax return—but he also taught me a lot more because he wasn't just a green-eyeshade accountant.

He taught me that listening was more important than talking. He taught me the value of street smarts, and the importance of trusting my gut feelings about people and my hunches about business ventures. Above all, he showed me that accounting wasn't just about crunching numbers. There is also an emotional side of the business. The numbers we work with signify more than just quantities of money; they also reflect the personal things our clients tell us, and sometimes what they *don't* share but only imply. Ultimately, the numbers are about living, breathing human beings and their struggles, needs, desires, conflicts, and everything else that makes up the day-to-day drama of their lives.

These crucial insights were important building blocks in the development of my own unique approach to accounting. As I mentioned in the Introduction, all accountants are trained to use their brains— not their whole brains, mind you, just the part that calculates and analyzes—but their training does not typically include the heart. Their training is also heavily weighted toward the past. But tough business and financial decisions have to be based on the *future*, and the future is not just a logical extension of the past. The future is uncertain and hard to predict, and we imagine it largely on the basis of hope—the stuff of which dreams are made—and often clouded by fears and anxieties.

My father was a good teacher, and I was an equally good student. More than that, I was a terrific business associate. At home and in school I wasn't exactly the kind of son parents brag about, but at work I was a blessing. I worked hard, I learned quickly, I got done everything I was supposed to, and I did it perfectly. All that earned my parents' approval, and I craved that as much as any other kid. Mom and Dad gave me precious little positive attention at home, and they didn't have the skills or personalities to give me a whole lot of affection. But at the office I got what I needed from them. I not only didn't mind being good at work, I enjoyed doing what was expected of me. Work was my refuge. Working was an escape from school, where other kids beat me up and picked on me. Doing well at the office balanced out all the wrong I did—and all the wrong that was done to me—everywhere else.

Another benefit was that I was spared something many young people agonize over: deciding what to do for a living. To say I was born to be an accountant is an understatement. I never once considered any other occupation. I never even *fantasized* about doing anything else.

With the benefit of hindsight and my therapy with Dr. Jones, I came to realize that I missed out on the opportunity to just be a kid. But I made up for it by loving my work so much that even now I begin each day with the enthusiasm of a twelve-year-old. And, as my wife Harriet will tell you, I'm making up for lost time by acting like a kid much of the time.

Chapter 4
What Ever Happened to the Class Nerd?

*D*r. Jones says I was "the classic definition of a workaholic," even as a child. I don't know if it's possible to be *born* a workaholic, but if it is, I'm the textbook case. Work came easily and naturally to me. I kept on working at my parents' office all through my school years. "That was the place where you could get positive attention from your parents," Dr. Jones told me. "That's where you felt useful and received positive feelings, because you had such a genius knack for the work." My therapist helped me see that my parents did not know how to nurture. In effect, they never let me be a child. They were more comfortable treating me like an apprentice, and later as a business partner. It took a toll on me, but it would have been a lot worse if I didn't love the work so much.

After I was liberated from the military academy, I attended Paul Revere Junior High, a public school, and I worked for my father the whole time I was there. After that I went to Palisades High School. Pali High, as it came to be called, was only one year old when I entered. The spanking new campus, nestled on a hillside canyon with the Santa Monica Mountains above and the vast expanse of the Pacific Ocean below, cost the L.A. school district the then-princely sum of $8 million. Being a student there was considered a privilege. To me, it was the place I had to go to five days a week, whether I wanted to or not. I made the best of it by turning high school into a workplace at every opportunity.

In my three years at Pali, when I wasn't in a classroom or working with my parents, I filled my waking hours with work. I got to school an hour earlier than everyone else and put in about a half hour at the switchboard in the administrative room of the principal's office. This was one of those old-fashioned switchboards you now see only in period films, where an operator answered a call and plugged the cord for that line into the appropriate hole to connect the caller with the person they were trying to reach. When the regular operator arrived, I went to the school store and worked the cash register for twenty or thirty minutes, taking money from students buying supplies, candy, tickets to games, and other items. During "nutrition," the twenty-minute snack break between the second and third periods, I was like an ATM. I took dollar bills from kids who didn't have the exact change they needed to buy a piece of cake or a banana or a drink, and gave them change from a coin machine. At lunchtime, I worked in the faculty cafeteria as a cashier. When classes ended for the day, I was back in the student store.

I didn't get paid for these jobs at Pali High. The only time I got paid was when I sold tickets at the stadium before football games. The rest was all volunteer work—a workaholic nerd's equivalent of extracurricular activities like the school orchestra or athletics or the chess club. There were fringe benefits, though. Working during nutrition period earned me a free snack. At the faculty dining room, after the teachers had been served, I got a free lunch, and the food was a whole lot better than the meals in the student cafeteria. I ate alone, but who cared? I probably would have eaten alone in the student cafeteria anyway, and I wouldn't have had any peace. All in all, I thought this was a pretty good deal, and I made it profitable by pocketing the food money my parents gave me. In fact, most days I also kept the bus fare they gave me, by walking the twenty minutes to school. The walk to school was probably the only exercise I got in those days, but that wasn't the incentive. I was motivated by watching my secret savings pile up.

Mostly, I worked because I loved it. Work also served two emotional needs I didn't recognize at the time: (1) unlike life at home, it brought me regular doses of positive feedback from grownups, namely the teachers and administrators who appreciated my efforts, and (2) it was a very good way to avoid other kids. Most of my classmates either ignored me or tormented me. At my ten-year high school reunion, one guy came up and apologized for picking on me all the time. I didn't even remember him, because *everyone* picked on me back then. At least it seemed that way. I was in my own little world when I worked, and I enjoyed that world because I was successful. In fact, I liked working so much that, in my senior year, when we chose electives, I elected to receive class credit for putting in extra time in the student store. I think it's safe to say I was the only student in my class of 500 who chose working as an elective—just as I was the only boy who wore a white shirt and tie and carried a briefcase every day. (I must have had my fill of that outfit back then, because now I *never* wear white shirts. I wear colorful dress shirts and ties to work, and wear a colored shirt even when I don a tuxedo.)

Overall, I estimate that I worked about seventy hours a week during high school. That's not a typo. I know most people couldn't handle a seventy-hour work week even without the added burden of attending classes. But I did, and I loved it.

Lessons from the Pharmacy

I spent at least forty of those hours at Bay Pharmacy, where I actually got paid. On weekdays, when my after-school duties in the Pali High store were completed, I walked down Sunset Boulevard to the pharmacy and put in a few hours. On weekends I put in even more. I wasn't supposed to work that many hours. It was, in fact, against the law for someone my age. I was supposed to work twenty-eight hours max, but the owner, Mr. Briller, said, "We'll sneak it by." That was fine with me. I started out scooping ice cream, selling sweets from the well-stocked candy counter, and manning the cash registers. In time, I moved up to more sophisticated duties. I never had an official title, but Mr. Briller said, "You're really my assistant manager." I was also his only Jewish employee, so I worked on Christmas Day. We were the only store in Pacific Palisades open that day, and we did great business selling last-minute presents from our big selection of gift items. In the summers, of course, I worked there full-time.

Working at Bay Pharmacy had many fringe benefits. For one thing, I got to eat a lot of ice cream. I was a pudgy kid, and Mr. Briller teased me by saying, "Don't eat all the profits." He meant it too. When *he* wanted ice cream and I was at the counter, he'd actually pay me for it. I didn't follow his lead. I just ate the ice cream, because when he was feeling generous he'd say, "Take something once in a while." I don't think he would have liked my definition of "once in a while."

Some of the fringe benefits were more important than ice cream. In the five years I worked at Bay Pharmacy—three years of high school and two years afterward, when I attended Santa Monica Community College—I learned a tremendous amount about business and life. I learned that making money can be fun. I learned you can relate to people from a position of mutual respect and mutual benefit, and that is different from the social context of teenage life, which was a toxin to me. I learned about sales. I learned what it was like to run a business, how to make a profit, and how to deal with customers and suppliers. I even learned a few things about accounting, because at one point I started toting up the books at the end of the day.

I also learned how *not* to treat the people who work for you, because Mr. Briller treated his employees badly and paid them poorly. He was greedy, selfish, and cheap. I had to beg him for raises. A few times during the period I worked for him we did this little dance together. I'd ask for a raise. He'd say no. I'd say "I quit." He'd give me the raise—maybe not what I asked for, but something. To me it was part of the fun, but I was a kid with no overhead and no family to support. In truth, I would have worked for free, but I sure wasn't going to tell him that. From that experience I gained a lifelong tendency to take the side of the underdog and a commitment to treating employees decently and fairly. With the help of my partners, our firm, RBZ, has earned a reputation for doing just that.

You'd think working for a pharmacy and my parents' business would be more than enough for a teenager who didn't have to work to put food on the table or a roof over his head. But for me it wasn't enough. At times I'd also put in hours on weekends and week nights selling Fuller brushes door-to-door. During the holiday season I sold Christmas cards. I never saw any of those jobs as an obligation, nor did I experience them as drudgery. And I didn't do it just for the money, even though I was proudly building up quite a nest egg. My pharmacy salary, the cash I made selling door-to-door, and the long hours I put in with my father at minimum wage all added up to a princely sum for a teenager, especially one who had no interest in clothing, record albums, entertainment, sports, dating, or any of the other things kids my age spent money on. I would rather save than spend.

The fact is, while I liked seeing my savings grow, I loved working, and looked forward to it every day. Work was my my escape. Some of my classmates did drugs. I did work. In a sense, work was my drug of choice. In truth, this was the easy part of my life. Sitting in classrooms and taking exams and dealing with classmates—that was the hard part.

The Class of '65

I was in Pali High's second graduating class, the class of 1965, which was destined to become famous. In January of my senior year, *Time* magazine ran a cover story titled "Today's Teenagers." Pali was the centerpiece of the story. The school was selected by the editors to illustrate their theme, which was stated this way: "In the mid-1960's, smarter, subtler, and more sophisticated kids are pouring into and out of more expert, exacting, and experimental schools." I'm not so sure Pali students were any "smarter" than those in other high schools, but they *were* subtle and sophisticated—also, with glaring exceptions like me, stylish—largely because they were privileged kids from families in Brentwood, Bel Air, and Pacific Palisades. *Time* made a big point of our affluence, emphasizing that Pali students lived in $100,000 homes—about 1.1 million in 2013 money—and most of them drove more expensive cars than their teachers. Among my classmates were the children of Hollywood stars like James Arness, Betty Hutton, and Karl Malden.

Time dissected our class's social structures and trends, touching upon activities that foreshadowed the sex-drugs-and-rock-and-roll counterculture that would soon erupt. But the main message presented us as the cream of the crop of the largest, healthiest, best-fed, best-housed, best-educated generation in history. We were "on the fringe of a golden era," the article said, and youngsters like us would lead the way into a glorious future.

Ten years after we graduated, two of my classmates, Michael Medved and David Wallechinsky (son of the famous writer Irving Wallace), tracked down thirty members of that privileged group to see what had become of their lives. The book that resulted, *What Really Happened to the Class of '65?*, became a surprise bestseller. For us, the fifteen minutes of fame Andy Warhol allotted to everyone was multiplied many times over. The jacket copy read: "They talk of their dreams and disappointments, their initiation into drugs and sex, their reactions to the Kennedy assassinations, the Vietnam war and the music of the sixties. Their stories are candid, compelling and often startling." The stories included drug busts, exotic adventures, racism, and suicide. The characters profiled included a lawyer, a minister, a model, a spiritual seeker, a mental patient, a welfare recipient, and an unwed mother. Plus one highly successful nerd with a predictable, conventional life: me.

The Champion Nutseller

I was shocked when Medved and Wallechinsky called me out of the blue and said they wanted to interview me. I was even more shocked when they told me why. They'd already interviewed a number of my former classmates, and many of them, when asked who they remembered most from high school, mentioned Harvey Bookstein. Me? I was about as unpopular with the other students as a surprise quiz. Here's how much of a social outcast I was: in my senior year, a fellow student named Bob Karp talked me into running for class treasurer. I kept saying no, but he persisted. "You're perfect for the job," he said. "You're the only one in school who knows about money. You have all the skills. No one else even comes close."

If Bob wasn't the only friend I had in high school, he was certainly the best, and he was definitely my only confidant. We weren't like most high school buddies, who ran with a pack, messed around with drugs and drink, played and watched sports, went to parties, and chased after girls. We talked and played cards—nonstop gin rummy—and sometimes we slept over at one of our houses. Bob had a lot of other friends. Sometimes I would tag along with them, but I never really felt I was part of things. I was more like Bob's guest.

I trusted Bob, and he must have been very persuasive because he was able to talk me into running for class treasurer. Come to think of it, he also talked me into the only other political campaign I was ever involved with: he got me to volunteer for Eugene McCarthy's run for the 1968 Democratic presidential nomination. In any event, I announced my candidacy for treasurer and started campaigning. I even spent some of my own money on signs and banners. How many of the five hundred seniors voted for the best qualified candidate? Six, including Bob and me. That's how popular I was. The election defeat was just one more in a long series of high school humiliations.

But I guess even if you're a complete loner with a zero popularity rating, if you're also the only kid who wears a white shirt and tie and carries a briefcase every day, and works the cash register in the school store, and if you've been voted Class Nerd three years in a row, people will remember you and wonder what happened to you. That's why Michael and David turned to the Accountants section of the West Los Angeles Yellow Pages and found this entry: Bookstein, Harvey, 1801 Avenue of the Stars, Century City. And that's why I ended up in their famous book.

My chapter is called "Harvey Bookstein: The Cashier." It opens with a quote from the December 14, 1962, edition of the school newspaper, *Palisades Tideline*: "'I really enjoy selling,' says Pali's champion nutseller." That's me. I had sold 121 cans of nuts at a dollar apiece to raise money for a new football scoreboard. Not that I gave a damn about football. I just liked selling—and the feeling of outdoing all the other kids, most of whom could barely sell six cans. Here's how my fifteen-year-old self explained how I accomplished that stellar feat: "I went all around the Pacific Palisades area, from the ocean to 'the center.' I only sold about six cans to people I knew—teachers and family. I took home several cases each day, sold them that night, and brought back the money the next day."

The article concludes with evidence of what I've been saying about my work habits: "Harvey is a member of the Tritons, the boys' tenth grade service group. He also works in the student store selling school supplies before first period, operating the change booth during nutrition and lunch, and then selling candy after school." What the article didn't say was that my homeroom won the prize for the most nuts sold, thanks to my work ethic. At the party to celebrate the victory, my appreciative classmates gave me a couple of presents, including a ceramic rat with a penny attached to it and HARVEY printed on it. I still have those gifts. In *Class of '65* I called that homeroom recognition "the nicest thing that happened to me at school."

What was the *worst* thing that happened in high school? As I told the authors, it wasn't being picked on by other kids. It was the time I was accused of stealing ten dollars from the student store. I'd been working there for a year and a half, and one day the total cash tallied by the student store manager came up ten bucks short. I was the obvious suspect. My parents were called in, and right in front of them and the principal I was accused of stealing. That night was hell, because I didn't do anything wrong, yet no one believed me. Fortunately, I was vindicated the next day when the bank found a deposit error. In the book, I was quoted as saying, "I'm sure it must seem insignificant to other people, but to me it meant an awful lot." I find it revealing to read that statement now. My parents had always drummed into me the importance of honesty and integrity, and to this day those virtues mean more to me than almost anything else about doing business.

Seventeen Going on Forty

This is how the classmates interviewed for *Class of '65* remembered me ten years after graduation:

- "I see a very short, pudgy guy with dark hair and a very Jewish-looking face, standing somewhere in the back of gym class having trouble doing calisthenics."
- "He was very much a little businessman who enjoyed working in the student store every day. … He would never break the rules for you. He wouldn't sell you a candy bar after the bell had rung."
- "Harvey was seventeen going on forty."
- "I remember Harvey always walking around trying to balance everything with that huge briefcase on one side of him."
- "My memory of him in a black suit is so strong that I can't remember him taking it off to shower or to sleep."
- "He was the brunt of a lot jokes, a lot of adolescent cruelty. Yet even though he didn't fit in and everybody made fun of him, I felt that he was a person with some concept of himself. He felt himself to have a place within the scheme of things."

The people quoted had no idea what had become of me in the intervening decade, but almost all of them made the right call about my occupation. "He was always dealing with money somehow," said one. "We used to call him 'Booky.' I would think that today he would be a certified public accountant." Another said, "In the student store, he knew where everything was and usually what the closing balance was. I imagine that today he's an accountant. He should be." Remembering how much my boss at the pharmacy liked my gung-ho attitude, a third classmate said, "He was kind of the typical accountant." And the guy who remembered me in black suits with "several pencils and a pocket protector" said, "Everything that you say about an accountant could have been based on Harvey Bookstein. I would imagine that by now he is the super accountant of all time. I think he will ultimately be handling all the accounts for the planet."

Well, not quite, but by 1975 I did have a lot of clients.

My classmates sure had my number, except for one thing. I am *not* a "typical accountant." I wasn't then, and I'm even less so now. But they had no way of predicting what kind of accountant I'd become. Neither did I. Overall, their observations about who I was in high school, and their predictions about what I would become, were so accurate that when I read the book I realized how lucky I was to be doing exactly what I was meant to do. I never had to give a single thought to age-old questions of youth, like "What should I do with my life?" and "How should I make my living?" As I told Medved and Wallechinsky, ever since early childhood I wanted to do what my father did. "Other kids wanted to be policemen or firemen, but I always wanted to be an accountant," I said. "I was put on this earth for that purpose."

I was honest with them about what my high school years were like emotionally. "I stuck around with the crowd that always got picked on," I said. "I remember I used to come home very depressed. Sometimes I used to go home and cry. I could have understood not being liked if I had been a nasty, mean person. But I wasn't like that, so it just didn't make sense. My world didn't stop, though. I had my own little world to escape to, where people's reactions didn't make any difference. I had what I considered my happiness."

As I said, the world I escaped to was work. I told Medved and Wallechinsky what my schedule had been like in high school, and they put it in the book. I'm sure people who read my chapter thought, "That guy worked more hours in one week than I did in four years." No wonder I found so many surprises in *Class of '65*. Back in high school, I was not only rejected by anyone with an ounce of coolness, I was too busy working to know what was really going on with *any* of my fellow students.

One thing I learned, for instance, was that the hot dog stand directly across Sunset Boulevard from Bay Pharmacy was the site of a lot of drug dealing. From the store I would see crowds of people gathering at the hot dog stand, and a parade of cars and trucks stopping by, but I had no idea they were buying more than hot dogs. I was that clueless and left out.

But while some people focused on getting high and falling in and out of puppy love, I was making big bucks by high school standards. As I revealed in my interview with Michael and David, when I was in the eleventh grade I took $1,300 from my savings—a whole lot of money for a seventeen-year-old in those days—and invested in the stock market. A year later, when I was a senior, I sold that stock for $11,000. I had a nose for high-yield deals even then.

You may wonder how I found time for my homework. The truth is, I didn't. I was a lousy student. When it came to academics, I was a willfully disobedient underachiever who couldn't care less about grades. No wonder I ended up in the lowest tenth of my class. The only subjects I was remotely good at were math and business-related courses, because numbers came as naturally to me as writing did to my bestselling classmates, Medved and Wallechinsky. That's still true to this day. Joe Ruvolo, one of my partners in real estate investing, said recently, "I don't think I've ever met a person who is as quick with numbers as Harvey. His grasp of numbers and finance and economics is truly remarkable. We'll meet somebody, and two months later Harvey won't remember his name, but he'll remember every single economic detail they discussed, and he'll remember it for years on end. He simply does not forget."

Plenty of smart kids don't live up to their academic potential, of course, but it's usually because they're goofing off or obsessed by sports or sex, or doing whatever it takes to be popular. I was one of the rare birds who slacked off on schoolwork because he was too busy earning money—not because I had to, but because I loved working more than most grownups do.

Some Things Change, Some Don't

Reading that chapter now, thirty-seven years later, I see how little I've changed in some ways. Michael and David described the first moments of our reunion this way: "As we shook hands at the door he stretched himself to his full five feet four inches, then scurried off to settle himself behind his enormous desk. He spoke with great candor, and spat out his words with such unnatural speed that at times it was difficult to understand what he was saying." I still talk a mile a minute, and most of what I say is, in fact, candid.

What I said about my then-new accounting firm is still true to this day: "There is no question of the fact that any person we do work for is going to get the best service available." And my radar is still tuned in to good opportunities, as it was when I said goodbye to my interviewers.

"I really wish you luck on your book," I said. "In fact, I hope you make a million dollars. Because if you do, believe me, then you'll need a good accountant." Michael, who became a well-known conservative talk show host, did not become a client. But David did, for several years. In the picture of him and me at our ten-year reunion in *Class of '65* (I'm sporting a gaudy shirt and a thick mustache, typical of the 70s), he's holding his bestseller, *The People's Almanac*. The caption says I'm advising him on his tax return (not true).

But in some ways, the Harvey of 1975 has changed dramatically. For example, one statement I made then seems totally ludicrous now. It's embarrassing to reproduce it, but here goes: "I'm very much a male chauvinist. I don't believe in women working. At least not my wife." I was referring to Kathy, to whom I had been married for four years at the time. She felt differently about that issue, and she wisely ignored my wishes and kept on working. By the time I married Harriet, my second wife, I had gotten over that antiquated attitude. I'm proud to say my company has earned a stellar reputation for hiring and promoting women, and for having zero tolerance for sexual harassment or sexual discrimination of any kind.

I also said this in *Class of '65*: "I've got the wife I want; I've got the house I'm going to live in for the rest of my life." Not quite. As we've seen, my first marriage was destined to end, and I gave up the house. But if I were interviewed now I'd say exactly the same thing about my marriage to Harriet and our present home. In fact, I would shout it with the strong conviction that comes with maturity and many hours of excellent therapy. Above all, I'm extremely glad one statement I made in that 1975 book came true a few years later: "Hopefully, someday I'll have the children that I want." That I do, and I couldn't be more grateful.

Chapter 5
The Education of a Born Accountant

*I*n my high school yearbook, as reproduced in *What Really Happened to the Class of '65?*, the caption under my graduation picture read:

Harvey Alan

Bookstein

U.S.C.

Accountant

As everyone at school knew, the chances of the accountant part coming true were as close to 100 percent as any prediction could be. I knew accounting. I was good at accounting. Accounting earned my father's acceptance, and sometimes even his pride. Some boys get that paternal recognition with good grades, athletic prowess, or proper behavior. I got none of that. In my eyes, I failed my father as a son, as a man, and as a human being—but at work I was a champion. He wanted me at the office because I was useful, not just to keep an eye on me like a babysitter. There, I did things right, whereas everywhere else I did things wrong. As a future accountant, I was, in my father's eyes, a star in the making, and I felt it. Did I *like* accounting? I don't know, because the question never entered my mind. Accounting was what I did and what I excelled at. I was comforted by the knowledge that I'd be doing it the rest of my life.

As for the U.S.C. part of my yearbook entry, that would have been a bad bet. I didn't even apply. The University of Southern California was an expensive private school with a reputation for recruiting great football players and preparing children of the wealthy elite for professional careers. I not only didn't think I'd fit in, I knew there was no way an academic underachiever like me would *get* in. Plus, my parents thought I should pay for my own college education, and I was too good an accountant to go deep into debt for something I didn't want to do in the first place. The truth is, I had no interest in going to *any* college. I didn't see the point. I was a bad student because most of what I was required to study bored the hell out of me. Nor did I need four years to discover my passions and talents, or explore my career options. All that was crystal clear before I even set foot on the Pali High campus.

Besides, I thought my future would be better served if I kept on honing my skills and expanding my knowledge by working *and getting paid,* rather than paying for the privilege of trudging through four more years of school. I was more comfortable learning on the job than in a classroom, and I certainly didn't need any help developing a strong work ethic. I had more work experience at eighteen than most people do at twenty-five. Maybe even thirty. I could earn an awful lot of money in those four years, which would give me a big leg up on everyone else my age. As for the other things eager freshmen look forward to—the fraternities, the parties, the football games—I couldn't care less, and I wouldn't fit in anyway.

The Road to CPA

My father had other ideas. He wanted me to go to college for one reason and one reason only. The master plan had the two of us becoming bona fide business partners. The company would be called Bookstein & Son, and the son would be a CPA, with all the privileges and opportunities that come with certification. My father knew from long experience what a difference that could make. Without a CPA, Bookstein & Son could not be a full-fledged accounting firm; it would be limited to the simple services my parents had always offered. They had made a big success of that kind of accounting, but the scope was too restricted and the future prospects for such a limited practice were no longer as bright as during the postwar years. So the plan wisely called for me to become a Certified Public Accountant. But this was the kicker: for that, I needed a bachelor's degree. Harvey had to go to college.

In retrospect, I believe my father also knew I'd be frustrated if I could only practice his kind of accounting. The world was clearly becoming more complex and global every day. With a college education and a CPA license, I could provide more services to high-end clientele. I would also stay interested in my work. Boy, was Dad ever right about that! In *What Really Happened to the Class of '65,* I was quoted as saying, "I wanted to be a real accountant, an *all-around* accountant. I wanted to help small clients make something of themselves. You just feel good. You pat yourself on the back when you see a small company that has bad records and nowhere to turn, and they call you up and you make a few right decisions and they really make a go of it. You feel kind of proud. You feel like a piece of them." I still feel that way today.

Despite my qualms and some active resistance, I eventually came to understand my father's reasoning. I didn't like it, but rules are rules, whether or not they make sense to me. If I was going to become a CPA—and it was obvious that I should—I needed a piece of parchment with "BA" printed on it. But where would I go to get it? With my rebellious streak, my distaste for book learning, and my insanely busy work life, I had totally screwed up any chances of getting into a top-notch university. Fortunately, I found a good option in a most convenient location: Santa Monica City College. SMCC was a two-year school. I could earn an associate's degree there while continuing to work for Bay Pharmacy and my father, learning my trade firsthand. If I got through those two years with decent grades, I could move on to a regular college and complete my bachelor's degree. And that's what I did.

SMCC also had the great virtue of being affordable, and I'm proud to say I paid for the entire two years myself. I also lived apart from my parents, although it wasn't exactly a declaration of independence. When I graduated from high school, in June 1965, I moved into a furnished studio apartment on Lincoln Boulevard in Venice. The modest apartment was above my parents' office in the building they owned, and free rent was essentially part of my compensation for working in the family business.

From SMCC to CSUN

For the class nerd, SMCC was a brand-new life. I wasn't picked on there. I was with new people who didn't know me and with whom I had no shared history, instead of mingling with kids who had me pegged as a target ever since junior high. Plus, the students at SMCC ranged from eighteen years of age to over fifty, so as a group they were more mature than most college freshmen and not the type to indulge in adolescent bullying. Still, I spent the absolute minimum time I needed to on campus, and I did not make any friends. I went to class, I went to work, I went to sleep, and I munched down quick meals when I needed to. Between my father's firm and Bay Pharmacy I probably worked eighty hours a week for those two years—more during tax season. By then, I was doing bookkeeping for my dad and some traditional accounting as well, such as tax preparation, financial statements, and bank reconciliations. I was paid a little over minimum wage, except when I did tax returns under the same commission deal as the temporary CPAs my father hired. In fact, at one point I negotiated for a little more: forty percent of what the client was billed, whereas the CPAs got one-third.

I got involved with my studies at SMCC more than I ever did in high school, mainly because I took courses in accounting, economics, and business (there were also classes in the early computer languages, in which I did okay). I didn't need much studying to do well in accounting because most of what we learned was a repeat of what my father had already taught me. I was so indifferent to schoolwork that I mostly scraped by with Bs and Cs. I made it through, though, and I graduated with an AA degree in June of '67.

Before graduation, I had to make an important decision. Where should I go to finish up my four-year bachelor's degree? My top choice all along had been the nearby campus of UCLA. The university was much easier to get into back then, and like most California residents with mediocre grades from a two-year city college, I was accepted. Unfortunately, that very year, UCLA dropped its accounting major. If you wanted to be an accountant, you had to major in economics and then go on to get a master's degree in accounting. Not me. I wasn't about to spend a minute more than I absolutely had to in a classroom. In the end, the sprawling, conveniently located UCLA campus in Westwood would just be a place I glimpsed when driving down Sunset Boulevard.

Surprisingly, I was also accepted at Berkeley, although I wasn't exactly the Berkeley type. The campus had been the center of student radicalism ever since it erupted in what was called the Free Speech

Movement, when Vietnam War protests were in their infancy. By 1967, Berkeley had become a living symbol of the youth counterculture. Me? I was a conservative kid who wore jackets and ties. Drugs? Free love? Protests? Not in my repertoire. Even if I wanted to attend Berkeley, my father would have vetoed it. Not for social or political reasons, and not because he was worried I wouldn't fit in. He just didn't want to lose my help at the office. I had to stay in L.A. if I wanted to keep apprenticing with him and building the foundation of Bookstein & Son.

My choices were limited, to say the least. But once again I found a terrific alternative: San Fernando Valley State College. The school that became California State University, Northridge (CSUN), flew way under the radar compared to high-flying UCLA and USC, but at least one of the majors it offered had an excellent reputation: accounting. They had an outstanding program then, and it's even better now (thanks in part to the contribution I made in 2005, as we'll see in a later chapter). CSUN's entire business school is good, but the accounting program is consistently ranked among the top five in the nation. Major firms actively recruit its graduates. My decision was made: I'd fulfill my college requirements about a half hour up the 405 freeway from my parents' business.

Lies My Father Told Me

The summer of 1967 was an eventful one for my generation. The Beatles' breakthrough album, *Sergeant Pepper's Lonely Hearts Club Band* was released around the time I graduated from SMCC. Then hippie kids flocked to San Francisco for the famous and infamous Summer of Love. I was totally oblivious to all that. I spent the summer working full-time for my parents and the rest of the time at Bay Pharmacy, enjoying the work and squirreling away just about every cent I made because I lived rent-free, ate cheaply, and didn't spend a nickel on dates, booze, and other things guys my age dropped their paychecks on.

That September, I started classes at CSUN. My attitude toward school hadn't changed a bit; I still didn't care much for it. But with my eye on the diploma and the CPA certificate it would lead to, I rose to the occasion. Predictably, I received straight As in accounting, and I got As and Bs in business classes. I also did well in philosophy and psychology. That might sound surprising, but those courses emphasized logical thinking and I found the enquiry into human nature interesting. As for other subjects, suffice it to say I was uninspired and my grades reflected that attitude. No matter: I learned what I needed to learn, and I did what I needed to do to earn a bachelor's degree.

My CSUN years were eventful in another way as well: I discovered love and sex. During those two years, I lived in a dorm in Northridge, except between January and April 15, tax season, when I stayed in the studio apartment above my parents' office, so I could work long hours (as many as a hundred a week) without wasting time commuting. At those dorms, during my second year at CSUN, I met my first wife, Kathy Nilsson.

Until then, I had spent my entire adolescent and teenage years avoiding girls. I was afraid of them, or perhaps it's more accurate to say I felt intimidated by them. I attribute this in part to self-consciousness about my height (or lack of it) and my well-earned reputation as a nerd. I didn't know anything about sex, and I assumed—no doubt incorrectly— that any girl I'd want to be with would be more experienced than I was. Thinking I'd inevitably embarrass myself and be teased or ridiculed, I just avoided the whole thing.

But there was a more unusual, and tragic, reason for staying away from girls: my father. As I've said, Dad was an incredible business mentor. I admired his intelligence, his incredible work ethic, his personal charm, and his people skills. But as a father he could have done a lot better. Among other things, he gave me mixed messages about women. On the one hand, he was an exceptionally kind, generous, loyal husband. He could not have treated my mother—or my stepmother after my mom died—any better. In that sense, he was an excellent role model. On the other hand, to say he had a sexist, male chauvinist side would be a gross understatement. He had apparently been quite the ladies' man when he was young and single in the 1940s in Detroit. According to his younger brother, my Uncle Marvin, he had a long series of girlfriends from an early age, and they were all a few years older than he was—as were my mother and my stepmother. He was less than 5'7", but he made up for his short stature with good looks, charm, and an exceptional gift of gab. He must have sown all his wild oats by the time he got married, because, as I said, he was a prince of a husband.

The sexist in him came out when he spoke to me, his only child, about girls. I wasn't even thirteen when he started urging me to have sex, and as time went on he would tease me—and sometimes torment me—because I didn't. He let me know he was disappointed in me. He'd say things like, "When I was your age I already had six notches on my belt, and you haven't even kissed a girl." He actually defeated his own purpose, because he was so crude that he made me want to have nothing to do with girls. The worst instance, one that's deeply etched in my mind, was when he said, "Harvey, you've got to understand, if they're old enough to bleed, they're old enough to butcher." Butcher! He actually used that word. I can still hear it today, and it makes me shudder. He was equating sex with butchery. No wonder I avoided it. I didn't want to be a butcher, and I figured if I kept my distance from what my father depicted as livestock I would never have a chance to be one.

When I finally broke through that fear and became sexually active, I was determined to be more like the mature, grown-up Harold Bookstein—the faithful husband who treated his wife like a goddess— not the man who talked to me about sex in such a vulgar way. In the long run, the experience probably made me a better man. With one exception—a blind date between my marriages with a seductive, sexually aggressive Russian woman who did not speak English and had put away a lot of vodka—I have never slept with anyone else for whom I did not have genuine feelings. I would never just have sex; I would always make love.

I Finally Play the Dating Game

I didn't go out on a single date in high school, or during my two years at Santa Monica City College. I went on my very first date when I was a college junior, in my first year at CSUN. She was a nice Jewish girl named Beverly, who lived at home with her parents. We went out for three or four months, but we never even came close to having sex. I wanted to, and I thought I was finally ready to, but she was the product of a more conservative, old-fashioned era, when good girls saved themselves for marriage. I slept over at her house a few times, and her parents actually let us sleep in the same room—the living room, on separate couches, where they could keep an eye on us by making random appearances. I managed to experience my first real kisses, though. Most guys my age considered that getting to first base, at best. To me it felt like a grand slam. Beverly never pressured me about marriage, but she clearly had her sights set on that, and I did not. I don't remember how we broke up, but I do remember thinking the relationship was going nowhere. In any event, it ended, and the next girl I dated would become my wife.

I was living in a privately owned dormitory next to the CSUN campus. There were two sides to the dorm, one for men and one for women, and to accommodate more women they had recently converted part of the men's dorm into a new row of women's rooms. One night I was walking across an outdoor quad next to that new women's wing, when a group of African American students, who had been drinking and smoking marijuana, started calling me "whitey" and other epithets. It was in the latter part of 1968, only a few months after the assassinations of Bobby Kennedy and Martin Luther King, Jr., and racial tension in the country was high. The taunts quickly turned violent. They knocked me down and started kicking and punching me. At that point, one of the co-eds in the women's wing of the dorm opened her window and yelled, "I'm calling the police!"

My tormentors dispersed. The girl who had saved me was Kathy, and the first time I saw her face was when she took the screen off her window and helped me climb into her room, overruling her frightened roommate, who didn't want to get involved. A fellow student drove me to the school's medical clinic, where they bandaged my wounds and sent me home. It was quite an adventure and the perfect opening for a happily-ever-after love story—only it didn't turn out that way.

Around that time I started to have a somewhat normal social life. I got to know some of my fellow students, and while I wouldn't exactly call them "friends" I did at least have acquaintances and people I could talk to. That included my three roommates in a dorm suite with two bedrooms (two guys in a room) and a common bathroom. Kathy's room was just around the corner from mine. She and I became part of a group of student buddies who would go out together.

The first time we did something that cost money, I managed to alienate the other men in the group. Six of us, three girls and three guys, decided to go to dinner and a drive-in movie. We weren't three couples on a triple date, but six friends who happened to be men and women. Still, I had certain ideas about the sexes, so I said to the other guys, "Let's pay for the girls."

"Are you crazy?" they said. "We're not dating them. We're not getting any action out of them. Why would we possibly pay for them?"

"Because it's the right thing to do," I answered. "It's proper."

They wouldn't give in, so I shocked everyone by picking up the check myself.

Now they thought I was not only only crazy, but dumb as hell.

I cite this story for a few reasons. One, it shows how naïve I was. I never socialized, so I didn't know what was normal and expected. I always saw men paying for women, and we were three men and three women: end of story. The difference between a date and an outing with friends had never registered to me. This was also an early example of two personality traits that remain with me to this day. First, I can be highly principled, and I stand firmly behind my principles. I'm proud of that, but I've also learned that when you take good qualities to an extreme they can become problems, and sometimes barriers to good relationships. In my case, standing up for my principles has at times been viewed as obstinate, petty, or unfair.

Picking up the check was also an early sign of a second trait: I love giving things to people, especially when I can surprise them. I loved surprising Kathy, and I still love surprising Harriet with gifts. I spend a lot of time plotting and doing research to pull off a good surprise. I've done it for other people too, just because it makes me happy. I once surprised my Uncle Marvin and Aunt Goldie in Michigan by having a picnic table and chairs delivered to their home.

Another time, I bought a painting by an artist my aunt admired, as a gift to her. I don't say this to brag. I've never understood why I'm more comfortable being a giver than a receiver. Getting gifts makes me so uncomfortable it has led to tension with my family and colleagues. Dr. Jones says I never felt worthy of gifts. It's also true that I always felt that accepting a gift meant I had to reciprocate, and I hate being forced or coerced into doing anything. Not accepting gifts meant I didn't have to deal with such obligations. That's why I don't like celebrating my own birthday.

My resistance to being given anything used to bother Harriet. On one of the occasions she joined me at a session with Dr. Jones, she complained that I never let her buy me anything, and if she buys me something anyway I make her take it back. Dr. Jones said, "You don't understand, Harriet. When Harvey gives *you* something, he's giving *himself* something also, because it makes him happy." Harriet got it. As we were leaving the office, she said, "Dr. Jones, I'm going to let Harvey be as happy as he wants to be." Sure enough, she stopped complaining that I didn't let her buy me anything, and let me lavish her with presents. Months later, she told Dr. Jones, "Harvey has made himself very happy."

Back to those college dorms and my group of friends. At one point, Kathy started dating someone. This triggered a strange new feeling in me. I don't know if *jealous* is the right word, and I would have adamantly denied being jealous at the time, but seeing her go out with someone else upset me so much that I lost touch with one of my greatest assets: rational thinking. One night, Kathy and this guy, whose name I can't remember, were going to a movie. I convinced her roommate, Rory, to go to the same movie with me. The guy bought tickets for himself and Kathy, while Rory and I managed to sneak in. We sat right behind them. About halfway through the movie, I tapped Kathy on the shoulder. She whispered to her date, "Someone's touching me." His response was, "Don't worry about it." I did it again, and they saw who it was. I kept doing it. Eventually, my rival—who didn't know he was my rival—started getting mad. Afterward, the four of us went to a diner for milkshakes. That's when he *really* got pissed—not because I annoyed them during the movie, but because Rory told him we'd sneaked in. That he'd paid for two tickets while I got in free—that *really* set him off. Now I knew he didn't deserve Kathy and I would find a way to get him out of the picture.

I essentially mounted a propaganda campaign. I dug up unflattering things about the guy, and I told Kathy everything I learned. But I couldn't get through to her, and she kept going out with him. Then, one night, a bunch of us went to a party, where I had three or four drinks. That was three or four more than I usually drank, so I must have been agitated deep inside. When I returned to my dorm, Kathy was there with my roommate and two or three other people. I lost it. I ripped the sheets off my roommate's bed, stuffed them into the sink and turned on the water. I have no idea why. I must have done other idiotic things as well, because my roommate got so mad he left the room and took the others with him—except for Kathy. She stayed to make sure I was okay.

And I said, "Kathy, I love you." Both of us were shocked. I didn't know where those words came from. I'd never consciously had the thought, and I'd never even kissed her. The words just came out. And they had an impact on Kathy. She told me she'd stopped seeing the other guy a week earlier. I successfully eliminated him by exposing all his flaws—

some of which I probably made up out of whole cloth—and Kathy and I were free to start dating. That night was the last time I ever got drunk.

Going All the Way

An attractive brunette, Kathy was a year and a half younger than I was and two inches shorter—5'2" to my 5'4". Other than a shortness gene, our choice of colleges, and the fact that we were both only children, we had little in common. She grew up in a church-going Lutheran household, where she was exposed to the classic stereotypes about Jews. She actually ran her hand over the top of my head once, to feel the horns. She figured they were probably little bumps, not pointy things. Her father was a carpenter, and her mother was a homemaker who brought in additional money by doing laundry and ironing for other people. Kathy and I were oriented to different halves of the brain: she was artistic in temperament and skill; I was logical, rational, and mathematical. But when you're young and in love, differences like those seem unimportant.

The sexual revolution of the 1960s was moving ahead rapidly, but Kathy and I dated as though we were living in the fifties. We were a pair of innocents, taking things slowly, getting used to being a couple. At some point we felt we were ready, and we lost our virginity together, in my apartment in Venice. My dad used to call it my "bachelor pad," and it looked like one, with red carpeting and functional, single-guy furniture. Now, it finally *became* one. At a time when most college guys had roommates or lived with their parents, having a place of my own to bring a girlfriend was quite a luxury. I also had a car—a shiny new yellow Camaro my parents gave me as a high school graduation gift—so Kathy and I could shuttle between the Valley and Venice. This was an ideal, hassle-free set-up for first-time lovers. Everything was easy, except the sex itself.

We were as nervous as little kids who had to sing and dance for an auditorium filled with grownups—without rehearsals. We did what we thought nature designed for males and females, but it didn't work. The gates were closed, the passage was narrow, the door didn't open—name your metaphor, the bottom line is, Kathy was so nervous she couldn't take me in, and I was such an uptight rookie I didn't know how to ease her anxieties. I had enough of my own to deal with.

The first time was disappointing for both of us. But we'd broken the ice in many ways, and we figured this wasn't an unsolvable problem. Kathy talked it over with her best friend, who was, shall we say, more experienced. The friend was happy to offer step-by-step instructions: "Do this, then do that." The next time we were in my apartment, Kathy did this, then did that ... and it still didn't work. Then her friend gave *me* a tip: give Kathy a drink to help her relax. So, one day, I made her a mix of Tang—the artificial orange juice supposedly invented for astronauts—and vodka. "Drink it straight down and relax," I said. She did, and my makeshift screwdriver worked—too well. She was dizzy in minutes. In fact, she started to act so drunk that I said, "Let's not do it. You're too far gone."

"No, I want to," she said. She probably knew the time was right and the alcohol would ease her fear and relax her. She was right. We were able to have intercourse for the first time. But it wasn't without trauma. She felt pain, and I climaxed in a nanosecond. The next thing we knew there was blood everywhere. I grabbed a handkerchief and started wiping it up. Kathy was terrified. "What do we do?" she cried. "Do we have to go to the hospital?" This was not the brave, resourceful girl who rescued me from a beating the night we met. But the pain didn't last long. The bleeding stopped, and the panic eased. We both felt awful, and guilty, and inadequate. Then it got even worse: Kathy got alcohol poisoning, and we had to go to the hospital after all.

This wasn't the best way to experience lovemaking for the first time. Fortunately, we got over it. We learned the ropes, mainly through on-the-job training, and nature took its course. After that, we made love whenever we could. When it was inconvenient to drive to my apartment, we did it in my car, usually while parked in an alley near her parents' house.

Then nature took its course. Kathy got pregnant. I had used condoms, but not every time, and she refused to take the pill. She was a good Christian girl, but she didn't hesitate to say she wanted an abortion. This was before Roe v. Wade, and abortions weren't easy to obtain. We found a place through the grapevine—not in Mexico or some back alley, and not with an amateur abortionist with a clothes hanger, but an actual clinic with an actual MD, somewhere in L.A. I forget how we found it. We probably had to lie on some forms or exploit some loophole, but it was a legal abortion.

In the waiting room, I was shocked to find I was the only man present. No husbands, no boyfriends, just pregnant women and their friends, sisters, or mothers. I couldn't believe the men who had impregnated those women were not present. I felt so guilty, so responsible, so ashamed, that I couldn't *not* be there. In retrospect, I think I must have acquired my father's better traits, as a loyal, responsible gentleman for the woman he loved. I also wanted to pay for it. Kathy objected to that. She insisted it was her responsibility. But I sidestepped her objections and took care of the bill.

We'd been dating for about six months when we decided it was time for me to meet her parents. I drove to their modest home in Van Nuys, in the San Fernando Valley, maybe ten minutes east of where I now live. Kathy was living at home then, but still attending CSUN. The instant I laid eyes on her father, a tall (6'2" or 3"), well-built man in his sixties, I knew he hated me. From everything Kathy had told me, anti-Semitism ran deep in the Nilssons' souls and was reinforced by their church. I had hoped her father could overcome it at least long enough to get to know his daughter's boyfriend, but that was not to be. I was rejected and despised before I even rang the bell.

Soon, Kathy's father laid down the law. I was forbidden to date his daughter. I was not to set foot in his house. His second command was obeyed, but not the first. Kathy would tell her parents she was going out with friends, and I'd pick her up at school or some other meeting place. We dated behind her parents' backs the rest of my time at CSUN and the first part of my life as a full-time working adult.

Chapter 6
A CPA in Training

I graduated from CSUN in January, 1970. About eight months before that rite of passage, I started interviewing for jobs with CPA firms. I didn't want to. I felt perfectly prepared to start working full-time with my father. But the master plan for Bookstein & Son was for the son to be a full-fledged CPA, and one of the prerequisites for this was a two-year internship at a CPA firm. The certification board wasn't about to make an exception just because I'd been interning with my father practically my whole life. So I started looking for the right job to step into after graduation. Well, not exactly *right* after graduation. I presented every prospective employer with one stipulation: I would not start work until May 1. I had promised my father I'd finish one more tax season with him, and I wouldn't budge from that commitment.

In *Whatever Happened to the Class of '65*, I'm quoted as saying, facetiously, "I liked the free lunches, so I interviewed with almost every company there was." The truth is, I couldn't care less about the lunches; good food never meant a whole lot to me. I interviewed with fifteen firms because I wanted to find the right one for my skills, interests, and personality. I had many suitors, because those years with my father gave me a big leg up on other candidates, even the ones whose college grades were much better than mine. Fourteen of the fifteen companies asked me back for a second interview at their offices, to meet their people and eat that free lunch. Thirteen made offers. I thought it through systematically, making graphs of their advantages and disadvantages. In the end, I accepted the offer from Kenneth Leventhal & Company.

Being Recruited

At the beginning of my selection process, Leventhal was actually at the bottom of the list because they didn't do much normal accounting. They specialized in real estate accounting, and conventional wisdom said it would be hard for a young accountant to take what he learned at such a place and move on to a general accounting firm. But their Human Resources person was unbelievably persuasive. "Anybody can count widgets," he told me. "Anybody can confirm bank statements. But how many people know about lot book reports? How many people know about construction costs? How many people know about financing? Working here can be a big step in your future. What you learn here will be valuable anywhere." He added that because of my work experience I already knew what I'd learn in the first few years at a general accounting firm. If I spent time at Leventhal, he said, I would not only know what everyone else knew, but I would have a unique specialty that would carry over to other kinds of businesses.

He convinced me. At the time, I thought, "If I work at Leventhal I'll bring more value to Bookstein & Son." I had no idea an education in real estate, about which I knew nothing at the time, would lead to a whole new passion and, eventually, a lucrative business in real estate investing.

Leventhal had other things going for it. One was a reputation as the hardest-working accounting firm in Los Angeles. Hundred-hour weeks were not unusual. That appealed to me because it fit with my work ethic. I was already accustomed to working long, hard hours, so why not be at a firm where hard work was the norm and everyone else would be nose-to-the-grindstone too?

I also liked what I heard about the company culture. They were very entrepreneurial; accountants could carve out their own niche, specializing in whatever appealed to them, as long as their work produced bottom-line results. Plus, rewards and promotions were based on performance rather than seniority. Productive accountants could move up the ladder without getting stuck in a bureaucracy that rewarded only time of service. Other firms at the time were more regimented, with standardized roles for the employees. Having a wider range of options and more freedom to operate my way sounded attractive. So did the prospect of advancing on my own merits instead of moving up in lockstep with the rest of my "entering class."

The job was mine for the taking. The firm said they'd respect my commitment to the family business and let me start in May instead of January. I also had the *chutzpah* to demand more money. Their initial offer was $775 a month—a fine starting salary in those days—but I said, "It's not enough."

I figured I was worth more than the typical start-up guy because of all those years with my father. And with twelve other companies ready to hire me, I was in a good negotiating position. They gave me $850 a month for a forty-hour week. I could also earn time-and-a-half for every hour over that, and for every extra hour I worked I'd gain more sick time and vacation time. For a workaholic like me, this was like owning a money tree. Earning extra pay for extra time would be as easy as pocketing the bus fare and lunch money my mom and dad used to give me.

My First Job as a Grownup

I started working for Leventhal in May of 1970, and it turned out to be a better decision than I realized at the time. The HR person was right: I'd already had so much on-the-job training that starting at a general accounting firm would have been redundant. I wouldn't gain much new knowledge or learn many new skills. At Leventhal I would learn a completely new field, real estate accounting, which turned out to be incredibly valuable to my career.

I owe much of that education to my first supervisor at Leventhal, Steve Berlinger, who had started at the firm a few years before I did. Early on, I bumped up against something I couldn't figure out, and I put the question to Steve. His response was, "You know what to do? Get the hell out of here and figure it out." As a supervisor, Steve was the epitome of tough love. When you were down, he'd kick you in the teeth, but he made sure you learned something valuable by the time you got back up. He and I became close friends, and after he left accounting to become a managing partner at Highridge, a hugely successful real estate investment company, I became his company's accountant. Over the years we've worked together on many business deals.

My advantage in experience compared to the other junior accountants paid off big-time when the economy succumbed to a major recession about eight months after I joined the firm. All the CPA firms laid people off, and because Leventhal was hit extremely hard by the real estate market crash, I expected to be let go. In most businesses, when layoffs occur the policy is to give preference to senior employees. I was not only one of the last hires, because I started in May instead of January, but I was also paid more than the other newcomers. But I was spared, thanks to the extra value I brought to the firm.

"Compared to other junior accountants at the time, Harvey was a superstar," Steve said when he was asked to recollect those days. "He had a vast amount of accounting experience from working for his parents. He had a deep knowledge of taxes and a great facility with numbers. I would say he was one of the best numbers guys I've ever known. On top of that, he worked harder than anyone. That love for accounting—his passion for doing it right—was of a much higher magnitude than other accountants."

I include that statement not to brag, but to point out how much I had going for me at that early stage of my career, thanks to my lifetime apprenticeship with my father. My background gave me so much raw confidence that I must have come across as cocky. For one thing, I didn't hold back when I had an opinion, even if it meant disagreeing with a senior accountant, or even one of the partners. "When issues came up, he would present a very honest, clean view and would stick by his guns," Steve remembered. "He would take positions, and he was passionate about them, and you couldn't push him around."

People think accounting is so black-and-white there would be nothing to argue about. Numbers are numbers, and arithmetic is arithmetic. But accounting is more an art form than a science. As in law, there are rules and standards and codes, but interpreting them opens the door to a wide range of possibilities. That was especially true when I was starting out. "At that time, there were very few accounting rules," Steve said. "A lot of it was done by custom. There were certain principles called APBs—Account Principle Board opinions—and they set the rules for doing this or that. The rest was by custom and what you learned in school." Now we have thousands of pages of rules and standards set by the American Institute of Certified Public Accountants—and they're still subject to interpretation.

The point is, accounting is not as cut-and-dried as people think, and real estate transactions are often highly complex. So, at Leventhal, we would have long discussions about, say, whether certain earnings should be recorded or *how* they should be recorded. These were often judgment calls, and the well-informed, well-intentioned, highly skilled professionals in the room didn't always agree. Sometimes I came down strongly on one side or another, and unlike most junior accountants I wasn't afraid to voice my judgments. Steve explained it this way: "Harvey would have well-reasoned opinions. He would objectively look at something and then, either through deductive logic or inductive logic, come to what he thought was a rational conclusion. He *didn't* do what some people do: decide what answer they want and backtrack to build up a case. He was fact-based, not outcome-based. And he had the courage of his convictions. He would stick to his guns, no matter what, unless new facts were brought to light. If he was overruled, he moved on, but it wouldn't change his opinion if he thought he was right, and he usually was."

Moonlighting

I was lucky to report to guys like Steve, who didn't mind disagreement. They understood that a little tension can be a good thing because it puts different perspectives on the table. But my strong opinions sometimes rankled other people, who would rather have everything go smoothly and every decision be unanimous. Uniformity makes things easier, especially in situations where there might be litigation down the road. But smooth and easy doesn't always bring out the truth or lead to the best results, and that's why I was willing to risk being a pain in the neck.

My confidence came out in other ways too. I'll give you an example of just how much swagger I had. I'd been working at Leventhal for about two years when I was assigned to a job in San Leandro, a Bay Area town just a short hop from the Oakland airport. I said I would do it only if I they would fly me home every other weekend—and let me bring my parakeet on the plane with me. That meant the company had to pay for two round-trip air fares every two weeks. They agreed to it, because in my two years at the firm I had proven my value in spades, and they knew I worked harder and longer than anyone else. In fact, it was around that same time that I broke a record that had stood for twenty years. I billed 218 hours in a two-week billing period. And that was just the billables! I probably put in thirty hours in *non*-billable time on top of it. As was the case when I worked for my parents, or at Bay Pharmacy, I liked the extra cash, but I *loved* the work.

I loved it so much that during tax season, when all the hard-working accountants at Leventhal were putting in longer hours than usual, when we finally called it quits at the end of the day, I would head straight for my father's office and work some more. At times I put in as many as 120 hours a week. Two of my Leventhal colleagues, Ted Roth and Dave Zaslow, wanted to earn extra money too, so at a certain point, I brought in additional troops. It was quite an adventure for the three of us to work our tails off in Century City all day, then zip down Pico Boulevard about six miles to moonlight at the family business. In the process, we discovered we had a lot of personal and professional compatibility, in addition to a shared capacity for hard work—good ingredients for a productive partnership. Eventually, Ted and Dave would become the R and Z to my B in the public accounting firm RBZ.

CHAPTER 7
Tying the Knot

I had been working at Kenneth Leventhal & Company for about a
year when I decided to propose to Kathy. She graduated six months
after I did and was working in the art department at May Company, a
large department store with several branches around L.A. She was still
living with her parents and I felt we'd been sneaking around behind
their backs long enough. Now was the time to grow up, settle down,
and have a family. And, in the value system I had absorbed, I *had* to
marry Kathy because I had taken her virginity—or deflowered her, to
use the vernacular of the time.

I felt no reservations about being ready. Unlike most guys at age
23, I had no inclination to play around with other women or travel the
world; my career choice was already in place; and I had no concerns
about my ability to earn a living. In that department, I was way ahead of
the game. I not only loved to work, and was good at a well-compensated
profession, but I had a pile of money socked away. Forty-five thousand
bucks, to be exact. That's about $340,000 in today's money. I didn't tell
Kathy, because I didn't want money to enter into her decision whether
to marry me.

I kept quiet about my savings for a long time, in fact. *Whatever
Happened to the Class of '65?* quotes me as saying, "I didn't tell Kathy
about the money. I told her I had been in the stock market and lost

everything. Then the second year we were married, I gave my wife the passbook as a gift. She was shocked! It was really neat to watch her reaction." In truth, it wasn't a gift to Kathy, as such; it was for the family. But she did react with shock and awe, in the best sense of the term.

That Kathy's parents despised me was not an issue. In fact, it might have made the prospect of marrying her more appealing, just to stick it to them. As for my own parents, my father was more or less indifferent, and my mother disapproved because Kathy wasn't Jewish. I said, "I don't care. I'm going to marry her." They had married against my grandmother's wishes, so they were my very own proof that you can build a successful marriage under the cloud of parental disapproval. My parents quickly came to accept my choice. Kathy's parents never accepted hers.

I plotted the proposal scene carefully, as though I was directing a film. For the location I chose a restaurant on top of a high-rise office building in Westwood. I made a reservation for dinner and went there the day before so the maître d' could help me choose exactly the right table with just the right view. At dinner, the view was a rare one for L.A.: a thunderstorm with flashes of lightning. With a beautiful diamond ring in my pocket, I waited for the right moment. We had drinks, which was unusual for both of us, followed by a sumptuous meal, and then I got on my knees as though I was looking for something. Kathy looked under the table to see what I'd dropped. That's when I opened the ring box and asked her to marry me. She was surprised, but she recovered quickly and said yes.

Stumbling Upon a Secret

What should have been a joyous time quickly became a drama. To obtain a marriage license I had to show both our birth certificates. Kathy didn't have one. The county court had no record of her birth. We couldn't ask her parents, because they believed I was long gone from Kathy's life and we weren't ready to tell them we were engaged. So I went to see Kathy's aunt, a lovely woman in her late 70s or early 80s. Like Kathy's parents, she was a religious person, but she had no prejudice, and was probably a more genuine Christian than anyone I've ever met. She was the only person in Kathy's family who knew we were still seeing each other, and she accepted me. Her explanation for the missing birth certificate was matter-of-fact and shocking. Kathy had been adopted. When I told her Kathy didn't know, it was the aunt's turn to be shocked. "I'm sure her mother and father told her," she said. But they never had.

I could no longer put off revealing the truth to her parents. I went to their home and told her father, "I am marrying your daughter. I need her birth certificate, and I found out I can't get it because she was adopted." That's how her parents learned we were engaged. To say their minds were blown is an understatement. They thought they'd gotten rid of me for good, and suddenly they found out I was going to be in their lives forever. And their secret about Kathy's origins was out of the bag too. I thought Bill Nilsson might punch me. He was nearly a foot taller than I was, with an upper body made strong by swinging hammers all his life. That he was nearly forty years older didn't matter. But I stood my ground. "If she wants her certificate, have her come here and get it," he said.

I wasn't sure what to do. This was long before I discovered therapy, so I went to the only person I could think of who might have good advice: a rabbi. "What do I do?" I asked. "If I tell Kathy she was adopted, she'll be angry that I told her, and if I don't tell her, she'll be pissed because I held a secret from her." This felt like a lose-lose proposition. The rabbi didn't hesitate. I had to tell her. The only alternative was to have her go to her father for the birth certificate and force him to reveal what he should have told her years before. I chose to tell her myself, because I didn't trust her father. Kathy was stunned. I don't believe she ever forgave her parents for not telling her she was adopted, and she may not have forgiven me for telling her.

That wasn't all. She never learned who her biological parents were. She knows the woman who raised her wasn't her birth mother, but she never found out if Bill Nilsson was her real father. He would never speak about it. Bill died about ten years after Kathy found out she'd been adopted. I tried to get her to pry the truth out of him before it was too late, but she wouldn't do it. Nor would she speak to her mother about it before she died some years later. For legal reasons, the adoption bureau would not open the file. We hired detectives to look into the mystery, but we never got the scoop.

I believe this was a big source of the anger Kathy carried inside her, like a bleeding wound. The abandonment trauma common to many adopted children, plus being lied to about it, plus not discussing it after the lie had been exposed—everything added up to rage. And, just as I feared, years later, after we were divorced, she told me I had ruined her life by telling her the truth.

Wedding Guests and Absentees

Kathy and I got married on Sunday, December 26, 1971. Why did we choose that date? It had nothing to do with Christmas, or the availability of reception halls, or the fact that schools were out, or that many of our guests wouldn't have to go to work the next day. Believe it or not, I wanted to get married before the end of the year because there was a huge difference between what I would pay in 1971 taxes as a married man as opposed to being a single man. Kathy wanted to wait until February or March, but I knew how to win arguments when money was involved, and in this case the numbers were all on my side. By getting married in 1971, I saved more than enough to pay for the whole wedding.

Why would a young man in his mid-twenties pay for his own wedding? Because Kathy's parents not only wouldn't spring for it, they didn't even attend. The fact is, they didn't want their only child to marry *anyone*. They were in their 60s, and they expected her to remain free to care for them as they aged. On top of that, they despised the man Kathy had chosen to marry. But even if they liked me personally, they would have disapproved. She could have chosen Jonas Salk, or Neil Diamond, or even Sandy Koufax; Kathy would still be marrying a Jew, and that was just not acceptable. To her credit, Kathy didn't inherit her parents' prejudice. In fact, she knew more about Judaism than I did because she took religion classes at CSUN, including one with a rabbi. In the years we were married, she cared a lot more than I did about observing Jewish holidays as a family, and she insisted on having our kids attend Jewish Sunday School classes. "They need some religious foundation," she said, "and my church will never accept someone named Bookstein, so the kids won't have a shot there."

She was right about that. Once, on Easter, I went with Kathy to the church her father, the carpenter, had worked on when it was being built. The sermon was the most anti-Semitic rant I'd ever heard in a public setting. Kathy was shocked. She kept looking at me in disbelief and embarrassment. I shrugged it off, and we never went back. Years later, the church was damaged in the Northridge earthquake and tried to raise funds to rebuild. I asked Kathy if she wanted us to help out. She did, and I gave the church a personal loan at zero interest. To protect my risk I took a lien on the church property. At the time, one of my business associates said, "How stupid can you be? What if they don't repay the loan? You won't be able to foreclose, because the headline would read, 'Jew Forecloses on Lutheran Church.'" But they did pay me back. Sometimes, generosity is the best revenge.

Our wedding took place in a restaurant called The Fox and Hound on Wilshire Boulevard in Santa Monica (it's no longer there). We tried to get the rabbi whose CSUN class Kathy had taken to officiate, but he wouldn't do it unless Kathy signed a contract agreeing to raise our children Jewish. She had no objection in principle, but refused to put it in writing. I didn't blame her; I wouldn't have signed it either. So we found a rabbi in the Yellow Pages, and we got hitched without a hitch in front of about seventy guests, including my mother and father.

But not Kathy's. Her parents' refusal to attend the wedding was heartbreaking for her, especially coming on the heels of the adoption bombshell. Her aunt came, and that took some of the sting out of it, but Kathy, who was an only child like me, walked down the aisle by herself. She said our wedding day was the happiest and saddest day of her life.

Her parents' stubborn, bigoted behavior aroused the vengeful little boy inside me. I vowed to get back at them, and two years later I found a way. My mother-in-law had a mini-stroke. Kathy was still so angry she didn't even want to visit her. She hadn't seen or spoken to her mother since before our wedding. But I insisted we visit—not just because it was the right thing to do, but also because I'd thought of a way to get even. It happened to be Christmas time, and I gave her parents a present: four framed photographs from our wedding. I got them to place the pictures in strategic locations, so they'd never forget they turned their backs on their daughter's big day.

There is one last point to make about that wedding. The event was memorable not just because of who was absent, but because of who was there. One of the guests was Harriet Miller, who was married to one of my accountant friends and was pregnant at the time. She is now my wife, and the girl in her womb is now my stepdaughter, Roni.

The Newlyweds

The series of traumas and mishaps continued into our honeymoon.

We planned a two-week trip to Europe, first stop London. Kathy got sick the first day with a severe inner ear infection. She vomited a lot and could hardly stay upright without losing her balance. She ended up in the hospital. When the symptoms subsided enough for the hospital to release her, we found we couldn't extend our stay at our bed and breakfast. This was the peak season and they were totally booked. So was every other place we called. So we flew back home after a distressing, and very expensive, three-day trip. But the money part more than balanced out. My colleagues at Kenneth Leventhal & Company, especially Steve Berlinger, were happy I returned unexpectedly. They were in the middle of an important job, and my help was indispensable. Instead of a honeymoon, I worked even longer than normal. I guess that's what some people call karma.

Kathy and I settled into a two-bedroom rental in the Palms section of West L.A., near Culver City and Venice. The apartment was a new one, on two levels with vaulted ceilings, and I think we paid $235 a month. We didn't have our own washer and dryer, but otherwise it was great, and very convenient, with me working in Century City and Kathy working at the May Company store in the Westside Pavilion shopping center on Pico Boulevard.

But we stayed there only for about eight months, because Kathy kept getting bronchial colds from the damp night air. As a Valley Girl, she was used to dry heat, so we decided to move to the Valley, where many young couples lived because real estate was cheaper and the schools were better than in the city. We bought a house in Sherman Oaks. This was my first important real estate deal, and I made a good one: 3,000 square feet for $69,000, and I put so much money down that the monthly payments were less than I'd been paying in rent. That's the house I told the authors of Class of '65 I'd live in the rest of my life. Well, we lived there for almost ten years and started bringing up Michelle there, before we moved to Tarzana, which is where we were when the earthquake hit.

The early years of my marriage seemed typical and ordinary to me. We argued a lot, but it wasn't dramatic or hostile. I assumed these arguments were normal. We were just two young people carving out a life together, with one exception to the norm: I worked longer hours than most husbands. Kathy put in a normal forty-hour work week, sometimes a little more, and I worked my usual eighty. Since recreation and entertainment didn't matter a lot to me, and since I was always a pleaser who enjoys doing whatever the people I care about like doing—assuming it's not something I find distasteful—I went along with whatever gave Kathy pleasure. As it happens, she was into collecting dolls, and I chose to support her in that. So, in our non-work time we would often go doll-hunting at swap meets, antique stores, and doll shows (yes, there are such things). In retrospect, it's kind of amazing how busy that doll-hunting kept us. We spent hours just looking at antiques and dolls.

Time rolled on that way, with one major exception. I was married less than a year when we discovered my mother had a virulent form of ovarian cancer. Told that her only hope was surgery, she agreed to the procedure. Sadly, by exposing the interior of my mother's body to air, the operation hastened the metastasis of the cancer cells. The doctors said there was nothing more they could do. My father and I didn't tell my mother she was dying. The decision was consistent with how the medical community thought at the time; they felt the truth would be too great a burden for a terminally ill person to bear. It's different now, of course; the dying and their loved ones are forewarned and able to prepare for the inevitable end. My mother died in November 1972. She was only fifty-three.

In addition to the grief loved ones experience at such times, the tragedy led to a family upheaval and a major change in how I practice my profession.

Grief and Shock

My parents had never done any estate planning. No wills, no trusts, nothing. Following the cancer diagnosis we had five or six months to put the family's financial affairs in order, but we didn't want to make my mother's remaining days any more miserable than they were. In hindsight, we should have done certain things. If I had a do-over, I would've had my parents set up AB Trusts, which establish a two-step process: when the person dies, half of their joint assets go into a trust for the surviving spouse to live on, and the remainder goes where the deceased individual wants it to go upon the death of his or her spouse. That's the typical AB trust scenario. My parents didn't do that, or anything else. The upshot was that, by law, everything in my mother's name automatically went to my father. It also meant if my father remarried and made no other legal arrangements, upon his demise everything he owned would automatically go to his spouse.

I didn't think much about this at the time of my mother's death. But, to my astonishment and great consternation, my father remarried six weeks later. As if that wasn't shocking enough, he married his own aunt. Marlene, his new wife, was the youngest sister of my grandfather (my father's father). She was only about six years older than her nephew (my father). Marlene and her late husband Eddie had been fixtures in my life, because they socialized a lot with my parents. It was only natural that my father would turn to Marlene for comfort when my mother died, because she was both a close friend and a relative, and as a widow she knew the pain of losing a spouse. Evidently, friendship turned into something more romantic, and with shocking speed my father asked Marlene to marry him.

My Uncle Marv, my father's younger brother, remembers it this way: "Harold needed a woman in his life. He wasn't the type to be left by himself. And the woman he was closest to was Marlene. I'm positive nothing ever happened between them while Celia was alive, but after she was gone the two of them struck it up. Marlene wanted to wait, but my brother was a salesman and he pushed the issue. He called me to talk it over, which was very unusual because we never had long conversations about anything outside of business. He said, 'I'm not going to listen to what other people say. I'm going to be happy with this woman. We care for each other, we get along, and I don't want to lose her. We're not hurting anybody.' A lot of people felt it was wrong. They thought they should have waited longer. Harvey was one of them. He resented it, and he was certainly hurt."

I sure was. I reacted strongly. I understood my father didn't want to be alone. There was no question he needed companionship. That was obvious to me at the time, maybe because I'm that way too. Harriet always jokes that if she dies before I do, I'll be interviewing for a new wife at her funeral. I like being coupled. So did my father, but I didn't understand why he couldn't have companionship without jumping into marriage just weeks after my mother's death.

To her credit, Marlene came to me and said, "Your dad wants to marry me and he doesn't want to wait. How do you feel about that?"

"It would mean a lot to me if you would wait," I said. "It just doesn't seem right. Suspicions arise."

"I understand that," she said. "I'm going to give you some time."

When she told my dad about our conversation, he reacted as strongly as I had. Basically, his attitude was, "Screw Harvey. It's our life. Who is he to say whether we get married or not? What business is it of his?" Marlene's commitment to wait was tossed aside. To me, that was a major betrayal. After they got married, I held it against Marlene—not so much the marriage itself, but the broken promise—for quite a while.

Where There's No Will, I Find a New Way

My father's hasty remarriage caused a lot of residual damage. Relatives on my mother's side were so angry they cut themselves off from my father and me. I never saw my aunts and uncles again. Despite all the emotional upheaval, my father and Marlene were happy together, and I eventually got over my resentment. The financial end of it also turned out fine. The fact that my parents had done no estate planning could have had bad consequences for me and my family, since I had effectively been disinherited. My mother's assets automatically went to my father; my father's assets would automatically go to his second wife if he predeceased her; and, upon her death, everything she owned would go to her children. But Marlene had no children of her own. In the absence of direct heirs, everything she had when she died went to me. So, in essence, it all worked out as if my parents had planned an inheritance for their only child. As it happened, I didn't need the money, but 99.99 percent of the time, it wouldn't work out that way.

In the aftermath of my mother's death and my father's quick remarriage, I came away with a lesson that changed my approach to accounting. I could easily extrapolate this experience to other families and other circumstances. If someone as financially astute as my father, a professional accountant, could neglect planning for his and his wife's eventual death, imagine how easy it is for other people to do the same. No one likes to think about dying; it's much more pleasant to live in denial of that inevitable end. Plus, other families are bigger than ours was, with more people and more complex relationships. And most offspring are not as well off as I was at that age, so the consequences of bad planning can be disastrous. My wakeup call when I realized my parents hadn't planned for death wasn't about the money I might lose out on—I knew I could take good care of myself—but the idea that my mom's wishes might have been ignored. She would want to be sure neither my father nor I would suffer financially. But what if my father had married someone half his age instead of an aunt who was six years older? What if his second wife had children of her own, or if they had children together? I, my mother's only child, could have been left out in the cold.

I decided to be the kind of accountant who didn't let that happen to his clients. When I had my own firm, which I knew would be soon, I wouldn't just do the usual tax returns, financial statements, bookkeeping, and the like—all the humdrum stuff that involves looking back at yesterday. I would also help clients plan for tomorrow. My thirst for a nontraditional kind of accounting was now in the forefront of my mind. I wanted the excitement of being involved in people's lives with a wider horizon than just crunching numbers.

I started researching everything I could find on estate planning. I'm certainly no expert on the subject, but I did become knowledgeable, and I know exactly where to get the answers I need. Ever since then, I've used my family's story as an example. My story is a personal way to let clients know what can go wrong if they don't plan properly. In my case things worked out the way my mother would have wanted, but there's no reasonable expectation that that will happen for everyone. "Part of your job as a parent," I tell them, "is to have a will and/or a trust to protect your children and other loved ones, or your charity, whatever it may be. You can't assume that after your death your spouse will do what you would have wanted done."

"Have you prepared your wills and trusts?" became one of the items on my checklist, along with typical questions like "Did you file your tax return on time?" and "Do you have your extra money in a savings account instead of checking accounts?" I don't tell them what provisions they should make for their assets upon their death. Whom they leave what to is entirely their business, although I'm happy to weigh in when they ask me to. The important thing is to think through what you want and to have your wishes properly documented. If you don't, you may jeopardize your loved ones' future.

That was the beginning of my journey to becoming a therapeutic accountant. Over the years I got involved in more and more nontraditional projects, covering a wide variety of concerns. For instance, I work with clients to prepare for near-term retirement, not only by helping them sell their businesses, but also by helping them plan for what they'll do after the sale. I work with clients who have new business concepts they wish to develop. I help clients form strategic alliances, often with other clients of mine, or with foreign investors searching for opportunities to invest in worthwhile U.S. companies. I identify real estate and business opportunities for investors. I'm proud to say my concern for estate planning has led many of my clients to have so much trust in me that they've made me—not the firm, but me personally—their executor or trustee. I take care of a multitude of trusts today, and I've also trained some of my partners to take on that role; it's not only a good money-maker, but more importantly we provide a vital service by removing a potential source of anxiety and aggravation from our clients' lives.

I'm incredibly grateful I can work with my clients, my associates, and my staff the way I do now. Every business day is exciting, varied, and important, because I never know exactly what might crop up. Strangely enough, I owe much of my professional satisfaction to my father's expert training—and some of it to his careless neglect.

Chapter 8
Off to a Great Start

*K*enneth Leventhal & Company was a fairly small local firm when I
started there. But it was the Cadillac of real estate accountants in
that area of expertise, and on the fast track of growth. During the time
I was with them, the company added an office in Orange County and
then another in San Francisco. All three branches grew rapidly, and
eventually they were replicated in Dallas, New York, and Washington,
D.C. Being part of a growing firm with an outstanding national
reputation was exciting, and for many young accountants it was the
kind of place to set down roots and build a stable, affluent career. But
for me it was not enough. I wanted to do my own thing, be my own
boss, and put my own thumbprint on a new, creative accounting firm.

I ended up staying at Leventhal for four years and eight months,
more than twice as long as I originally planned. I had two reasons for
staying. First, I was expanding my horizons with real estate accounting,
which I found both exhilarating and a perfect companion for my style
of accounting. I wanted to keep learning as much as I could. Eventually,
that new passion led to a lucrative business in real estate investments.

The second reason I stayed was that I kept failing the CPA exam.
Specifically, I failed one part of the five-part exam—not once, not
twice, but *five times.* You may be wondering how that's possible after
everything I've said about how good I was and how much more I knew

than all the other junior accountants. It comes down to the difference between getting things done in the real world and taking an exam—two activities that require different competencies and different mind-sets. Studying bored me. Rolling up my sleeves and doing the actual job? That's a different ballgame, and it's the game I love to play. If my income depended on taking tests instead of getting real work done, I'd still be living in the studio apartment on Lincoln Boulevard. Plus, the part of the exam I kept failing was the only segment that involved essays instead of multiple choice questions. I had trouble with those essays.

When I took that section of the test for the sixth time, a lot was riding on it. If I failed again, I'd have to take the *whole* exam over, even the four parts I'd passed long before. I'm not sure I would have chosen to go through that again. I might have decided to move ahead with Bookstein & Son without being a CPA, at least in the short run. Clearly, if I failed one more time my whole life might have been vastly different. But I passed the exam—probably by the skin of my teeth.

The Odd Couple Partner Up

My life took an unplanned turn anyway. My time at Leventhal made it obvious I could accomplish more on my own than I ever could working with my father. To his great credit, my father also recognized that. And so, by mutual consent, we gave up the dream of Bookstein & Son. That led to January 1, 1975, when Ted Roth and I left Leventhal and started Roth and Bookstein Accountancy Corp.

Ted and I contemplated the move for a long time and planned it for six months. He arrived at Leventhal about five years before I had, and for most of my tenure there we didn't know each other well. But I knew him by reputation. He was known as a straight shooter, a man of integrity, and an outstanding technical accountant. At one point I was assigned to a job in San Diego, with Ted as my supervisor. When you work together for two intense weeks, as we did, you learn a lot about each other—and we both liked what we saw. I gained tremendous respect for Ted, and I like to think the feeling was mutual. We were different in our skills and temperaments. Ted was steady as a rock; I was more mercurial. Ted was quiet and reserved; I was a blabbermouth. Ted was an expert technician; I was not, and I didn't care, because I had other gifts, like my business acumen and my entrepreneurial instincts. I thought we'd make a good match.

I 'd seen other accountants leave large CPA firms to start their own businesses, and most of them failed. They were good accountants, but they tended to partner with their buddies. They'd get along great and have fun together, but they were like twins when it came to skills. They had the same strengths and weaknesses, and usually the same areas of expertise. Their businesses failed to take off partly because they didn't have enough range, balance, and flexibility. Those failures didn't give me a moment's hesitation. They meant nothing when it came to my own prospects; I was convinced I could avoid the common mistakes, and I felt confident I had what it took to build a successful business. And in Ted I knew I'd found exactly the right guy to balance my personality and provide essential skills I didn't have.

My friend and colleague Steve Berlinger once said, "Oddly enough, as a technical accountant, Harvey was, and still is, very average. He's really a businessman. For him, accounting is a tool, and that tool serves him well in business." He went on to explain: "On one level, accounting is a lot of technical gobbledygook. It's very dry and boring, and Harvey was never much into that. He had to know it, but it wasn't his passion. Applying accounting knowledge to business transactions— that's another skill set, and Harvey had the acumen for it right at the beginning."

That's why I needed someone like Ted. One day I said to him, "I'm going to leave Leventhal. It was always meant to be a steppingstone for me, and I'm going to start my own practice. Do you want to join me?"

He didn't say yes. But he didn't say no either. I was happy to see that the prospect of going into business with me was appealing enough for him to contemplate it. His hesitation was more than understandable. This wasn't about our personalities; like me, Ted knew those differences could be good for business. "Harvey had a lot of qualities I didn't have," he once said. "I thought that would help us become successful. I thought, 'This guy can bring in business.'"

The reason for Ted's reluctance was that starting a business was a bigger risk for him than for me. The potential rewards of a successful independent accounting firm were huge, in terms of freedom, independence, and wealth. For me it was a no-brainer. But Ted was already a manager at Leventhal. He could potentially have become a partner. He also had a wife and three children. Giving up a secure position with a mapped-out future was not something to be done without due diligence. Ted had to think through all the risks and rewards, and he had to talk over all the ramifications with his wife Lillian. The process went on for weeks. Finally, to her great credit—and my everlasting gratitude—his wife said, "Let's go for it." I had apparently earned her confidence.

Well Begun Is Half Done

And so, the Roth and Bookstein Accountancy Corporation was born. Why the name? Why not Bookstein and Roth? I've been asked that a thousand times over the years. It's not because Ted is older, or because he made placing his name first a condition of partnering with me. The truth is, we were in my house one night discussing our plans, and the subject of the name came up. We each had our opinion, and you can imagine what they were. We needed a simple, fair way to end the stalemate. I suggested we cut cards. Ted agreed, probably because he couldn't think of a better way to go about it. I'm a card player and a risk-taker. Ted is neither of those things. If we'd been in his house there probably wouldn't have been a deck of cards to cut. So, it was my house and my cards. But this wasn't a skill game; it was pure chance. I pulled a three. Ted drew a king. Ergo: Roth and Bookstein. It was as simple as that.

Ted and I gave notice to Kenneth Leventhal & Company. We arranged a line of credit from a bank in case we needed cash at some point (we never did), and I found a low-cost way to get office space. In fact, a *no*-cost way: we got two rooms from a Century City law firm in exchange for accounting services. We bought some basic furniture from a Leventhal client who was going out of business, and we stuffed all our papers into one four-drawer file cabinet. We had no secretaries, and no assistants other than the law firm's receptionist, who answered our phones and greeted visitors. I did all the typing. I processed all the bills. I did the invoicing. This was a real mom-and-pop start-up, with Ted and me playing both mom and pop. That low overhead was a huge plus in getting us off to a good start.

Of course, we also needed revenue. This was especially true for Ted, whose personal overhead and family responsibilities were much bigger than mine. Fortunately, I was able to bring over my biggest client from Leventhal. He was a wealthy real estate investor who needed a lot of hand-holding, and one of Leventhal's partners recognized I could provide a level of personal attention a large firm could not. He was generous enough to do the right thing and let the client go. In addition, because we opened the new offices at the beginning of the busy tax season, Leventhal asked Ted and me to help with certain accounts we were each familiar with. Plus, we kept on moonlighting at my father's company.

With all that business in hand, we hit the road running, working as many hours as we ever had, if not more. At the same time, we started developing our own clients. That was mainly my job. I was the hustling entrepreneur; Ted was more at home working the technical aspects of accounting. My father referred clients to me. Companies that were too small for places like Leventhal found us. And I could tell people I knew, "Now's the time. I'm ready for you. I have my own company, and I can give you the service you need."

That was a nervous year, but we were doggedly determined to meet the one and only goal we set for ourselves: to earn at least 75 percent of what we had earned in 1974, our last year at Leventhal. We set an ambitious goal for a start-up, but I was so confident in our prospects that I made a bet with Ted that we'd exceed it and earn as much as we had the year before. We did. In 1975, the company's total revenue was $106,795, more than twice what we had projected, and Ted and I made 137 percent of what our combined salaries had been the prior year. Plus, I got a $500 bonus—the amount Ted had to pay me on our bet. That first year's performance was a booster shot to our confidence, which was already high. We were off and running.

Freshman-Year Lessons Learned

There were lessons to be learned from our first year of operation, and some of them contributed big-time to our future success. One was the importance of setting clear, specific expectations, while also remaining flexible enough to constantly reevaluate those expectations. That first year we had only the one goal I've mentioned: make as much money as we did the year before at Leventhal. We were so focused on one objective that the future was off the radar screen. We didn't set any meaningful expectations about how the firm would grow. Perhaps we were foolish not to look ahead and plan for future growth. On the other hand, maybe we wouldn't have had such a great start if we'd been thinking long-term. Once the initial year was behind us, we immediately began setting multiple broad-based goals. Over the years, long-term planning and goal-setting have been keys to our success. The number of partners and staff grew, and the size of our offices, our administrative costs, and other aspects of doing business all multiplied, along with our revenues.

For example, staff training wasn't an issue when Ted and I started out, since we had no staff. We also performed a limited range of accounting services. As we grew, we took on clients in a variety of industries and locations, including many with international concerns. Meeting their needs required hiring the right people and creating appropriate training procedures, so the staff (and the partners) would always be up to date and able to handle today's complexities. Every step of the way, we invested a great deal of time and resources in establishing standards and setting new expectations. We communicated those standards and expectations to everyone concerned, so they had a way to measure results.

However, we also knew there are times when it's better *not* to set specific expectations, because you can get locked in to them and miss new opportunities. I've seen many clients fail to seize a great unexpected opportunity because it didn't fit their current goals. What I tell my clients is: set clear expectations and use them as a guide, but *only* as a guide and not as an absolute. You have to remain flexible at all times so you can adapt to the inevitable changes that arise.

Through it all, the company has had one overarching goal: to keep growing while also improving our ability to service clients. I'm proud to say we've succeeded in doing exactly that.

Another takeaway from that first year was that Ted and I were 100 percent right in predicting that our different personalities and skills would perfectly complement each other. Here's how Ted described our teamwork in those early days: "We're different kinds of people, and we appealed to different kinds of clients. Harvey likes dealing with a client's personal issues. He spends time with them, listening to them, advising them, making decisions with them. He knows how to find out what they're interested in. When he talks to someone, he can empathize. He always had that quality. I think he learned it working with his father. Some of his father's clients were folks with small businesses. Bigger companies have financial experts working for them; they don't need outside accountants to do certain things. But with small businesses— little restaurants, a plumbing supply store, places like that—if you do their taxes and some bookkeeping, like Harvey's father did, you're involved with every part of their activities. You learn how to deal with basic business and personal issues."

He went on to contrast me with him: "Harvey is socially friendly with many of his clients, while I try to avoid that kind of stuff. We both do it intentionally. I like to keep my personal life and my business life separate. Not that I never socialize with clients, because I occasionally do, but I don't go out of my way to do it, and I try to limit it. I don't give clients my cell phone number or my home phone number. Harvey does. Harvey's fast-talking and affable, and I'm quieter and more laid back. He's a big-idea, risk-taking kind of guy, and I'm more careful and conservative."

We learned early on that my personality appeals to some clients, while his is right for others. Some people are excited by my business style, while others are scared by it and prefer Ted's calmer, more predictable ways. And, as I described earlier, we also have different professional strengths as accountants.

Of course, we also have different shortcomings, many of which are a matter of taking our strengths a little too far. "Sometimes I don't deal with problems quickly enough," says Ted. "I cogitate. I'm a thinker, and I can think about things too much and over intellectualize. Harvey is much more emotional, which can be a great advantage. But sometimes it means he doesn't think *enough*. He can react too quickly. He can be very impulsive and not think things through."

Ted is absolutely right. I've become so emotionally attached to certain employees, for instance, that I couldn't bring myself to terminate them when it was obvious they weren't performing well. I can also overreact emotionally when someone does one small thing that irritates me or offends my sense of right and wrong. Both tendencies have created problems, and they would have created more issues if I didn't have Ted's calm, clear-headed thinking to balance my personality.

Then again, without my passion, my interpersonal skills, and my willingness to take calculated risks, the company would never have become the success it is. With that lesson in hand, as our firm grew and our success multiplied, we made sure to add new people whose particular skills and personalities added value to the firm and met our current needs.

The Third Musketeer

At one point during that first year we were forced to move into new offices. The law firm whose space we were using moved out and subleased their offices to young entertainment lawyers. Next thing we knew, there was a piano in the library. Almost every day, late in the afternoon, the sound of musicians banging on the piano wafted into our offices, along with a cloud of marijuana smoke. We quickly realized this wasn't the appropriate environment for an accounting practice. We leased space in the building next door, 1801 Avenue of the Stars. Now we were actually paying rent. We also hired our first employee: a receptionist named Sunny. She's still with us, having become our indispensable office manager.

In our second year of operation, we made an even more significant addition: Dave Zaslow. Dave had moved from Leventhal to start his own firm before Ted and I left. He was on his own, and we all rented office space together. About a year and a half later, Dave suggested to Ted and me that we'd all do better in business if we joined forces. We changed the name of the company to Roth, Bookstein and Zaslow, the predecessor to our current name, RBZ. The outside world saw us as partners, but economically we really weren't. We split the overhead two-thirds and one-third, but Ted and I kept what we earned and Dave kept what he earned. Another year and a half later, we took the next step and became an actual partnership.

Dave fit right in. A perfect complement to Ted and me, he was between us in temperament—more outgoing than Ted, but less so than me. As a business trio, we were as harmonious as the Kingston Trio or Boyz II Men. One reason for that was the fact that all three of us had worked both for Leventhal and for my father. One company was a large, well-structured firm with wealthy clients; the other was a small, informal storefront operation serving ordinary people and small businesses. We didn't appreciate it at the time, but that combination added up to a uniquely valuable set of experiences. Here's how Dave explains what we learned from working with my father:

"A lot of the traits we got from Harvey's father were used in building our own practice. I'm saying this because this is how we were trained, and Harvey is still the same way today. We learned how to work long hours—sometimes three weeks straight without a day off. We learned how to be efficient and frugal. Harvey's dad would reuse the adding machine tape. The roll of tape would come out of the machine onto the floor, and after he used one side he flipped it over and used the other side. Being frugal was very important when we first started out in Century City. For example, we bought parking stickers by the month, and we figured out how to share one parking sticker.

"We also learned ways to be super efficient from Harvey's father. The faster we could do something, the more we got done, and the more the client appreciated it. I not only learned how to work as fast as I could, I also learned to talk fast. If you talk fast, you can say twice the amount in the same period of time, and clients like that because it saves them billing time. Harvey is the fastest talker of all. That mindset stayed with us, and as our own company grew, we found ways to stay frugal and efficient even when we were super successful.

"I also learned how to take every possible tax deduction and tax credit available, because clients want you to save them every cent you can. So, for instance, Harvey's father taught us to ask the client if he had a lawnmower. Because, if they owned a gas-operated lawnmower they were eligible for what's called an 'off highway gas tax credit.' We would always ask, and if they had one we'd apply for this tax credit and save the client a few dollars. He also taught us not to keep work papers in our files. Instead, return all documents to the client. That way, if the client needed some information during the year, we didn't have it. It's a way of making the clients responsible for their own papers.

"Another thing I learned from Harvey's father was how to market. He would write little bits of personal information about clients on index cards, so when a client came in, even if he didn't remember him whatsoever, he could pull out this index card and he'd know things. So he'd say 'How's your son, Joe? He's three years old now.' And the client would be so impressed that his accountant remembered this. That personal touch was very important as a marketing tool going forward. Harvey is a master of it, and he doesn't need index cards. He remembers everything."

Growing and Diversifying

Our company thrived. We steadily expanded in size and increased the range of services we offered. At first, because we had all worked for Leventhal, the bulk of our work covered real estate accounting. As time passed, we realized that real estate is a cyclical business; every few years, the market goes into a downturn, and we might represent companies that take a big hit. So, we decided to diversify our client base to reduce the risk. Diversifying also allowed us to spread the work out over the whole year. Because of tax regulations, the fiscal year for most businesses ends on December 31, and of course taxes are filed on April 15. For us, that meant we worked our tails off at certain times year, but during others—mainly the summer and fall—things were so slow that our employees weren't fully occupied. They were fully paid however, and the rest of our overhead remained basically unchanged. So, as we diversified our clientele we also looked for calendar diversity. As an example, we went after non-profit organizations, which generally have June 30 year-ends. That's one reason Tom Schulte was brought in; one of his specialties was working with nonprofits. This idea worked out so well that Tom is now one of our fifteen partners. Clients like those nonprofits filled in the calendar gaps, making us more of a twelve-months-a-year operation.

With a diversity of clientele, you need a diverse staff to match, and that has always been a big part of our personnel strategy. To this day, the majority of accountants we hire are recent graduates. We coach them and bring them up through our system, giving them a variety of assignments. After a few years, we sit down with them and jointly decide which accounting specialty would be the best fit. We also brought into the firm senior level people whose skills and client base could integrate seamlessly with ours. Some of them came in as partners, merging their boutique accounting firms with our larger company. In most cases, I was the one who made the initial inquiries and decided whether a merger would work out well for both parties. This kind of thing is quite common in the accounting world. Most small firms don't have the resources to grow or the talent and inclination to operate a fully-functioning business. Providing professional accounting services is one thing; running a company, with support staff, secretaries, receptionists, telephone systems, office equipment, and all the rest, is quite another.

Fortunately, Ted, Dave, and I have both sets of skills. We've been able to run our business efficiently without missing a beat when it comes to providing excellent services. The proof of that pudding is that our employees are highly competent, and some have been with us for twenty or thirty years. As a result, some small firms have been thrilled to merge their operations with ours, because it frees them to serve their clients without having to deal with day-to-day managerial and administrative hassles. Being part of a larger operation also frees them from worrying about what would happen to their business if they were to become ill or die. For all those reasons, we were able to add highly skilled, successful people who had specialties we lacked.

Eventually, we changed our name to RBZ, LLP. I'm often asked why we switched from our names to initials. Two reasons: one, it's easier to answer the phone with "RBZ" than with "Roth, Bookstein and Zaslow," and two, the name change made it easier for unnamed partners to solicit business. As I write this, in the fall of 2012, we are fifteen partners strong. Of the twelve who are not R, B, or Z, some had their own small firms and decided to join forces with us, while the others rose up through our system. This has worked out great for everyone, and I couldn't be prouder. As Steve Berlinger put it, "What RBZ accomplished is remarkable. There is a high attrition rate among accounting firms, as with law firms. So accountants move around a lot, and companies come and go. RBZ has been stable. It's survived during good times and bad times, and it's kept growing. One big reason is, the talent stays."

We had no pre-established blueprint for building the firm. We never had a long-range plan. Things evolved naturally, and we reacted creatively to the changing world each step of the way. We made our share of mistakes, of course; you can't be in business without making mistakes. We've had major setbacks too, like the emotionally wrenching time we had to terminate several good people at once. And we've had our share of conflicts, as all partners do. But we learned to manage our disagreements in a mature way, without letting our egos overwhelm our judgment and deceive us into abandoning sound business practices.

If I had to name one key to our success, I would say we've done an excellent job of finding the right people at the right time, empowering them, and integrating each newcomer into the firm without compromising the harmonious environment we worked so hard to create. As a result, surveys consistently name RBZ one of the top companies in L.A. to work for, and we often sit alone atop the list of best accounting firms.

Chapter 9
Married with Children

*T*he first few years of my marriage to Kathy seemed ordinary to me. In my eyes, we were a typical young husband and wife making a life together, except that I worked many more hours than most husbands. Domestic life was basically nondramatic: no big fights, no major conflicts. Sure, we argued and bickered a lot, but I didn't think there was anything unusual about that, and I didn't feel any great discontent. In light of how things turned out, I'm probably wrong. As I said earlier, I was so out of touch with my feelings that I didn't really know what I felt.

One thing did bother me during those years. I really wanted to have children. Becoming a parent was probably the main reason I got married, and I felt ready to be a father. But Kathy wanted to wait while she pursued a career in the art world. I didn't understand that at the time; I was stuck in an old way of thinking, where the husband was the breadwinner and the wife took care of the home and children. That any married woman would put work ahead of having kids seemed bizarre to me, especially when she didn't *need* to work, since her husband could support the family in style.

Kathy worked a forty-hour week, first at May Company and then at Disney, where she painted watercolor backgrounds for animated cartoons. I worked about twice as many hours, if not more. So we didn't exactly have a normal social life. As I said in an earlier chapter, it gave me pleasure to participate in Kathy's passion for collecting dolls. We went doll-hunting in antique stores and fairs; we went to doll shows; and from time to time I surprised her with a doll gift. Other than that and the occasional dinner with friends, we didn't do much outside our jobs. That didn't bother me, since I had no real interests other than work.

A Daughter and a Son

Seven years into our marriage, we finally had kids. The window of opportunity opened when Disney decided to computerize its animation department and move it overseas.

Kathy was laid off, along with most of the animators. Rather than look for another job, she said, "Okay, now it's time to have children." Michelle was born on October 3, 1978. I was elated, I was proud, I was joyful—emotions that didn't often come my way.

The birth wasn't easy. Kathy's labor lasted more than twenty hours, and the doctors finally had to perform an emergency Caesarean. I had taken the Lamaze training, and practiced the method to perfection, only to end up banned from the delivery room. Back then, fathers couldn't be present for C-sections. For me, this was a big letdown; for Kathy, of course, childbirth was a painful ordeal, made worse because she didn't have someone beside her to rely on.

After a brief period of joy, we went through a major aftershock on the Jewish high holidays, when I was in the synagogue. To be honest, I wasn't there for religious reasons. I attended at the request of my most important client, an elderly man whom I had come to love. He was almost a surrogate father to me, and we'd become so close that he treated me like one of his own sons—and in some ways *better* than he treated his sons.

I went to the temple out of respect for him. A leader of the congregation, he asked me to keep him company. That was good enough for me, even if it meant fasting all day and sitting in a stuffy synagogue from early morning to sundown. Kathy stayed home with newborn Michelle. There were no cell phones in those days, but we had a baby beeper—a device like a pager for parents of infants, so they could contact one another in case of emergency. My beeper went off during the service. Kathy was in excruciating pain. It seems that when they opened her up for the C-section, she got a staph infection, and now it had spread.

I dashed out of the temple and rushed home. Kathy looked like a ghost. I picked her up, helped her to the car, and sped to the Encino Hospital emergency room. They took one look at her and went to work. They cut her open and found pus everywhere. Virtually her entire abdomen was toxic. Thankfully, the medical staff did everything right and the emergency procedures worked. But Kathy was left with a big hole in her abdomen. For the next two months, I had to come home from work twice a day to pour a solution of medicine into the raw opening in her belly. The thought of it turns my stomach to this day. At the time, I didn't think about it; I just did what had to be done, like anyone would. We survived a big scare, and eventually the wound healed, but not completely; Kathy will always have an extra little indentation to remember it by.

I had the daughter I'd dreamed of. People always assume that new fathers secretly wish for sons. Honestly, I was hoping for a girl. Why not? I was never into sports, so I didn't long for a little boy to toss a ball with or take to Dodger Stadium. No, I wanted a little girl to plop on my knee and shower with affection. I wanted to buy her clothes and watch her get excited putting them on in front of a mirror.

A few years later, I was ready for another child. Marc was born on August 27, 1982, on my father's sixtieth birthday. I can't imagine a better birthday present than a grandson. This time, we had no surprises or emergencies. We knew in advance Marc would be delivered by C-section, and the procedure was performed right on schedule. This time I was allowed to be present. I even got to cut the umbilical cord.

I quickly discovered that not being a jock or a sports fan wasn't a drawback for the father of a son. I could be as affectionate with Marc as I was with Michelle. Even when he was as old as fifteen, we'd walk down the street holding hands. To this day, I can't believe he let me do that.

Parental Ignorance

I thought everything was just fine. I thought I was a success as a husband and father. What else would I think? I had a talented wife and two great kids, and we were living the American Dream in a big modern house in an affluent suburb. Life inside that house was more contentious than *Ozzie and Harriet*, but I knew the difference between a sitcom and reality. But I didn't recognize was my own ignorance. I was so oblivious to my own feelings, and to those of Kathy and the kids, that I didn't realize how much anger and resentment festered beneath the surface. I also didn't realize how much I didn't know about being a good parent. My close friend, Stella Kleinrock, the psychotherapist who recommended therapy with Dr. Jones, believes I didn't know how to parent because my own parents didn't know either, and therefore couldn't model it for me. "It was a very dysfunctional family," Stella said. "They had you working when you were ten years old. They never encouraged you to have friends. They never treated you like a child. They seemingly had no idea how to be parents."

She may be right. I've said a lot about my father already, and how he was more a business partner and mentor than a dad. Well, my mother wasn't exactly warm and wise like June Cleaver. At one point after I started therapy, I asked Dr. Jones if seeing a hypnotherapist would accelerate my understanding of my relationship with my mother. Dr. Jones referred me to a qualified therapist trained in hypnosis. I had a few sessions, and in one of them I was taken back in time to when I was three or four months old. What came up was a clear picture of my mother trying to suffocate me. She placed my plastic bib over my face and held it there so I couldn't breathe. My face turned purple. I saw myself in an ambulance, where an emergency squad brought me back to life.

Most of that actually happened. When I was three or four months old, something caused me to stop breathing and turn purple. An ambulance did come, and I did almost die. The part about my mother trying to suffocate me? That I don't really know. Obviously, it could have been pure imagination. Maybe some kind of accident took place, and I interpreted it subconsciously as a deliberate attempt to kill me. Maybe nothing like it actually occurred, and I converted some long-buried anger toward my mother into an image that seemed like an actual memory. Dr. Jones told me it doesn't matter whether that exact incident—or something like it—ever really happened. What matters is that, to some extent, my life was influenced by the unconscious assumption that I was so unwanted and unloved that I felt my mother may have wanted me dead.

Until that moment in hypnotherapy, I always thought my acting out as a kid was because I was born as a bad seed. Dr. Jones said no one is born bad, and that when kids behave badly and unleash the kind of vengeance I did, it's because something has happened to them. Whether the image that came up was literally true or not, hypnosis revealed something deep in my psyche that formed the basis of my difficulty trusting others and my negative behavior.

I don't know all the reasons I came up short as a father. I just know I did. I also know Kathy wasn't a great mother. In her case, the absence of parental role models was obvious. Good parents don't hide the fact that their child was adopted, and they certainly don't refuse to reveal her true parentage once the secret is out. I've always suspected Bill Nilsson had an extramarital affair with a woman who got pregnant and didn't want the child, and his wife was forced to adopt her. In my scenario, Lillian Nilsson, already in her forties, didn't really want the job of raising a constant reminder of her husband's infidelity, and Kathy felt that rejection and resentment every day of her youth. This makes sense to me, but we never found out for sure.

Besides those deficiencies in our upbringing, we were both pretty naïve. I won't speak for Kathy, but I had no idea what being a good parent entailed. I had some mighty big lessons to learn, and I didn't even know it. I learned those lessons the hard way when my kids were teenagers.

How My Children Saw It

While I was working on this book, Michelle and Marc sat down for a conversation about growing up in the Bookstein household. I'll let them tell their stories themselves.

"We didn't see our father very often," says Marc. "He left every morning at four-thirty to go jogging, and he would come home around ten or eleven at night after we were in bed. So the only time we really spent with him during the week was if we were able to stay awake at night. Sunday was our family day. But family day was not always a good experience. Most of the time there was arguing, bickering, fighting—not just my parents, but all four of us."

"That was the routine, especially during tax season," Michelle adds. As the older of the two, she also remembers this: "When the marriage started getting harder and harder, Dad started working more and more. He was unhappy, and work was his way of forgetting about everything else. I remember it getting kind of bad when I was around ten years old." That would have been 1988, six years before the Northridge quake.

"The arguing just seemed to escalate," Michelle says. "It seemed that they were disagreeing more often, and the more my mother wanted him around, the more he seemed to push her away and go to work. He'd keep himself busy and come up with excuses."

Michelle's memory is accurate. As things between Kathy and me grew more and more unpleasant, I started treating every season like tax season. I worked long hours every day, and I was AWOL from home much of the time. To a lesser extent, so was Kathy. "Our mom wasn't necessarily around a lot either," Marc recalls. "She was big into antiques and doll collecting, so she was out antiquing, or meeting people for dolls, or working on her collection."

"We were raised a lot by a housekeeper," Michelle adds. "We had a live-in from the time Marc was born." She's referring to Gladys Ramirez, a remarkable woman who lived in our home and worked for us for more than ten years. Marc and Michelle call her "amazing," and she was. "She was very caring, very affectionate, and she always made sure we were fed and well taken care of," says Marc. "And she didn't put up with our crap. We couldn't manipulate her the same way we could manipulate our parents."

"For the most part, our mother would pick us up from school and drop us off at the house, and then we'd go hang out with Gladys," Michelle explains. "She was like a third parent. We watched TV together, we played games, and we went swimming. And she kept the house clean and put us to bed."

Michelle also had another refuge. "I found escape in going to my grandmother's house," she says, referring to Kathy's mother. "I was very, very close with her. I went to see her as often as I could. She and my mother did not have a good relationship, but once I was born she was very much in the picture. She was already in her seventies then, and she became more present now that she had a baby granddaughter. When I was very little, my mother would drive me there in the morning, and Grandma would walk me to nursery school and then come and pick me up, and I'd stay there until my mom picked me up. So we had our alone time every day. And as I got older, I started spending some nights there, and sometimes weekends—basically as often as I could." Michelle and her grandmother (Kathy's mother) grew very close. I believe that hurt Kathy a great deal, because she was never close with her mother.

Michelle explains why she needed sanctuary: "There was always an underlying tension in our family. I didn't know much at ten years old, but I just remember feeling kind of uncomfortable. And we didn't see a lot of demonstrative behavior—not a lot of handholding or even pecks on the cheek between our parents. It was different from what I saw at friends' houses, where the parents were affectionate, and on TV shows. I could never quite understand why our family was so different."

Because he was the younger of the two, Marc has a slightly different take. "I thought fighting and blowups were normal," he said. "Normal to me was arguing and slamming doors or yelling across the house. I thought my friends' families were weird because they didn't do any of those things." Unlike Michelle, Marc did not find refuge with his grandmother. She was older by the time her grandson came along, and Marc's little-boy energy was too much for her to handle. "I was a little terror," Marc says, "so I was always jealous of Michelle's relationship with our grandmother." Michelle had that advantage, but she had the *dis*advantage of being old enough to know what was going on as her parents' marriage deteriorated. The bickering got louder and angrier, and the blowups occurred more frequently. As a result, both kids piled up a lot of anger and resentment.

Our family wasn't all bad, of course. We shared a good deal of warmth and affection as well. As Michelle and Marc remember it, the closeness was the reverse of the usual gender dynamic. "Michelle was Daddy's little girl and I was Momma's boy," says Marc. "We both had completely different relationships with our parents." What he describes next is something I was oblivious to at the time and came to regret very much: "I was always angry with my father because he couldn't take me to my baseball games or soccer practices. My mother took me everywhere I needed to go to. Dad would show up every now and then, but on Saturday he could get more work done instead of being at a baseball game. Every now and then he'd promise, 'I'll be there,' and he'd show up an hour late or even miss the game altogether. So I was always upset with him. My buddies' dads were there. Their whole families would be there watching them play, and it was just me and my mom."

Making things even worse for Marc, Michelle got to spend more time with me. Because she was older, she could stay up late enough to see me for a little while when I finally got home from work. "Also, my mother and I both had hobbies that involved collecting," Marc adds. "She did dolls and I did action figures and Hot Wheels. So we shared a passion for collecting, even though we were collecting totally different things. She drove me to all the toy stores, and we did trade shows together. My father wasn't interested in any of that stuff. He didn't understand it. So it was always me and my mom."

Of course, the main issue was that I was a classic workaholic who didn't make time for my children. Even Michelle, who felt close to me, didn't get to spend enough time with her father. Unfortunately, that meant *two* parents didn't pay much attention to her. "I always felt left out," she said. "Dad was always at work, and I felt that Mom loved Marc more than me, so I was like, okay, my parent is Gladys." Gladys and Kathy's mother filled the spaces in Michelle's life where her parents should have been.

I knew enough to *tell* my kids I loved them, but not enough to *show* it consistently. "I grew up understanding that you know somebody loves you if they buy you something," says Michelle. "Dad would say, 'I love you, I love you, I love you.' I'd hear it all the time, but he showed it with gifts, not his presence."

Adolescent Anguish

Michelle started acting out when she was twelve or thirteen. "I guess I figured it was payback time, and I was going to do my own thing," she recalls. "I started drinking and smoking pot and hanging out with a promiscuous crowd. Most of them were older than me. I guess I wanted attention. I was sick of being ignored." Her friends had access to drugs and alcohol, and to some extent so did Michelle. Kathy and I didn't drink, but we had a fully stocked bar in the house for company. "I would just get liquor from our bar," Michelle says, "until my brother ratted me out when I was fourteen."

That was an important moment. I wish I could say everything changed after that, but it didn't, and in some ways it only got worse. For me, this began a long period of education in parenting. Marc says he squealed for typical adolescent reasons: he wanted to hang out with his older sister and her friends, and they wouldn't let him, so he got revenge. "They were drinking in the driveway," he recalls, "and Michelle left in a car with an older guy who was drunk. I took the cup she was drinking from to my parents and said, 'Smell this. This is what Michelle was drinking, and she just left in a car.'"

That was a wake-up call, and we answered immediately. As Marc puts it, "They were actually decent parents when it came down to certain things." These were the pre-cell phone days, but fortunately we had given Michelle a pager for emergencies. We paged her and told her to come home immediately. Marc says, "My dad sat her down in the bedroom and made me sit there and watch so I would learn from it. Michelle was a vegetarian. She doesn't eat red meat. And Dad said, 'I want you to think about sausage, I want you to think about bacon.' He was trying to make her nauseous, so she'd throw up the alcohol. He dragged in a big trash can, and he made her puke into it. I was forced to sit there and watch even though I had nothing to do with it, to learn a lesson. And I did. I didn't try alcohol, or any kind of drugs until I was sixteen." He made up for lost time in a big way, but I'll get to that later.

Michelle says that night was a blur. "I remember throwing up, and I remember my parents made me sleep in between them that night, as if I were a three-year-old. You know: a total punishment."

Unfortunately, the family dysfunction ran deep, and we all had to go through a lot of hell before anyone learned what had to be learned. The deep anger Michelle felt did not go away. She kept on needing to escape. "I was pissed, and alcohol is numbing," she says. "When you're intoxicated, you don't have to think about all the crap. I would sneak out my window, jump off the roof, climb down the tree, and meet my friends to drink and smoke. I don't think my dad and mom ever knew the extent of it, although they had the cops over a few times to lecture me on the choices I was making and how I was going to end up."

Those visits by the local police were acts of desperation. They didn't work. In fact, they may have made Michelle act out even more. Marc recalls one night when he might have saved the house from burning down. "Michelle and a friend were smoking pot in the backyard," he says. "We lived on a hill with brush behind the house, and they lit it on fire. I ran barefoot up the hill from the pool with a bucket of water. I made like five or six trips before the fire went out, and they just sat there stoned, laughing at me. The whole house could have gone up in flames."

Things continued that way, with Kathy and me at a total loss for a solution. Michelle went to a public high school for one semester, then we transferred her to an expensive private school, hoping the more disciplined environment would straighten her out. Michelle calls it a joke, and the joke was on us. "They sent me to this prep school in the

Valley," she says. "Well, there were more drugs there than in Hollywood." About a year and a half later, with our daughter's life deteriorating even further, we told her, "You're going to boarding school." She didn't take us seriously, and for good reason. We'd threatened to send her away several times before and hadn't followed through. "I never believed they'd actually do it," says Michelle. "They'd always be threatening me and thinking up new punishments. Like, they'd take my personal phone out of my room. So, I'd go downstairs and unplug one of their phones and take it to my room. I'd keep switching out phones until they basically had to take out every phone in the house except the one in their bedroom. Sending me to boarding school was just another threat, so I laughed it off."

But this time we meant it. In 1994, shortly before Michelle's sixteenth birthday and shortly after I moved out of the house for what I thought was a temporary respite, we sent her to a strict therapeutic boarding school in a remote part of Northern California. That was far from the end of my troubles with my two children, however. In fact, Marc's difficult period hadn't even begun.

I Take Refuge at RBZ, and RBZ Takes Off

The tension between Kathy and me grew stronger by the day, as did our exasperation over Michelle and our concern for Marc. My business life went in the exact opposite direction. Throughout the eighties, the company diversified and expanded. So did my business interests outside the firm, and that success often enriched RBZ clients and my partners as well. My personal worth and the company's profits kept growing. As I've said, I worked ridiculously long hours all my life. Now, with things being so bad at home, I worked even harder. This pattern was the reverse of most people's lives: home was toil and trouble, and the office was my sanctuary.

I want to emphasize, however, that work was not an escape. I didn't work long hours just to get away from home, the way some guys escape to bars or casinos. I *loved* my work. I had *always* worked long hours, and I still do even though my home life now is deeply satisfying and my family is the most important thing in my life. I spend all that time at work because I love doing what I do, and I do it exceptionally well. And I get paid exceptionally well to do what I love. How lucky can a guy get?

It's like getting paid to do your hobby. The truth is, I can't imagine life without the passion I bring to my work. (More on that in Chapter 15.)

RBZ's success was built on a strong combination of proficiency at accounting and smart management policies, which added up to an extraordinary corporate culture. "Harvey did something I consider remarkable, building that firm the way he has," Steve Berlinger said. "I would say he is as good as Kenneth Leventhal was, or better, as an 'accountant businessman.' He's built a very fine, good-sized regional accounting firm. There are bigger firms, and there are much smaller firms. But RBZ is considered one of the best companies to work for. I think the way the firm is managed, the way they motivate their people to work, and how they compensate them is unique. In most firms, the top guys are like pigs at the trough when it comes to splitting the profits. Harvey's compensation plan is the opposite, and it comes out to be a very fair system."

I'll explain that system later. Here, I want to emphasize that we set out to create an environment that would attract and keep great talent, and we accomplished exactly that. In 1985, for example, we brought in the first of many younger accountants. Tom Schulte had been with Arthur Andersen LLP, which at the time was one of the "Big Five" national accounting firms and probably the best known of the lot (except for maybe Price Waterhouse, which tabulated the Academy Award ballots). Tom became RBZ's managing partner, a position he filled with great agility for ten important years. He is a great example of the importance of finding people with skills we needed, and then empowering them to do their jobs well.

Tom is also a great example of how a little notoriety can go a long way. We were casting around informally for new blood, and Tom was interested in us because he'd heard we were a small niche firm that wanted to diversify its offerings. As Tom put it, "I was looking for a way out of a firm where I had to work six days a week and show up on weekends whether I had something to do or not, just to make the right appearance because I aspired to be a partner." After meeting with Ted and Dave, he was interested in RBZ but not quite sold. Then he came to meet me on a Saturday at my house. The first thing he said when he walked in the door was, "Are you the Harvey Bookstein from *What Really Happened to the Class of '65?*" I couldn't believe my ears. It turns out he'd read the book about ten years earlier, and the character he remembered most was the class nerd who was tormented by his classmates and went on to do exceedingly well for himself. To him, I was almost a celebrity.

"You're too young to have read that book," I said.

"I'm an old soul," Tom replied.

Our rapport was instant. Here's how Tom remembers that initial meeting: "We spent a lot of time talking about our different high school experiences. I asked him about all the different people from the book. This was more interesting and enjoyable than the usual interview." One reason it was interesting was because we were total opposites in our high school years. "I was the class car guy, a jock and a surfer," said Tom, "like the guys who tormented Harvey. Only I was a little bit different because, for some reason, I always took care of the underdogs. I was always making sure they didn't get jammed into lockers by other guys. I stood up for them: 'Don't dump their books unless you want to dump my books first.'"

Something about the rapport we established in my home convinced me that Tom was the right guy for the job. What was the job? Mainly, growing the firm's client base. This worked out incredibly well, but it was rough going at first because Tom's arrival touched a lot of raw nerves inside RBZ.

We'd just gone through a rough patch, and we'd been forced to lay off some good people. Here's how Tom recalls his welcome: "I wasn't greeted with open arms. A lot of people had lost their friends in the layoff, and all of a sudden they're bringing in somebody who's probably well paid and appears to be taking the place of those people. My picture was posted out front, with 'Welcome Tom Schulte' on it, and somebody ripped it off the wall and put it in the urinal. They weren't very happy to see me."

The reaction was understandable, but what those resentful staff members didn't comprehend was that we brought Tom aboard precisely *because* business hadn't been good. We were still primarily a real estate firm, and while specializing is a great idea, being a one-trick pony in a fast-changing world is not. It was clearly time to diversify, and I sensed Tom had the right mix of technical know-how and entrepreneurial spirit to drive that process. That he was daring enough to walk away from a partner track at one of the top five accounting firms in the country was a big plus. One reason he was willing to take his chances with us, Tom said, was his sense that RBZ "lived and breathed the entrepreneurial approach." In that spirit, we were willing to invest in Tom at a time when we had to let other people go. We needed to broaden the niche we occupied, and he was the right person to help us do it. He had done both technical work and marketing at Arthur Andersen, and was eager to do more of the latter. His mandate was to bring in more business, and he did just that, despite the rocky start with some of our employees.

"Without Harvey supporting me through all that, it would have been tough to continue," Tom recalled. "But he made it very clear that I had his vote. And he told me to do whatever I thought it would take. He didn't micromanage me. He just said, 'Go out there and do it, however you need to do it.' That's what allowed me to get done what I had to get done."

The process came down to teaming up with the right people and trusting them enough to let them be themselves. As for the people who were antagonistic to Tom when he arrived, some came around and adapted well to the new direction the company took; others quit or were fired. At one point, we gave Tom the authority to recruit and hire new people. He remembers it this way: "Harvey said, 'I'm not going to be around as long as you will, so hire the kind of people you want to work with for the rest of your career.' So I got to bring in people who had both the right and the left sides of the brain going at the same time. They could do the technical work, but they also had the personalities to help market the firm and create a different kind of culture around here."

That new company culture eventually became one of RBZ's distinguishing features. Our culture is why we enjoy such a stellar reputation among accounting firms, and some of the policies and practices we developed have been widely imitated.

Oddly enough, the bond Tom and I shared with *The Class of '65* has remained a boon through all our years of working together. "Harvey and I aren't always on the same page," says Tom. "But I always think about the poor high school nerd getting stuffed into a locker, and I think, 'Man, he's come from a different place than I came from, and look at what he's done.' For some reason, that always grounds me a little bit in dealing with Harvey."

Coincidence? Good luck? Karma? Whatever it was, I'm grateful we had what it took to convince a great guy with the right skills to join our team. This was one of many examples of things going just right in business, at the same time things at home were going down the tubes. Throughout the eighties and the first half of the nineties, my personal life stayed on the opposite trajectory of my business life. If you charted my level of happiness and fulfillment in each, the arrow would point sharply uphill in business and steeply downhill at home.

Chapter 10
When Harvey Met Harriet

In October, 1994, about three months after I moved into my apartment, I walked into an office building in Sherman Oaks. As I entered, someone I knew was leaving through the same door. Her name was Harriet Miller, and she was about to change my life forever.

I'd known Harriet since 1970, when I worked at Kenneth Leventhal & Company and she was married to one of my co-workers, Michael Miller. Kathy and I often ran into them at company functions and other social events. In fact, they attended our wedding. Even after Michael and I left Leventhal, the two couples remained friends. We spent a weekend in Las Vegas together in 1972, and in the 1980s we were part of a gourmet cooking group that met every other month to share a special meal together. When Harriet and Michael separated in 1990, our friendship basically ended. I remember running into Harriet in 1994, shortly after the earthquake, when I was with my family at the Cheesecake Factory. After that, Harriet and Kathy spoke occasionally, in person and on the phone. Harriet later told me that Kathy shared with her that our marriage wasn't going well. They also got together after I moved out, at which time Harriet expressed the hope that Kathy and I would work things out and get back together.

Harriet and I were bound to meet again, but the way we bumped into each other that day had an element of kismet to it. She worked in the building and she was leaving through an exit she didn't normally use, because her normal route was blocked by workers doing earthquake repairs. Later, I always thought that was perfect, because I was busy at the time doing earthquake repairs to my psyche and Harriet would end up playing a major role in that process. Our exchange was brief and casual—the usual "What's going on? How are you doing?" kind of thing—but I ended by saying, "I'll call you." Harriet says her thought at the time was, "Yeah, okay, whatever."

I called her the next day. I can't say I had romance on my mind—not consciously anyway—even though I'd always found Harriet attractive. I just knew I wanted to talk to her. I'd always liked her. She was a smart, solid, no-nonsense person who understood where I came from and the world I inhabited. Not only had she been married to an accounting colleague, she herself is a trained, highly competent bookkeeper. Plus, she knew Kathy, she'd met my kids, and she recently went through a divorce herself. Sure enough, talking with her was as easy, comfortable, and natural as any conversation I'd ever had.

After the initial phone call we spoke from time to time. I called her, and sometimes she called me. I remember her calling around Thanksgiving to see how I was doing, because she knew how difficult that time of year can be when you're recently separated. In fact, Thanksgiving was the worst day I'd experienced during my separation. We talked about everything, from the important to the trivial, from the profound to the ridiculous, and we laughed about our lives. "I was just trying to be supportive of somebody who was having a difficult time, because I'd been down that road myself," Harriet says about that period. "I wasn't thinking about anything else."

Our First Date

In February 1995, just over a year after the earthquake, and four months after we'd become close friends on the phone, I called Harriet and said, "How would you like to go out on a real date?" She said yes. "I kiss on the first date," I told her. Harriet replied, "I only hold hands on the first date." We laughed, and set a date for February 21. I know that was the date because I recorded it in the journal I'd started keeping a few months earlier, at the suggestion of Dr. Jones. The first entry in that journal reads: "I decided to start writing this diary, as I now need to attempt to observe my progress and try to understand my feelings and progress to overall happiness. The last couple of days have been probably some of the toughest ever." Harriet was a godsend in that troubled time.

I took her to dinner at an Italian restaurant on the Third Street Promenade in Santa Monica, not far from my apartment. Harriet confirms that even though I asked her out I still had every intention of going back to Kathy at the time. She remembers asking how I was doing, and my answer was, "Not great, but I think eventually I'll be going back home."

"That will be good for you and your family," she replied.

But going back home wasn't in the cards.

Harriet says she was excited and nervous before our date. "I had no idea what your intention was," she tells me. "It was just dinner. I don't recall having any ulterior motive. I wasn't thinking, 'I'm going to get my hooks into him,' or anything. But I was still very excited, because there was something about you that I always liked, and the anticipation was unbelievable." Our connection was so deep and warm and comfortable that when we left the restaurant I found myself wanting to hold her hand. So I did, and I swear I felt some sort of electrical or chemical reaction.

I invited her to come up for "a little bit," to see my beautiful penthouse with the ocean view. She said okay and that "little bit" became a lot. When she left, it was almost four in the morning. For the record, there was no hanky-panky. We just talked and talked and talked, with only one interruption: in a great role reversal, Harriet's daughter, Roni paged her at about two o'clock in the morning, because she was worried about her mom and wanted to know when she'd be coming home. Roni was twenty-three at the time. I can easily calculate her age because Harriet was pregnant with her at my wedding to Kathy.

Like Roni, I felt protective of Harriet, and when she finally left my apartment I asked her to call me when she got home. She thought I was being ridiculous, but I persisted until she promised to call. She did, and before we hung up the phone, I said, "I'll call you tomorrow." Harriet recalls thinking, "Yeah, sure." She adds: "I thought it would be like when you go to a disco, and it looks so great at night, with the ball turning and everybody having a good time, and the next day, when they're cleaning up, it's just a dumpy little place with crummy carpeting, and the magic is gone. I thought that's what it would be like when you woke up in the morning: 'What was I thinking? I'm not interested in her.'"

I sure was interested, and when I called she seemed genuinely surprised. I was shocked that she was shocked. "I told you I'd call," I said. She has since learned that I always keep my word.

Seeing What Had to Be Done

The mind works in strange ways. I honestly believed I had a 99 percent certainty of returning to my marriage. But it turns out that even before that date with Harriet my subconscious knew better. In my journal, I'd written that I hated being alone, but I'd probably be better off alone forever than staying in such a bad marriage. Dr. Jones's prescription for me—candlelight, soft music, sitting on my terrace and looking at the ocean, thinking about my wants and needs instead of my duties—had made me feel safer and more comfortable by myself than I'd ever felt before. Not that I liked it. I didn't. I knew I wasn't cut out for solitude or the single-guy lifestyle. But at least being alone was somewhat peaceful: no arguing, fighting, or screaming. I'd become accustomed to a life in which whoever screamed the loudest that day was the winner, and I realized such an environment is extremely toxic for kids. Kathy and I were causing Michelle and Marc so much psychological pain they'd probably be better off if we split up.

Nevertheless, even though I had those realizations, I assumed I'd find a way to reconcile with Kathy and go back home. Deep inside I was probably not convinced I'd be okay by myself. The truth is, I believed I was unlovable. I told myself: "Why the hell would anyone want to be with this short, little nerd?" I was afraid I'd end up a lonely old man. I remember saying to a client of mine, an architect named Herb Nadel, "Who's going to want to date me?"

Herb's reply was right on the nose: "You're living in high school. High school girls want the quarterback. But *you're* the quarterback now. You are the Six Million Dollar Man."

I wasn't buying it. "I'm nobody," I told Herb. "I'm nothing." My attitude was the opposite of "the grass is always greener." As difficult as my relationship with Kathy was, I feared I'd have *no* relationship if I divorced her—or, if I did, the new marriage would be even worse.

"You have no idea what you're talking about," said Herb. "You're going to find women begging to go out with you. You're successful.

You're kind. You're generous." He went on, telling me all the qualities grown-up women, unlike high school girls, want in a man, and insisting that I had those qualities. "You don't get it," he kept on saying. "You just don't get it."

He was right. I didn't get it. What he said made me feel good, but I didn't believe him.

The fear that no one would want me was a big reason I couldn't do what I knew I had to do: get a divorce. What if my life with Kathy was as good as it gets? Maybe I'd be dumb to expect any better. Thoughts like those arose in my weaker moments. But in my stronger moments, I knew the words in my diary were true: I'd be happier alone than staying in the battle zone that was my home.

Dating Harriet changed everything. Now I had concrete proof that Herb and Dr. Jones and others who cared about me were right: someone *would* want to be with me. Not just *someone*, but an attractive, strong, smart, kind, generous, compassionate, capable woman, who knew my weaknesses as well as my strengths. Harriet knew all about the baggage I brought with me. She even understood the profession I was dedicated to. What more proof did I need?

I felt like a kid with a crush on the best girl in class, and she surprised me by reciprocating. We went out two more times that first week, and each date was better than the last. One night we went to Old Town in Pasadena for dinner and walked around in the rain. Another night we had dinner with my dear friends Dan and Linda Rosenson—the same Linda who asked me why I stayed with a wife who treated me badly in public.

Perhaps symbolically, we dined in a restaurant called Truly Yours. Later that night, I said something bold to Harriet: "I'd like to have an exclusive relationship." I went on to say, in all honesty, "I don't know if I'm on the rebound. I don't know if this is real. I can't commit to anything else. I can't promise you anything, so don't put all your bets on me. My son Marc is having his Bar Mitzvah soon, and I don't want anything to get in the way of that. But I would like to have an exclusive relationship."

Harriet simply said, "Okay." Looking back on it now, she recalls, "Within those two or three dates, I could see myself being with you. Michael and I were separated in 1990, and divorced in '92. He had already remarried. So here it was, 1995, and I was open to having a relationship again. I figured I would take you at your word about wanting an exclusive relationship. I felt you meant it."

Letting Go

It's rare that I procrastinate on anything. As any of my colleagues will testify, in business I have a go-for-it mentality. I zero in, assess the situation, make a decision, and take action. I don't do a lot of mulling, and I sometimes lose patience with people who approach things more deliberately and cautiously. I make quick decisions, usually following my gut, and my track record over the years proves this rapid-fire style works for me. But telling Kathy our marriage was over was an exception. I knew what had to be done—move from separation to divorce—but I couldn't bring myself to move forward.

Then Kathy forced my hand. Someone she knew saw me out with Harriet. Kathy called and asked me outright if I was dating her friend. I said I was. That was it. No explanation, no details. If she'd asked whether I'd slept with Harriet, things might have been awkward, because I *had* slept with her but not in the way that expression implies. I'd slept in her bed, and she slept in mine. But we hadn't yet made love. We started out kind of old-fashioned in that way, and that was fine with me. I just knew I liked waking up with Harriet nearby.

Kathy didn't ask about that, but she was furious, and from the sound of it she seemed to be angrier at the prospect of losing her friend than losing her husband. Later, she would tell Marc and Michelle I had an affair with Harriet while I was still living with the family. I don't know if she truly believed it, or if she wanted to convince our kids it was true as an act of vengeance toward me. But it wasn't true. Honesty compels me to say that I *did* have two affairs while I was still living with Kathy. I was feeling unfulfilled, and when opportunities came my way I was weak enough to take advantage of them. I regret that, and I learned hard lessons from the experience. But it just wasn't so in Harriet's case.

I called Kathy a few days after she confronted me about dating Harriet. I asked her to meet me in a park in the Valley. The time had come to tell her I couldn't possibly return to the marriage, and I knew it would be easier to do in a public place than in the home we shared for so long. To say she wasn't shocked would be an understatement. She surprised me, however, by practically begging me to give her another chance. She admitted she was wrong. She said she'd been "sick"—

meaning emotionally distraught—and would work at trying to make things better. I appreciated that very much, but I knew I had to move on.

About a week later, Kathy informed me she'd filed divorce papers. I was relieved she'd taken that burden off my hands. She said the divorce proceedings would be completed in about six months. Yeah, right! It took about twenty months to finalize the divorce, and as we'll see later, that wasn't the final bell; negotiations over property and finances dragged on for another nine months. I would have a good laugh about how far off Kathy's prediction was, except the memory of bitter squabbles, tense negotiations, and through-the-roof legal expenses are so painful I can't find any humor in it.

Something about the reality of divorce triggered a period of rapid change and personal growth. Three months after Kathy filed the initial papers I moved from Santa Monica to an apartment in the Valley—Sherman Oaks to be exact—where I could be closer to both my son Marc and Harriet (Michelle was away at boarding school). I fell more and more in love each day, and before long I knew I wanted to share the rest of my life with her. But we had to settle for nights at either my place or hers, because I refused to live together while I was still legally married.

Closure and Proposal

The day I learned my divorce was finalized, November 13, 1996, I felt giddy as a teenager, and I concocted a special way of telling Harriet the news. I'll let her tell the story:

"I never pushed Harvey to get married. I didn't want to be in a position where he could come back to me one day and say, 'I really didn't want this, but I did it because of you.' In fact, he was always the one who would say he'd like to get married.

"On November 12, the day before his divorce was finalized, Harvey was acting strange. He had trouble sleeping. He was very restless. I kept asking him 'Is everything okay?'

He said 'Yes, there's just a lot going on. I've got this case, and I have to go to court and be a witness.'

The next morning, a Wednesday, I called him when I got to work to see how he was doing before he went into court. He heard my voice and hung up. But in those days there were so many bad cell phone connections, I assumed we got disconnected. I think I called twice, and then I just let it go and waited to hear from him. About ten thirty or eleven o'clock, I went to the restroom, and when I got back there was a policeman standing in the lobby. No one else was around, so I said, 'Can I help you?' He said, 'Yeah, I'm looking for Harriet Miller.'

"I got scared. I thought, 'Oh my God, why did I open my mouth?' So I told him I was Harriet Miller, and he said, 'Well, I have some paperwork I need to show you in my car, if you'll come with me.' So I got my glasses and walked with him down this long hallway. He asked me questions, a lot of personal questions. It was weird. He knew I had a son and a daughter, he knew what kind of car I drove, and then he said, 'And are you dating Harvey Bookstein?' At that point, I was done. No more questions. I said, 'What's this paperwork you have for me?' Out in the parking lot he walked to an unmarked car, and told me to stand in front of it. Then he took out an envelope and handed it to me. I opened it, and all I could see was 'Plaintiff,' 'Defendant,' 'Claims.' My head was spinning. I'm not well versed on legal documents, and I had no idea what he was showing me.

"He said, 'Maybe this will explain it,' and handed me an envelope. In it, on Harvey's personal stationery, was something like, 'My Dearest Harriet, I'm a free man.' I had no idea what that meant. Did they take him to jail? I couldn't wrap my head around what was going on. So I asked the cop, 'What does this mean?' He said, 'Harvey wanted me to tell you he is now divorced.' I was like, 'Oh, my God. You're kidding!'

"He said, 'No, and here's this long-stemmed red rose he wants you to have.'

"Harvey had hired a policeman to come to my office dressed in uniform and driving an unmarked car.

"I was stunned. I started to cry. I was beside myself. The guy said, 'That's quite some way to tell you, isn't it?' I'll say it was! He asked me if there was anything I'd like to say to Harvey. 'Just that I love him with all my heart.' And he said, 'Why don't you say it yourself, because there's a camera right over there.' He pointed to a van. Hidden inside was a guy with a camera. It turns out the policeman was wearing a wire and had recorded our entire conversation, from the time he came into the office. So I repeated what I'd said to the camera, and gave the cop a big hug goodbye.

"Meanwhile, my boss was concerned about me because he saw me with a policeman, so he was waiting in the lobby of the building. Not only that, the whole office stood at the windows watching what was going on. When I told my boss what happened, he said, 'Oh my God, that Harvey always has something going on.'

"I called Harvey at his office. He answered as if nothing had happened: 'Hi, what's going on?'

'What do you mean, what's going on?'

'Yeah, what's up? What's the matter?'

'I can't believe you did this.'

"He kept playing dumb. 'What do you mean? Did what?'

"It went on like that for a while. Finally, he said, 'I wanted you to have something to remember this day by. I didn't want to just tell you.'

"He had bifurcated his divorce, and he hadn't told me."

Let me break in here and explain what bifurcation means. There are three aspects to a divorce settlement: alimony and child support, division of assets, and legal divorce. In California law, a couple can come to an agreement on any one of those three components and close that particular chapter. It's a way of moving forward when there is difficulty reaching an agreement on the other aspects. Bifurcate essentially means, "Judge, I can't wait anymore." That's how I felt. I was eager to be divorced, and the contentious negotiation over assets threatened to drag on forever. Actually, bifurcating was Harriet's idea. She brought up the possibility at one point when I voiced my frustration with the proceedings. At the time I said, "I'll have to look into it." Neither one of us mentioned it again. Harriet didn't want to interfere, and once I decided to bifurcate I thought it best to keep things quiet until the deal was done, so I didn't raise false expectations. Plus, I'm a big fan of surprises. Back to Harriet:

"We were going to a charity event that night, and I met him there. Of course, he was telling everybody he was finally divorced, and of course the next words out of everybody's mouth were, 'So, when are you guys getting married?' He put his arm around me and said, 'Well, I don't know. I might want to try out this single life. I might like it.' I looked at him and said, 'Well, that's fine, but don't expect me to wait around while you enjoy yourself.' And he kind of laughed, and that was that.

Two days later, on Friday, we went out for dinner. He came to my house a little early, and while were getting ready to go, the doorbell rang. It was a limo driver. He said, 'Harriet Miller? I'm here to pick up the two of you for dinner.' There were a dozen long-stemmed roses in the back seat. We drove to the Twin Palms in Pasadena, and on the way Harvey said, 'I kind of like this. Maybe I'll start dating and hire limos to take me places.'

"'Whatever you want,' I said. 'If that's what you like doing.' He seemed nervous in the limo. He didn't let me sit too close to him. I found out later it was because he didn't want me to feel what was in his jacket pockets.

"In the restaurant we ordered drinks, and we were sitting and talking and having a nice dinner, and then they brought out this big chocolate dessert. Harvey knew I loved chocolate. I started eating it, and all of a sudden my fork touched something very hard. I felt around with my hand, and pulled out a heart-shaped box. Harvey dropped to his knee and proposed. Of course, I said yes.

"Before I opened the box, he stopped me and started to say something. I said, 'I know, if I don't like it I can take it back.' Whenever he gave me anything, it was always, 'If you don't like it, I'd rather you take it back. I don't want you to have something you're not going to use, or wear, or whatever.' But this time he said, 'This belonged to my Bubbe'—the Yiddish word for grandmother—'and I want you to have it.'

"It was an old antique-looking ring with little stones in a black mounting. It wasn't what I would have picked out as an engagement ring, but it had belonged to his grandmother, so I was thrilled. Then he said to me, 'Or would you rather have this?' And he slapped a second box down on the table. I didn't know what to say. 'This box comes with a condition,' he said. What was the condition? 'That we have an elopetion.'

"I said, 'What's an elopetion?'

"'We go away and elope, with just the family.'

"I said, 'okay, that works for me.' I opened the box and saw my beautiful engagement ring—a 2.78 solitaire diamond surrounded by baguettes, set in eighteen-karat yellow gold. We had seen the same kind of mounting in a store, and Harvey took a jeweler to see it, to make the ring exactly as we'd seen it. I was stunned.

"Meanwhile, people at other tables were looking at us, and someone sent over drinks, and the whole thing was recorded. Harvey had someone shoot it with a video camera, although the video portion didn't come out, just the audio.

"It turns out he concocted the story about his grandma's ring, just to have fun. It was actually a piece of junk with fake diamonds, and it looked a lot worse when we were out of the dimly lit restaurant. The truth is, I was so happy to be engaged to the man I wanted to spend the rest of my life with that I didn't care what kind of ring I got. But that's why he was nervous in the limo: he had the ring box in his pocket.

"We called my two children and my father from the restaurant. They were all thrilled. On the way home, we stopped in Tarzana and drove my father around for a while, just to celebrate with him. Later on, Harvey said, 'Actually, we don't have to have an elopetion. You can have this ring and you can also have a wedding.' And we did, the following July."

So, two days after my divorce was finalized, I was engaged. The next weekend, I moved into Harriet's house in Van Nuys, and the following Thursday I had the happiest Thanksgiving of my life.

Chapter 11
Building a New Family

*H*arriet and I were married on July 12, 1997, four days before her
fiftieth birthday. The wedding, black tie optional, took place on
an outdoor patio at what was then the Park Hyatt Hotel in Century
City. About 150 guests attended, including my two children (Michelle
was almost nineteen; Marc was almost fifteen), and Harriet's two
children (Roni was twenty-five and Joel was twenty). Marc and Joel
served as ushers, and Roni was Harriet's maid of honor. Michelle chose
not to participate in the ceremony; she felt it would be a betrayal of her
mother.

The event was wonderful in every detail, but the part almost every
guest brings up to this day is the pajama story. The officiant, Rabbi
Donald Goor, had to arrive on the late side because he had another
appointment, so we changed the usual order of things to have cocktails
and hors d'oeuvres before the ceremony. Since we wanted to observe
the tradition of the groom not seeing the bride in her full regalia before
she walks down the aisle, Harriet and I wore something special for the
pre-ceremony reception: matching cotton pajamas, one blue-on-white,
the other white-on-blue, and slippers—mine black velvet with a gold
emblem and Harriet's off-white with sequins. We made quite a picture,
with the bride and groom in pj's, surrounded by men in tuxedos and
women in fancy dresses. I should say this was an *unforgettable* sight,
since no one seems to have forgotten it.

Two other moments stand out in my memory. As part of the ceremony, Harriet and I would each take a small candle and light one common candle with them, as a symbol of two lives uniting as one. But the wind blew so hard we couldn't get the candles to stay lit. We treated the mishap more as an amusement than a problem, and moved ahead without the candles. The other unanticipated disturbance came from an earsplitting alarm that went off in the property adjacent to the hotel: the studios of 20th Century Fox. That alarm rang almost through the entire wedding.

We managed to get through the ceremony despite the distractions, and I said "I do" to my second wife almost exactly three years after I moved away from my first. In addition to making me a husband again, the marriage also made me a son-in-law, a brother-in-law, and a stepfather. Harriet's two great kids were still living with her when I moved in eight months before the wedding, and we became close from the start. I think having them in my life took away some of the pain I felt about not living with Marc and Michelle. I wasn't completely without children to serve as a parent. From the beginning, I let them know I was there to support them, like a third parent. I never attempted to take on the role of their father. Their actual father, my former colleague Michael Miller, stayed very much in their lives, and I made sure never to interfere with their relationship. To this day, the relationship between our family and Michael's remains cordial, and Roni and Joel have always stayed close to their dad. I became another older, wiser person in their lives—someone who cared about them and to whom they could tell things they wouldn't necessarily tell their mother or father. They quickly learned they would always get my honest opinion. They didn't always like my opinions, but they respected the fact that I wouldn't be a yes person. When they asked for guidance, I gave it, honestly and candidly, and always based on what I thought was best for them.

Before we were married, Harriet and I agreed we would treat our stepdaughters and stepsons like our own children. In fact, creating the strong sense that we are now one big family was so important to us that we took the unusual step of bringing three of our four kids with us on our honeymoon, a twelve-day cruise in Europe. It would have been all four, except Michelle chose not to come. In fact, Marc almost didn't make it either. Although she had approved earlier, at the last moment Kathy objected to him joining us, so strenuously and so stubbornly that

I had to take the issue to court. Thankfully, the judge ruled in our favor and Marc was allowed to come, along with Roni and Joel.

Successfully creating a combined family is one of the proudest achievements in my life. Joel lived with us until August 1998, when he went to the University of Nevada, Las Vegas. Roni stayed until the following June, when she was about to marry her husband, Jeff. As I'll describe later, Marc lived with us at certain points as well. I can't say it was always easy, or we were one big Brady Bunch. But we never wavered from our commitment to treat all four children as equals, and the various relationships among them, and between them and us, have worked out better than we could have hoped at the beginning. I take great pleasure in every greeting card Roni and Jeff send me; they're always addressed "to the most generous infuriating man we know."

Death and Divorce

As I write this, I've been married for fifteen years, and I feel profoundly blessed. At the time I separated from Kathy, I couldn't have imagined my personal life would ever be this fulfilling. I was wrong for two reasons. One is that Harriet and I are more compatible than Kathy and I. The second is that I became a different man. As I've said, the Northridge earthquake marked the beginning of a profound personal transformation. That process was still in its early stages when I married Harriet, and I often thought she was either crazy or a saint to marry the guy I was at that time. Of course, she isn't a saint, and she sure wasn't crazy; she was just an extremely perceptive woman with a heart of gold, who saw things in me I didn't know existed.

The transformation process was all for the good, but I'd be lying if I said it was easy. Change can be hard, especially if you're learning about yourself while also mending fences with people you love and cleaning up messes you helped to create. I was dealing with a lot of baggage during my first few years with Harriet.

In 1991, my father died a difficult death at age sixty-nine. His passing marked the merciful end of a long and painful process. He had diabetes, and over time he lost body parts and bodily functions piece by piece. A leg was amputated, then the second leg and a finger. Then he lost the use of his kidneys. He was on dialysis in a nursing home at the end, with his eyesight going fast. At one point, the doctors said there was nothing more to be done and recommended we take him off dialysis. His wife, my stepmother Marlene, consulted with me, and together we gave our consent. My father died about a week later. The loss was difficult, and I can still feel the tremendous influence he had on my life. In my heart, I work under the Bookstein & Son banner, even though that company never came to be.

I didn't make the grieving period any easier with my eulogy at my dad's memorial service. I spoke honestly and from my heart, and Marlene was hurt by some of the things I said. Specifically, I spoke about how upset I'd been when my father married her only six weeks after my mother's death. I also said my dad had certain shortcomings as a father. Even though I also praised him, especially for being a great professional role model, and even though I described how I grew to love Marlene after their marriage, the negative statements badly upset her. Later, I came to understand her reaction and to regret what I had said. Marlene and I grew closer than we ever were when my father was alive. I became her advisor and took care of all her financial affairs—without charge, of course—until she passed away on March 31, 2004.

The first part of my marriage to Harriet was blemished by my inability to finalize a financial agreement with Kathy. The process dragged on for what seemed like forever, and at times it got ugly. In Kathy's eyes I somehow changed overnight from an honest, trustworthy person to a greedy ex-husband trying to cheat her out of every penny. In a sense, I can understand her mistrust. After all, I was a financial expert by training and she could barely balance a checkbook. If I had wanted to cheat her, I certainly knew how. Ripping her off was frankly not on my agenda, but there seemed no way to persuade her that I wanted to be fair. I was accused of concealing my true financial worth, when in fact I put everything I owned on my list of assets and every cent I earned in my statement of income. But Kathy and her attorney assumed I would hide whatever I could get away with. For example, I had loaned my partner, Ted Roth, $200,000 because he needed a temporary infusion of cash. He quickly paid it back, and the deposit showed up in my bank statement. Kathy's lawyer used that deposit as evidence I was trying to hide income, totally ignoring the check I had written for the loan even though it appeared on the same bank statement as the deposit. We went through the same rigmarole over another loan too.

Kathy's lawyer was too smart and sophisticated not to have seen the deposits were loan repayments, not income. But he was a street fighter, and I'm sure he pulled stunts like that just to get his opponents so aggravated they'd either make a mistake or accept a bad settlement just to get it over with. I was not the type to be intimidated. I chose to fight back, and sadly, the hostilities escalated. It didn't have to be that way. Kathy's first attorney was a decent woman who wanted to settle our case agreeably and fairly. My first attorney was the same kind of person, and the two of them had worked out reasonable agreements in the past. But Kathy felt she wasn't being adequately protected, so she took on a more ruthless lawyer. I had to match fire with fire, so I hired a cutthroat attorney as well. That's how the income of divorce attorneys rises and their reputations sink.

As with many aspects of my personal life, I learned a lot from the divorce fiasco, and I integrated those lessons into my new identity as a therapeutic accountant. Now, when a client goes through a divorce, I tell them this: "Your spouse might end up with too big a share of your assets, but he or she can't take your brain. However, you can lose your brain all by yourself if you get caught up in the battle and start looking for revenge and victory at all costs. It's one thing to lose some of your assets; it's another thing to lose your dignity, your integrity, and your self-respect."

That's how I got through my nasty divorce. I kept telling myself, "She may get all your money, but she can't take your brain. So be careful, or you'll lose your brain anyway."

Now, when my clients get angry and bitter and vengeful, I tell them, "You're losing your brain." Sometimes they argue with me. They rant about their soon-to-be ex-spouses: "She's doing it!" "It's all his fault!" "She wants to take everything I'm worth!"

I say, "You may lose some money; you may lose some things; you may have to give away more than you think your ex is entitled to; but you'll be all right as long as you still have the brains to go forward."

I also tell them the freedom to start a new life is priceless. I will pay alimony to Kathy for the rest of my life, unless she passes away first or remarries. The truth is, I do not resent that obligation like many divorced men do. Each check I write to her is a reminder that divorce gave me the opportunity to have a new and better life. So, when men complain about alimony, I ask them, "How much would you pay for a new heart that preserves your life?" They have to admit there's no price too big for that. Which is exactly how I feel about my divorce.

I also often advise clients to use a mediator instead of divorce lawyers—not just because it's less costly, but because it reduces stress and strain. With the right mediator, you can save a fortune—not only in money, but also in time, energy, and emotional turmoil. Plus, with one person representing both sides, the process is totally transparent. There are fewer secrets, because virtually anything one party says to the mediator can be told to the spouse. But I didn't even suggest mediation to Kathy while our lawyers were going at it. There was one simple reason for that: I knew she wouldn't go along. I had so much more knowledge of finance, investments, and the law that she was afraid I'd take advantage of her if she didn't have an expert professional who could stand toe to toe with me.

The divorce was hell, but it all seemed worth it the day we signed the papers. Now I could get on with my new life with Harriet. However, I still had emotional turmoil to deal with and deep wounds to heal.

Heartbreaks and Mistakes

The hardest part of the divorce was seeing my relationships with Michelle and Marc deteriorate and eventually bottom out—partly because the kids digested Kathy's anger toward me almost daily with their breakfast cereal. Things became so bad at one point that I was in the dark about my own children's lives, because Kathy wouldn't answer my letters or take my phone calls. I had to appeal to the court for a remedy. The judge came up with a clever solution: Kathy was ordered to get a fax machine, so she could communicate without having to talk to me directly. That didn't work either. "No one ordered me to plug it in," Kathy said, so initially she wouldn't use the machine, which I paid for.

My ex-wife's anger was in many respects justified: I had broken my marriage contract, and as she repeatedly told the children, an honorable businessman like me should not arbitrarily ignore "for better or for worse" as if it meant nothing. Understandably, the kids came to see me as a selfish guy who betrayed their mother and broke up their family. Some of what they were told was false, and it was extremely frustrating to have to defend myself and set the record straight with my own children. But much of what she said was true, and hearing it from them was hard to bear.

The situation was compounded by bad choices made by the kids themselves. Teenagers often make reckless decisions, but Marc and

Michelle took that tendency to a destructive level. All in all, I came to realize what a clueless and negligent parent I had been. I'm eternally grateful I had the help and support I needed to change course and become a decent father.

As I said earlier, Michelle's teenage challenges began while Kathy and I were still together. We kept threatening to send her to a boarding school but never followed through. Well, one day we finally did, and Michelle went—literally kicking and screaming—to a school called Cascade in the small Northern California town of Whitmore, near Redding.

Completely isolated, the school offered a regular high school curriculum, but the main purpose was therapeutic. "We had group therapy, individual therapy, family therapy, phone therapy," Michelle recalls. "It was like a mini-jail. There were a lot of rules. We had to shovel snow. We had to chop wood. Everything was considered a privilege. If you wanted something, even something as simple as wearing jewelry, you had to write a letter explaining why you thought you had earned it."

There were no vacations, only earned leaves. Students were introduced back into their families gradually: a five-minute phone call, then a ten-minute call, then fifteen, and so forth. At a certain point, a student's parents were allowed to visit for a day. Eventually, the kids could go home for a few days. That's how it went for two years. I don't know if the program worked for everyone (the school closed in the mid-2000s), but it seemed to work for Michelle. At her graduation, I was grateful to hear her say, "Dad, I hated you for sending me here, but I think you saved my life." She says now that she left the school a better person: "I was clean, I had made lifelong friends, I felt better. If I hadn't gone, I think I would have ended up with AIDS, or pregnant, or seriously addicted to something." But it was hard to adjust to life outside. "That kind of school takes you away from the reality of the real world," she said. "There's a lot of brainwashing, and it's hard to get acclimated into society again."

Michelle was seventeen when she returned to L.A. in June of 1996. She lived with Kathy for a few weeks and then went away to Whittier College. For a while, it looked like she had straightened out her life, but she ended up dropping out a year and a half before graduation. "I got involved with an abusive guy," she recalls. "I was smoking pot, I started doing cocaine, and I was taking a lot of diet pills."

During that difficult phase of my daughter's life I dated, got engaged to, and married Harriet. "I had a *really* hard time accepting their relationship," Michelle says. "I don't know if it was because Harriet and her ex-husband had spent time at our house, or because she and my mom were friends at one point, but accepting it was a slow process. I attended the wedding, but the other three kids had a role in it, and I chose not to participate. It just took time to get used to it. I think I resented my father for breaking up the family."

Things got so bad between Michelle and me that we stopped talking to each other for four years. The break was precipitated by a blowup over money that became much more than a financial issue. Kathy's parents had created a trust for their grandchildren. As the appointed trustee, I invested the money well and increased its value considerably. Then, for reasons of her own, Kathy decided she didn't trust me. She convinced Michelle her trust was endangered, and they filed to have me removed as trustee. In court, the judge ruled it would be better for all concerned to have the trust managed by a bank. No harm was done financially. But the emotional damage from all the anger and mistrust was so severe that Michelle and I stopped talking to each other.

Marc's Turn to Turn Away

At the time, my relationship with Marc was as tight as ever. We had our father-son challenges, of course, and those challenges were more difficult because I was blamed for the breakup of our family. But we had always been close and exceptionally affectionate, and Marc seemed to be adapting to my new life. He treated Harriet well, and he got along with Roni and Joel when he stayed with us every Wednesday night and every other weekend, as per my divorce agreement. But he and Michelle had accumulated a lot of anger, and at times—no doubt compounded by their use of drugs or alcohol—it leaked out. Sometimes it exploded. Once, in the fall of 1998, when Marc and Michelle were living with Kathy, they fought so badly that Michelle called 911 and the police placed Marc in a seventy-two-hour hold before letting him go home.

Marc fought with Kathy a lot too. At one point things were so bad between them that a court made them attend anger management classes once a week, and they were allowed to see each other only at those meetings. That's why Marc moved in with Harriet and me in the fall of 1998. The following June he moved with us to the new house we bought together in Encino (where we still live). I enjoyed having my son with me full-time, and Harriet couldn't have been a better stepmom. But it grew more and more challenging, and after about a year everything hit the fan. Now I had *two* children I didn't speak to. Here is how Marc remembers that period:

"I got into pot, and I was drinking a little bit. I was also in a public school for the first time. I had been in private schools my whole life, but I got kicked out of three of them—two for bad grades and one for fighting—so I went to a public school for the tenth grade. I met some new people, and I met the first girl I ever really had a thing for, and we started smoking pot all the time. I was living with my mom most of that time, and at one point she couldn't handle me anymore. I was too out of control for her. So I lived with my father and Harriet.

"Harriet and I didn't really see eye to eye then. She was controlling—not in a bad way, but I *thought* it was bad because she didn't let me have my way. She made me clean up after myself, and she made me go to school when I didn't want to. I would come home late—eleven or twelve or one in the morning—and my father would be waiting up for me. He'd say, 'I don't want you running around with your gang anymore. You have to be home at night.' He gave me a curfew, and he said, 'Next time, I'm going to lock you out of the house.' But the next time came around, and he would let me in again. Then, one time, he said, 'Sorry, you're past your curfew. I don't care where you were, or what you were doing, you're done. You're not coming into the house.' So I left, and I snuck back into the house through the garage, and I went up to my room. My father came into the room and confronted me. 'I told you, you can't stay here tonight. You live by my and Harriet's rules or you don't live here at all.' I don't know exactly how it got started, but we actually got into a physical fight. He was much stronger than I thought he was. I had never lost a fight, but I lost this one. He got me in a chokehold, and I was out for the count. When I regained consciousness, I looked around and he wasn't in the room with me, so I made a run for it. And just as I'm running down the stairs, I see him coming after me. So I was, like, out the door. And I ran into the arms of eight or ten police officers. There were helicopters, police cars and the whole deal. Harriet had called the police."

That is a pretty accurate account, as I remember it. Harriet says that, prior to the blowup, Marc taunted us by opening and closing the garage door from his bedroom with the remote. Those details aside, I find it amazing that I, a lifelong nerd who couldn't throw a ball, much less box or wrestle, was actually driven over the edge to the point of having a physical altercation with my seventeen-year-old son. That's how bad things became. No one was physically injured, and no one was arrested. But I told Marc he could no longer live with us. When the police allowed Marc to call his mother, Kathy drove to our house and took him home with her.

Marc remembers the next period of our lives this way: "My father tried calling me once or twice a year to try to work things out. I ignored the phone calls. He sent me birthday cards. I threw them out. He didn't make a huge effort, but he made small gestures he felt comfortable doing. He's a stubborn guy, and I'm a stubborn guy. I don't know exactly how long it was that I didn't talk to him."

It was four years, with the exception of one brief interlude: we got together once and then stopped talking again because Marc failed to show up for a lunch we had scheduled and never explained or apologized. He's right about my being stubborn. I am, and I'm *very* stubborn when someone betrays my trust or lets me down. My friends have told me many times that holding people to high standards can be a virtue, but not if you take it too far—and I have learned, thanks to Harriet and Dr. Jones, that there were times when I did take it too far. In truth, I don't know if I could have done more in those years of estrangement to heal my children's wounds or to work out a way to reconcile. I'm not sure if anything I might have done would have worked at that time of our lives. Anguish. Guilt. Regret. Confusion. I experienced all those emotions, and I tortured myself with unanswerable questions: Should I try harder? Should I cave in and give them what they want? What else should I do? What else *can* I do? I'm just glad that in the end we were able to reconcile, mend the past, and create the loving bonds that parents and children should have.

The First Reconciliation

The reconciliation with Michelle came first, in fits and starts. At one point, she and I had lunch on Wilshire Boulevard, near my office. She had come to ask for money. I had by then grown wary of being seen by her as The Bank of Bookstein, and I had decided not to put up with it any longer. "I'm no longer your bank," I told Michelle. "If you need something we agree you need, I'll be happy to help out. But I'm not just passing out money anymore." She got so mad she threw down some money to pay for her lunch and walked out of the restaurant. She had never paid for anything before. I put her money in an envelope and kept it untouched for four years. When we finally reconciled I gave it back to her.

One day, in the spring of 2003, I received a letter from Michelle. The content wasn't exactly friendly. She wasn't reaching out to heal our relationship. Here's how she remembers it: "I had been living with a guy for several years. We were engaged, and were supposed to be married in August of '03. The date kept getting closer and closer, and my mom, who was always talking so negatively about my father, kept asking, 'Does your father know you're getting married?' She finally convinced me to tell him. I didn't feel comfortable seeing him in person, or talking on the phone, so I wrote a letter letting him know that I was getting married."

So much for the good news. She went on to say I was not invited to the wedding. Her brother Marc would be walking her down the aisle. I was not welcome in her life. As far as she was concerned, she no longer had a father. She explicitly ordered me not to write her back.

This came as a sharp blow to my heart. But I could not abide by her command. I wrote back, saying she was free to decide whether or not to speak to me and whether or not to invite me to her wedding, but she could not choose whether or not to have a father. Nothing could undo the fact that I was her father. Nor could she stop me from loving her. That was my choice.

Michelle wrote back. She began by saying, "I told you not to write back," but I had, so she let out more of her feelings. This wasn't the most positive way to break the ice, but at least it was broken. Communication had been established. I wrote back and suggested we get together. She agreed, and we had a nice dinner, just the two of us. A week later, we did it again, and that one didn't go so well. "Now that we're talking," she said, "Mom would like to know how much you're going to contribute to my wedding." I was prepared for that question.

"That's easy," I said. "Zero. If you invite me, I'll pay for dinner for Harriet and me. But if you're talking to me just because you want to get The Bank of Bookstein back, I'm not interested. That's not happening."

Michelle remembers that evening as "extremely uncomfortable." She's right. It was very tense, with a lot of anger and resentment simmering beneath the surface. I left feeling hurt, but at the same time oddly hopeful. We were talking again. Maybe there was a chance for a genuine reconciliation.

As it turned out, Michelle called off her wedding twelve days before it was to take place. She never married the guy, but I'm glad she almost did, because the wedding plans cracked open the wall between us. Slowly, we started talking again, and eventually she let me back into her life.

The Second Reconciliation

I didn't know it at the time, but Marc had trouble dealing with the fact that Michelle and I were mending our relationship while he and I were still on the outs. "One thing Michelle and I had in common," he recalls, "is that we weren't talking to our father." For me, speaking to Michelle again had an added benefit: I now had a reliable source of information about Marc, so I was able to find out what he was doing and how he was.

Marc and I had had one short-lived period of reconciliation in April, 2003, when Marc had a serious motorcycle accident. At first, no one informed me. "I was in the hospital for a week or two, and I didn't call my father," he says. "My sister knew about it. My mother knew about it. All my friends knew about it. I just didn't want him there, because my mother hated him, and she didn't want to be in the same room with him. I felt she deserved to be in the hospital with me, and I didn't want to make her uncomfortable by letting my father know and having him visit me."

When I finally learned about the accident from Michelle, Harriet and I went immediately to the hospital. Marc's memory of my mood is accurate: "He was very upset. He was hurt: 'How come nobody called me?' To this day, he says it's the worst thing I've ever done to him. My dad said, 'What would have happened if you had died? Would they have called me after the funeral?'"

This was one of those tragedies that bring unexpected benefits. Fortunately, it came at a time in both my life and Marc's when we could seize the opportunity. My son was no longer a teenager, and I was no longer the same stubborn father. "I realized how much he cared about me and how stupid our fights were in the past," Marc says. "I was young, and ninety-nine percent of it was my fault. I was running with a bad crowd, doing drugs, not following rules. But after the accident, I realized how much he cared. I could see it in his eyes, how hurt he was that I was injured and no one had notified him."

During Marc's recovery in the hospital, we started to draw close again. Unfortunately, it was only a temporary respite that lasted until Marc had surgery. Harriet and I went ahead with our vacation plans, and when we returned I found Marc was very upset that I hadn't been there during his post-operative rehab. Between that and my own hard feelings about not being told about the accident, the brief thaw ended and the frost returned to our relationship.

Three more years passed before the wall separating Marc and me finally crumbled. "I was dating a girl who was a psych major at CSUN, and we would talk about our fathers," Marc says. "I had a lot of fond memories of him from when I was younger, and also a lot of *bad* memories. We used to talk about it, and I would get emotional. One day, she said, 'Why don't you try calling him and work things out?' I said, 'The ball's in his court. If he wants to call me, he can call me.' The very next day he called me. I was convinced my girlfriend had told him, 'It's time to mend things with your son,' but they both swear it was just a coincidence."

It was. As I said earlier, I tried calling Marc a number of times, but he wouldn't pick up the phone or return my calls. I'd pretty much given up and had come to believe we would never reconcile. Harriet believed otherwise. She saw the great pain I was in, and she tried to comfort me. "Watch, it will get better," she would say. "It's just going to take time." I thought she was just saying what a wife is supposed to say, but she really believed it.

So did Dr. Jones. "When are you going to do something about your son?" she would ask. "How are you going to get back with him? Are you going to call him?" I kept putting it off. I didn't want to fail again. But at one point I decided to take the risk. On the day after tax season, April 16, 2006, I called Marc on his cell phone. To my surprise, he answered.

"I answered the phone only because I'd been speaking about him the night before," Marc said.

I asked if he'd like to get together. He said "I'm not sure."

"Okay," I said. "The offer's there. If you want to, I'd love to get together with you. I still care about you a lot."

To my eternal relief, he said, "Okay."

We met for breakfast at Jerry's Deli on Ventura Boulevard, near my house. What I thought would be an hour meeting lasted for four hours. I don't remember much about what was actually said, but I know it was one of the most important conversations of my life, and I remember the tremendous love and gratitude I felt to lay eyes on my son and hear his voice again. Everything changed that day. We were able to put the past and all our bitterness behind us and let the love we always had for one another rise to the surface. As Marc says, "We've been getting closer and closer ever since."

At Long Last, My Family Is Whole

During those years of estrangement, it wasn't easy to stick to my version of tough love. Being apart from the children I adored was a constant heartache, but I stuck it out because I knew there were lessons they had to learn, about maturity and responsibility, and they wouldn't learn those lessons if I continued supporting them while they engaged in irresponsible, self-destructive behavior. People were astonished I had the discipline to stick to my guns when the separation was causing me such immense pain. My friend and client Michael Rosenfeld remembers it this way: "Harvey essentially said, 'Look, I love you. I'm your father. But I will not support what I consider to be wrong action, and if that means I can't have a relationship with you right now, then that's what it means.' I'm very close with my children, and what he did was beyond my comprehension. It broke his heart, but he knew the best thing that he could do for his children was to hold them accountable and treat them as the adults they were becoming. I don't think I could have done it. But I learned from watching him do it that making them confront their own issues and take responsibility for their own outcomes may look like abandonment, but it can be one of the most giving things you can possibly do. You're giving them a skill they will need in life. I admire Harvey tremendously for taking such a huge risk. If something tragic had happened during that period, he might have spent the rest of his life in deep regret."

I'm not sure I deserve that much admiration, but Michael is right that it was difficult to stick to my guns and insist that the children

I loved more than anything else in life be held accountable for their behavior. He says "it paid huge dividends" in my life, and he's probably right about that too. Of course, I wish I could have had the family life I now have without going through all that agony. But to the extent that everything happens for a reason, the result in this case was my children matured into responsible adults. I'm grateful I was able to see that happen up close and personal.

I essentially missed four crucial years of my children's lives, and I was determined to try to make up for lost time. Little by little, Marc and Michelle became an integral part of my new family. Like many brothers and sisters, they had their difficulties throughout their younger years. But they are now about as close as grown-up siblings can be; for some time they lived in neighboring houses in Woodland Hills, about a ten-minute drive from Harriet and me. Marc became a graduate gemologist at the Gemological Institute of America in Carlsbad, California, and he now works in that capacity for M. Kantor and Associates. Michelle completed her college degree at the University of Phoenix and then became a teacher at the Jewish Community Center in the Valley. She went on to earn a master's degree in social work at my alma mater, CSUN. She married Jarret Lewis in August 2009, and I'm thrilled to report I gave away the bride and happily paid for the whole shebang. A year later, Michelle gave birth to Jayden, my first biological grandchild (my stepdaughter Roni has two kids, and my stepson Joel has one). Becoming a good father took almost two decades of self-reflection and the everyday influence of Harriet, who is the best role model of excellent parenting I can imagine. But becoming an excellent grandfather took about two seconds.

As difficult as they were, the years between the breakup of my first marriage and my reconciliation with my children were also fulfilling, joyful, and transformational. During that period, I was introduced to parts of myself I had never been in touch with before. I became open to life experiences I didn't know I was capable of having. The stage was set for the next phase of my life and work. And none of it would have been possible without the insight and compassion of the two wisest women I've ever known: Harriet and Dr. Jones.

Chapter 12
The New Harvey

The changes in my life began with intense introspection after the Northridge earthquake. My evolution accelerated and found a sense of direction when I started therapy with Dr. Jones. When I fell in love with Harriet the process took off even more and began to solidify. I was double-teamed by my wife and my therapist. Those two women taught me more about how to live than anyone else I've ever known.

Harriet showed me what it means to love someone. Perhaps more important, she made it safe for me to *be* loved. She grounded me in ways I hadn't been before. She brought out aspects of me that were buried so deep I didn't even know they existed. She also showed me by example how to be a good parent. If you want to be a parent who is capable of unconditional love, care, and support, but is also practical and tough when necessary, you couldn't ask for a better role model than Harriet.

But I might never have been ready for a relationship with someone like Harriet if it weren't for therapy. I think if I'd have married her in 1971 we'd have ended up divorced, just as Kathy and I did. I just wasn't mature enough. Harriet always says, "You don't know that. We would have had a totally different relationship." She's right, of course. There's no way of knowing. But I do know I was infinitely better prepared to be a good husband and father twenty-six years later, and a big reason for that was my therapy with Dr. Jones. Without that, I might not have been ready to appreciate Harriet. I might have been too blind to see how perfect she was for me. I might have been incapable of listening to her and learning from her. I might have been unwilling to rethink my way of life, and she might have said, "I can't be with a workaholic like Harvey." Above all, I wouldn't have known what to do with all the love in Harriet's big heart. I never knew that kind of love existed. I never had that feeling—or any other feeling. I was numb. I was a robot. Deep down, I believed I was unlovable. The one-two punch of therapy and Harriet opened me up to loving and being loved.

The process of self-discovery was painful at times, but also incredibly liberating. Dr. Jones says the person I am now was inside me all the time; it just took a long time to peel back the layers of the onion. The skin was too thick, and rushing the process would have been a mistake. Therapy brought out parts of me that were always there, but were suppressed. For example, I was pretty reserved during most of my life, until I discovered I love being playful. One of my favorite things to do is surprise people, to spring something unexpected on them, whether it's the way I proposed to Harriet or a gift for one of my grandkids. I never knew that side of me before therapy showed it to me and Harriet pulled it out of me.

The way I've readjusted my thinking, my attitude, my day-to-day actions, and my long-term plans—to this day, I find it absolutely amazing. This is my usual routine: On Mondays, Wednesdays, and Fridays I get up at 4:10, arrive at the gym at 4:50, walk on the treadmill for ten minutes, then work with a personal trainer for an hour, then hop back on the treadmill for another thirty minutes. After the workout I shower and drive to work. On Thursdays, I play racquetball at 5:30 a.m. with Dan Rosenson. But I have my best workouts on Tuesdays at 7:00 a.m. That's when I see Dr. Jones.

Without everything I learned in my sessions with Dr. Jones, none of the changes in my life would have been possible. Most of all, I would not have been open to the love I share with Harriet. I could handle being admired for my achievements, because I always knew I was good at what I do. But having someone care about me as a person? Loving me? I found that unbelievable. I hadn't received that kind of love from my mom and dad, and I had no brothers or sisters, so the whole idea was foreign to me.

As I said earlier, the feeling of unworthiness was so strong that when I was going through my divorce I was terrified I'd end up penniless. Me, the guy who'd been dealing with money since he was seven, was afraid of being destitute. This idea seems ludicrous in hindsight, but the fear was so real that Dan and Linda Rosenson offered me a significant amount of money to ease my concerns. I said, "Why would you give me money? I might not be able to repay you." Linda said, "Where would I rather spend my money than on someone I really care about?" It was extremely difficult for me to accept that answer. Why would anyone care enough about me to make such an offer?

I couldn't even believe my children cared about me. During the time we were estranged, I'd say to Dr. Jones, "We're always talking about the kids in therapy, but I'm sure they're not thinking about me." She would reply, "You have no idea how bound you are to each other. You have no clue. Why wouldn't you think they'd be talking about you, and missing you as much as you miss them?" Why? Because I didn't feel important enough. But Dr. Jones would always say, "I'm sure it's inside them, even if they don't say it verbally. They're thinking about you all the time." She was right, of course, but it took me a long time to accept it.

As a result of therapy, I was able to accept love. I also reoriented my priorities so my family replaced work at the top of the totem pole. I still put in more hours than most people could tolerate, and I'm as passionate about my work as ever. But my life is far more balanced now. I actually enjoy my non-work time. I have more and better friendships. I take real vacations with my family on a regular basis. And my home is the peaceful sanctuary that busy businesspeople always yearn for. Most men my age won't believe this, but to this day, fifteen years after I married Harriet, the thing I enjoy most in life is watching her get undressed for bed. Sleeping in the nude with my wife is my single greatest daily pleasure.

Now I'm going to let the people who know me best describe the ways I've changed. This will be more convincing coming from them, and they can say it a lot better than I can.

STELLA KLEINROCK: "I think Harvey is a great story of self-invention. He had a lot to overcome. In his high school there were social stigmas attached to things like appearance, and who's in and who's out. It wasn't cool to be smart. It wasn't okay to be as geeky as he was. He needed to come to terms with that, and with his experience with his parents. It was a very dysfunctional family. They never treated him like a child. They never encouraged him to have friends. They seemingly had no idea how to be parents.

"Most children internalize a sense of security at about eighteen months, when they begin to walk away and the parent keeps reassuring them: 'I'll be here. You can walk away, and I'll be here when you come back, no matter how far you go.' That gives children a sense of internalized security. Harvey didn't totally internalize it. And then he married somebody who was really inappropriate for him. And as soon as his mother died, his father married his aunt. Harvey was so enraged he couldn't mourn his mom. And of course, he never learned how to parent, and he felt terrible that he did not have a better relationship with his kids.

"A divorce always causes one to reexamine what was going on. If you don't reexamine, you lose a fantastic opportunity. Harvey was also going through the beginning of middle age, and midlife crises are called crises because it's a time when we look at ourselves and say, 'This is what my life has been until now. What do I want from here on out?' Even though Harvey may not have been totally aware of that, he didn't want a life like the one he had with Kathy. He loved his work, but his home life was a wreck. He's a doer, so he had to do something.

"His life was a bit of a mess. He had a lot of rigidity from holding himself together. We would talk about personal stuff, and I thought as a friend that he would benefit from some perspective on his life. But I never tell people, 'I think you should see a therapist.' It's inappropriate. Then Harvey started talking about a therapist who flies into town for three days and has marathon sessions with the client and leaves. There were promises of dramatic changes. I listened for a while, and I said, 'Look, I don't normally interfere with people's therapists, but nobody is going to make any real changes with that kind of therapy. What you need is a good therapist who is here, whom you see on a weekly basis, as many times as you can manage it, and then you will see some changes.'

"I really encouraged him to do it. I tried to tell him he deserved it, that he needed to take the time to make his life more meaningful. He asked if *I* could see him as a therapist, and I said, 'No, but I can refer you to somebody.' Sylvia Jones was one of my colleagues, and I knew her work. I had a feeling Harvey would work very well with her. I wanted him to work with a woman because I saw he needed a connection with women.

"The changes started happening quickly. Harvey is like a sponge. He totally internalizes every therapeutic intervention. He had always been a little stilted, and now we were able to become much better friends. He started paying much more attention to his kids. He took much more of a personal interest in them. They went through a very hard time, and it's a credit to Harvey and Harriet that they're doing as well as they are. Harriet is a kind, good person, but she's not a softie. I truly appreciate her role in Harvey's life. I'm grateful for her."

DR. SYLVIA HIRSCH JONES (NOTE: I have given Dr. Jones carte blanche permission to reveal the process and progress of my work with her): "My work with Harvey has included an eclectic range of attention, mainly in-depth therapy with a psychoanalytic orientation. Later in the work, at Harvey's request, we opened it up to do family therapy. This is kind of unusual, but Harvey is unusual. I orient myself to the patient's needs, and it worked very well with him.

"Our work together developed over time as he gained more access to his feelings. In fact, Harvey didn't know he *had* feelings. Everything was black and white. So decision-making was based on something outside of himself because he didn't have access to his emotions. He was completely confused. He didn't know that he felt sad or that he was panicked. His life had gone awry, but he couldn't label the feelings. I hoped to be able to acquaint him with the emotional side of his life.

"I tried to help him feel safe with me—that I wasn't going to dismiss him, or make him feel insignificant or foolish. And then, over time, I got him to talk about his life, and I'd say, 'What might you have been feeling here or there?' or notice his behavior, or the look on his face, or the tone in which he would share these things with me. As the work progressed, Harvey began to trust me more. He started to feel connected to himself as the walls came down. He wanted more and more. Harvey really felt 'Oh my God, there's something here that I've been missing.' He really took to it, and it changed his life.

"It happened gradually, over time. There were tough periods, like going through his divorce and trying to work things out with his kids. He felt very alone. He didn't know he was connected. He didn't trust anyone, and when you're at that level of mistrust, you feel alone. You can't let anyone in, because they can dismiss you and reject you. He didn't trust that he was really cared about. He didn't understand how his kids could love him. I asked, 'Why would they not love you?' He shared his guilt about his absence from the home as he worked at the office obsessively. How he expected their mother to raise them, ignoring her apparent depression and her inability to care for or protect them. He was painfully able to acknowledge his participation in the estrangement with his son and daughter. In a certain way his detachment was his way of coping, and we had to look at how this way of coping was self-destructive and alienating.

"We worked on his childhood and his relationships with his parents. His mom and dad were aloof and undemonstrative. He felt ignored by them and insignificant to them. He felt punished by their detachment from him. His parents didn't like his behavior, and my guess is they had no idea what to do about it. They were not introspective enough to ask themselves if they were doing something that might be causing it.

"He described them as an extremely close pair, and he said he did not feel special in any way. This made him feel very alienated—unloved, unlovable, and really angry. As a child, he attempted to interfere with their relationship, to break them up in various ways in order to get attention. He was manipulative. He'd give the impression to one that something was going on, and tell the other one something else, in order to split them apart. He spent a lot of time scheming. He was a troublemaker. He was vengeful, and he learned how to manipulate and get back at people. I doubt his parents were able to see his negative behavior as a cry for help and intervene in a loving way. He was not a bad seed, but a lonely, alienated kid.

"Meeting Harriet was a new lease on life. It was a chicken-and-egg thing: therapy probably made it more possible for him to respond well to Harriet, and Harriet's presence may have opened him up further to the process. He started to believe he might be worthy of being loved. He began to work through the mistrust. He could risk wanting to be loved, and letting her love him, and having all the feelings that come with that: fear of it not working out, fear of him not pleasing her enough. They were normal feelings, and now he could tolerate the vulnerability, so he wasn't out there being the tough guy with that old kind of bravado. He was a soft, sweet guy who was a lot more accessible.

"A playful side of him emerged. He'd play tricks on Harriet, and surprise her in quirky ways with gifts. He derived a great deal of pleasure in seeing the light come into her eyes. It was very childlike, and wonderful to see. They were kids together in a certain way, but it was also romantic and fun. And a big change from the extremely difficult kind of communication he had with his first wife. He loved it, and I think he was really hungry for it. He didn't know how hungry he was, because he didn't know that kind of a relationship existed. It surprised him, but he went for it.

"The estrangement from his children was terribly painful for him. He didn't believe he was worthy enough, or the bond was secure enough, for him to fight for them. It wasn't about custody, it was about defending himself and trying to get through to them how much he loved them and how much their relationship meant to him. The kids were giving him a hard time. They were angry at him. They believed their mother was right, that Dad was bad and the breakup was his fault. Harvey was the one who left the family. The kids were torn in every direction, but children turn toward the weakest parent because they feel she needs protection. Harvey had to examine his guilt regarding his own absence from his kids, and his deep feelings of being unlovable and unworthy, before he could recognize they really cared about him and could love him. He had to risk trusting that repair was possible. Eventually, he was able to bridge the gap and cautiously but lovingly make contact with them.

"There were occasions when Harvey asked to bring one of his kids or Harriet to his therapy. I've never seen anyone approach such a session the way he does. He begins by asking each family member, 'Is there anything upsetting you about me? Dr. Jones will help me work on it so I can keep a deep, loving relationship with you.' It's extremely unusual. The usual scenario is that the client, between the lines, says he wants me to change his wife. At this point, Harvey has come in with every family member except his three youngest grandchildren, Katie, Jayden and Bryan. My most recent pleasure was to meet his oldest granddaughter, Sami. She calls him Gramps. Sleepy-eyed and holding his hand, she did not escape hearing his question: 'Is there anything I do that gets in the way of our relationship? If there is, I want Dr. Jones to help me with it.' She thought for a minute, and said, 'I don't think so.' Then she looked at me, hesitated, and told him, 'I'll tell you in the car.'

"Harvey's commitment to the therapy process and our work together has been remarkable. I think the access to his feelings woke him up, and became a kind of nourishment he never knew he could have. The *Therapeutic Accountant* idea is a metaphor for being fully present—not just in his work, but in his relationships. He's all there now. He's focused, so he can fully enjoy his life and really be in it. He has been able to work with his clients fully present, no holds barred. Along with success in his work, his life as a family man, husband, father, grandfather, and friend has also been a remarkable evolution. Therapy was a gift to him, and Harvey has truly been a gift to me. We met two sessions a week for a long time, then we cut back to once a week, and therapy is still ongoing. His appointment is at seven in the morning, and he doesn't miss a session unless he's out of town.

"Harvey has been one of my most memorable clients, because he's someone who's not going to give up. He's a persistent guy. He doesn't like to fail. He's right in there, soaking up everything he can about the experience. Really, it's been a privilege. I feel fortunate to have met him and to work with him." "

DAN ROSENSON: "Linda and I double-dated with Harvey and Harriet in the first week of their relationship. We had dinner together. Harriet was 180 degrees different from Kathy, and there was a vast difference in Harvey's behavior. He's always holding hands with her, always touching her. And she can stand up to Harvey when necessary. She knows how to pick her battles. She also brought a lot of good advice to him. Harriet gets things done in a very subtle, loving, caring way."

LINDA ROSENSON: "Harvey and Kathy were incompatible, and that brought out the worst in both of them. You could also say that by the time he got together with Harriet, Harvey was much better equipped to be a proper husband to somebody. He's also learned to be a true friend. When he says, 'How are you?' he means it, and he doesn't expect you to just give him a quick answer, 'I'm fine.' He wants to hear *why* you're fine, or why you're *not* fine, what's going on in your life. He wants to share the good and the bad with you. I think it took him a long time to get those skills. He smiles now. He's loving. He's caring. He's touching. He's engaging.

"Harriet is a warm, loving, caring, considerate person. She has a heart of gold. Very nurturing, and a great parent. I think she taught Harvey the importance of family life, and he has picked up those skills. He switched his real love from his profession to his family."

DAN: "If you take a look at his schedule, he's up before the sun comes up, and he doesn't leave the office until six or seven o'clock. But he always has dinner with Harriet, which I think is remarkable. It was always a challenge to get Harvey to reduce his work hours. He did not know how to stop and relax. I would say, 'You're coming of an age where you need to slow down and smell the roses. I'm trying to get you to realize there are benefits to not having to do something.' Now he devotes more time to family and travel and other things, so it's much better than it once was.

"I have a lot of friends, and Harvey is, without a doubt, my most trusted friend. After knowing him this long, I now understand his idiosyncrasies. We have a regular poker game, usually at my house. It's twenty-five cents, fifty cents, a dollar, so you can't lose much, and Harvey and I let our hair down. He could not have done that before. He was really a locked-up guy. He had a lot of insecurities. His 'safe zone' was his office, and he didn't want to be in the outside world, in my opinion. Now he's a lot of fun. What inspires me most about him is his passion to learn about himself."

STEVE BERLINGER: "Harvey has broadened himself. He's not as narrow as he was. He had the curse of many successful businesspeople: they become so focused on the narrow thing they do that they don't grow. To me it's a tragedy, because when you die no one cares how much money you have, and you're not going to spend it unless you have bizarre beliefs in the afterworld. So it's how broad you can be in doing things. That's probably the major change I've seen in Harvey. He's a businessman. And now he's active in giving back and building something at Cal State Northridge. And he's also very into his family.

"He can still be mercurial at times. He's still a complex and intense person. If you disrespect him, if you're rude, if you try to cheat him, he can get set off. And he has so many things going on at the same time that he runs on tight time schedules, so when you discuss something complex he'll jump right to an answer, sometimes without enough background. But it's much better now. Because of my relationship with him, I can say, 'Just shut up and listen for a minute before you get to the answer.'"

MICHAEL ROSENFELD: "Harvey used to be a twenty-four-hour-a-day worker who was very meticulous, very technical, and would meet you any time, any place to get the job done. His life was ninety percent business and ten percent other, although when I first knew him he was very close with his son, Marc, and he would sometimes bring Marc along when he had meetings on the weekends.

"Even though there's an age difference between us, we had similar paths. We grew up in households where expectations were high, and where we felt a need to succeed or perform to validate ourselves. Neither one of us gave any consideration to our own feelings or needs. It was just, Do whatever it takes, deliver on your word, work very hard, and if that means working all day and all night, you work all day and all night. We took care of other people, and later in life we came to understand that sometimes taking care of everybody and everything may seem like an act of altruism but is actually an act of control. I think we evolved and had some eye-opening experiences about our patterns of behavior and how they served us. Burying yourself in work keeps you from confronting your feelings. Taking care of everybody and everything keeps you from having to be dependent on anyone. These turned out to be defense mechanisms, even though we saw ourselves as being stalwart and noble and stoic and all those types of things.

"Many years later, at different times, we both came to the understanding that it actually takes courage to face your deficits, to face your fears, to trust other people, to allow others in. In many ways Harvey went before me. He made a commitment to face his issues head-on, to come to terms with his feelings and overcome things that were ingrained in him from childhood. That was an inspiration to me, and when he was going through his divorce—a really dark and questioning period for him—I spent a lot of time with him. I was honored to be able to support him as a friend, as I feel he has supported me as a friend.

"When he went into therapy and started to look at these things, he dedicated himself thoroughly to that process. And I think he found out that the things he was told about himself, and that he bought into, were not all true. The feelings he carried weren't necessarily valid. He became a very open person. He chose life. I think had he not gone through the challenges and the transformations, he would have missed the whole thing. He would not know the love he shares with Harriet. He would not know family as he has it today, which is really, I think, at the core of his existence. His relationships are so much more meaningful. He did not have to give up his values or his work ethic. He just gained so much more.

"One thing that distinguishes Harvey is that he genuinely wants to see other people succeed. A lot of people give lip service to that. Harvey will help people. He will give them his input. He takes great pleasure when he can play a role in helping people do well, even when there's no self-interest involved. He is a giving person. He loves to give. I think he was probably always that way, even before he went through his transformation. I think that's his nature. But he was a deeply wounded and dysfunctional person. He was not living life; he was going through life. I think the profound change that came about was his ability to see all the beautiful gifts he has, and to participate in the wonderful things that are available to him. It's been great to watch. He's my dearest friend."

JOE RUVOLO:

"I first met Harvey in 1977 or 1978. I was a real estate broker and he was the accountant for one of the guys I was doing deals with. We became business colleagues, and he ended up being my accountant for two years. Then we lost touch, and in January of 2003 we started doing real estate deals together. I offered him a certain kind of expertise he didn't have, and he represented a part of the real estate equation I was never strong in – bringing money into deals.

"Thirty years ago, I don't think we could have had the kind of business relationship we have now. He was different then, and so was I. Back then, he worked just as hard as he does now, and he was just as quick with his thinking, but he didn't have the social graces, so to speak. He was very abrupt, very matter of fact. Flash forward, and he has developed the ability to engage and really be interested in people.

"There are a lot of smart people out there, but being smart doesn't mean you're going to be successful. You need to have social skills in addition to being smart to get to the top of where you want to go, if that's something you strive for. There's nothing more important than how you engage in dialogue and communicate with people.

"That's really the biggest difference I've seen in him, and I think it's why our relationship has turned out to be the way it is, which is very good. I like talking to Harvey, because he listens and he helps, and you can tell he's seriously interested in your life – the good, the bad, and the ugly. He wants to hear about it. He'll make suggestions. He wants to see you and your loved ones happy. I can only spend time with people I like and have a high degree of respect for. Given how long I've been doing this, I can pretty much do whatever I want. I work because I enjoy being in the office and doing deals with Harvey.

"We have a high level of respect for each other, because of the way we see other people and how we think about family. If you're an investor in one of my deals, your money is more important to me than my money. I don't mind taking a loss in real estate; it's what I do. But you're an investor, you're not a real estate guy, so if you have a loss I can't sleep at night. Harvey's the same way.

"Recently, he started to do these Town Hall meetings, where he invites everyone in the office to come and hear him talk, and they can ask him any questions they like. At the most recent one, fifty or sixty people showed up, and they were emboldened; they're not threatened. They felt free to ask whatever they wanted to, and most of the questions were of a personal nature, not a business nature, about Harvey's marriage, about his kids, about being a grandparent, how he prioritizes, what's important to him – things like, 'What do you do in the morning? Do you work out? What time do you get up? What is your typical day?'

"Most people at the top insulate themselves from going that far. They're typically difficult to approach; for whatever reason, they don't want to be bothered with the people below them. Harvey's not afraid to go out there and say, 'This is who I am.' And I think that's the key component: not how much they learn about real estate or accounting, but what they learn about one of the founding partners who heads the company. When you connect the dots with his personal life, it has a huge impact. It's invaluable, and most people go their entire careers without getting enough of that. You can educate yourself about accounting practices, finance, and all the things they do here, but you don't learn the social skills and the personal engagement in college. When you can learn it from someone who has been successful, nothing is more valuable. I tell people, 'Go and listen, and if you can walk away with just one or two items that stay with you, those items will be yours for the rest of your life.'"

DAVE ZASLOW: "He's still hungry, he's still driven, and he's still a nut, but I think where he's changed is in realizing that personal relationships are very important to him. I think that's what drives him now more than anything. His priorities have changed. Success is important. It's way up there. But it isn't his top priority anymore.

"Because Harvey goes to extremes, his maturity could have taken him in a different direction, but he chose to take it in the direction of doing good things in life. Thirty years ago, I would never in my wildest dreams think he would be charitable, whereas today he is *very* charitable, not just with dollars but with his time. He recognizes his priorities, and those priorities are very important."

MICHELLE: "My father is a completely different person. He's more sensitive. He's more in touch. He's not as cold. He's not as rock-solid, like he needs to keep it together all the time. He's more open-minded. He jokes more. He's more relaxed. He's also given up a lot of his need for control.

"The first big thing I noticed was that he was home on a Saturday. It was like 'What! You're home on a Saturday? Are you sick?' As much as he worked, he always claimed family was very important to him. We didn't see it. Then I think he realized his children had grown up, and he missed out on a lot. We weren't kids anymore. We made a lot of decisions without him. We're close now, even though I can't talk to him like Marc does, because I don't understand taxes and trades and stocks and investments and real estate, and that's what he's passionate about."

MARC: "He understands now that you have to lead a balanced life. You can't be so compulsive about one thing. He has a good balance between friends, family, and work, where before it would be ninety percent work, five percent family, and five percent friends. He's really cut the pie evenly now, and I think it's incredible. He always said family was important. Now he *shows* it's important. He sees Harriet every night for dinner. During tax season, he might work a couple of Sundays, but for the most part he doesn't. I think we took vacations maybe every few years when I was a kid. Now it's a yearly thing. He wants to get away from work and be with family.

"I see another difference too. He still has a very strong presence. He always has, and that's not going to change. That's just who he is. But he used to have a harsh body language and tone to him. He's lost a lot of that. He's less intimidating.

"The biggest change, to me, is that he wants to work on himself, and he tries his best to be a better person. As good as he is, as smart as he is, he always tries to find a way to be better. Before therapy, it was always, 'What's wrong with everything else? My situation is messed up. It's not me.' Now, instead of, 'How do I change the situation I'm in?' he asks, 'How can I change myself to make the situation better?' Once or twice a year, he takes Harriet and all the kids to therapy with him individually, and he says, 'How can I be a better father?' or 'How can I be a better husband? What am I doing wrong? What am I doing right?' He's not looking for a pat on the back; he's looking for the truth. I respect someone who knows he has faults and tries to work on them. I'm trying to do that myself now.

"Our relationship has gotten progressively better. I think, for one thing, he never respected me as an adult, even five years ago, and now I feel like he has much more respect for me. This is important to me, because I respect him immensely now. I respect him in business, and I admire him as a person. We can have intelligent conversations. We can sit and talk about life, politics, and business. I go to him for advice— work advice, personal advice, relationship advice. I confide in him quite a bit."

HARRIET: "He talks about having changed so much, especially when he started therapy and so forth, but I didn't see that. He told me, 'If we had been together all those years ago, we never would have made it.' I don't necessarily believe that, because we're all different with different people. I'm not Kathy, and Kathy's not me, so maybe we'd have made it because our relationship would have been different.

"I don't think he changed who he is. I think he's basically the same person, in that he's always had a wonderful heart and a good soul. I feel his love for me, and he loves being around the family. He loves my children like they're his own. I think those are things he was looking for all along. People think he's changed because of me, because he takes a lot more time off now. He never used to travel or take vacations. Before we got married, he was invited to join an international accounting organization, and he asked if I would be interested in traveling with him. It would be an excuse. You see, he felt he needed an excuse. He couldn't just say, 'Oh, let's go to … wherever.' If we were going for business, that made it okay. Now we travel and take real vacations.

"He has a good heart. He's extremely ethical. Integrity is his number one mantra. He cares deeply about his family, and about his clients. He always puts everyone else in front of himself. He loves putting people together to make something work, and he never looks out for his own benefit. He just gets high from being able to get it done. In business, he's always interested in how things affect *everybody*. It's never just about him, and it's never just about the money—unless people don't pay their bills. He's hard-nosed when it comes to that.

"I know many accountants. None of them are like Harvey. He's got something they don't have. I told him early on, 'You don't get it.

Everybody can put those numbers in that form when they do those tax returns, but you have something up here, in your head, that the others don't have.' I think he finally got it."

* * * *

I sure did. I finally got a *lot* of things, as you can tell from those comments from the people who know me best. I recognize that having others speak about me might come across as a big ego massage. I hope you, the reader, understand that the point of doing it this way is not to boast, but to show how much I've changed. If I said all that myself, it *really* would have seemed like an ego trip. I'm proud of the changes I made in my life. They did not come easily or quickly, but they were profoundly transformative. As a result, my personal life is vastly different from what it was when the earth shook on January 17, 1994.

PART TWO

CHAPTER 13
A New Professional Identity

*T*he personal changes that flowed from my marriage to Harriet and therapy with Dr. Jones brought unexpected benefits to my business life as well. I felt free to be more creative, and I grew bolder in applying my unusual approach to accounting. For the first time, I truly understood what I'd been doing instinctively all along. Now the time was right to develop it into something special. In 1999, I gave my concept a name: *Therapeutic Accounting*®.

What prompted the need to name what I do was my decision to step down as managing partner of RBZ. I'd held that position for twenty-three years. It was time for a change. On a personal level, this change would give me time to enjoy the family life that had become so precious to me. Professionally, I felt I had run my course as a managing partner, and I felt I could serve my clients better if I let someone else take over that role.

I knew RBZ would be in good hands with my chosen successor, Tom Schulte, who was ten years younger than I was and highly qualified. I literally passed the baton to Tom at a partner meeting. I presented him with an actual baton—the kind that's used in relay races—inscribed: "From Harvey Bookstein to Tom Schulte, Transfer of Managing Partner." The baton idea went over so well that Tom passed the same one to Dave Roberts in 2008.

As soon as we made the change I realized I needed new business cards to replace the ones that read "managing partner." What should my new ones say? "Founding partner?" Not special enough. Just plain "partner?" A million other accountants had cards like that, including six at RBZ at the time. I certainly couldn't go with plain vanilla "CPA" or "accountant." To me, "accountant" brings to mind a Normal Rockwell painting on the cover of *The Saturday Evening Post*, with a guy wearing a green eyeshade sitting in a high chair, with a tilt-up table, doing the math on columns of numbers. With all respect to my fellow accountants, that didn't reflect what I was or what I did. I didn't want to be seen that way.

None of the usual terms came close to expressing my actual role. My task was what we now call "branding." I wanted to define what I do and brand it with something unique. I settled on Therapeutic Accounting® and had a batch of new cards printed. I even went through the process of getting the term trademarked and registering a url: www.therapeuticaccounting.com. I've used those business cards ever since, and I love seeing how people react when they read it. People who don't know me can't imagine what the hell a therapeutic accountant is, but people who know me immediately get it.

I now had the name, the freedom, and the awareness to step wholeheartedly into a business style I'd been practicing for years. It meant I could bring even more value to my clients and my firm, even though I was spending more quality time with my family. I had never felt better about who I was, or more comfortable with my life as a whole.

What's a Therapeutic Accountant?

Toward the end of 1999, shortly before my firm celebrated its twenty-fifth anniversary, I wrote an article for *The Bottom Line*, the RBZ newsletter. In it I described the services I brought to our clients and explained the new description on my business cards: "As I understand it, a therapist is an individual who helps another person find out where they have been, and then helps them move to where they really want to go. This applies to accounting because many accounting decisions are not strictly about profit margins and last year's tax returns. Many decisions involving money are extremely emotional, particularly when they involve planning for the future and looking ahead, services which now involve a good deal of what I call Therapeutic Accounting®."

I went on to explain that in serving my clients I often talk with them about deeply personal issues, such as marriage and divorce, charitable giving, estate planning, insurance, problems with their children, investment decisions, retirement, and of course, tax planning. Naturally, these all involve finances, but they are also deeply emotional. Feelings such as love, loyalty, confusion, disappointment, hope, frustration, anger, pain, and many others come up as people talk about these matters. I strive to understand my clients well enough to confidently advise them in ways that serve their personal needs as well as their financial interests. My apprenticeship with my father taught me to do that. Now, thanks to Harriet and Dr. Jones, I could do even more. I could now serve my clients with my heart as well as my head. That doesn't mean I allow emotions or sentimentality to influence my financial judgment. Nor do I act like a psychotherapist and inquire about aspects of people's lives that are none of my business. It simply means I understand my clients as complex human beings, not just a set of numbers. This approach actually allows me to be *more* objective about business and finance, because I evaluate situations based on a more complete perspective.

By bringing more of myself to my profession, I could work holistically with my clients and do far more for them than I could under the normal limits of accounting. I mentioned some of those nontraditional functions in that newsletter: "For instance, I'm working with clients to prepare for near-term retirement, not only by helping them sell their business but also by helping them decide and plan what to do after the sale. I'm also working with clients who have new business concepts they wish to develop. I'm helping clients form strategic alliances with different clients, and foreign investors searching for opportunities to invest in worthwhile U.S. companies. I'm identifying real estate and business opportunities for other investors. In moving between clients, professionals, investors, key employees, and financial institutions, I really enjoy finding new ways to bridge financial gaps, and to open new avenues into the future."

That word "enjoy" was not used lightly. As I've said many times in this book, I've always enjoyed my work. Once I branded myself a therapeutic accountant my enjoyment multiplied. So did my client base, and so did my company's revenues, because I could now do more for my clients than ever before. On more than one occasion, for instance, I said to a company, "Why don't you close your accounting department? You'll save a lot of money if you let our firm take care of all that for you." As a result, instead of billing that client, say, $25,000 a year, we might bill them $6,000 a month, for a total of $72,000 a year and still save them money. Or, take the example of a wealthy individual client. I might ask personal questions a tax accountant wouldn't consider asking, and in the process find out he hasn't changed his will in twenty years. "You're sixty-four years old now," I say. "If you don't want to do it, let me. Show me the old will, and let me tell you what I like and don't like about it, and what I think you should consider doing, based on what you've told me."

Twelve years later, at Tom Schulte's request, I wrote an article for *The Bottom Line* explaining my unique niche in the firm. "I realize that the term I coined back then was a perfect definition of the work I did in addition to my 'normal' accounting work," I said. "Today, the definition that I had come up with after being in therapy for a short time back in 1999 still defines my accounting style." I added that, having continued to grow, "I have learned how to listen differently and to not only answer the questions at hand, but to look at them from a complete life perspective." In other words, I became a better therapeutic accountant as I learned about myself and how to deal with my own issues. This process worked the other way around too: being a therapeutic accountant taught me a lot about myself. It still does.

Serving the Whole Client

I have to confess that not every potential client relishes the idea of working with someone who delves into their personal lives. Some people want a straight-ahead, number-crunching accountant who does the books and nothing more. We have excellent traditional accountants at RBZ, and I happily turn such clients over to them. Other people are intrigued when I tell them all the things I typically do. They're like people looking at the Cheesecake Factory menu for the first time, seeing dishes they've never heard of before. "I didn't know accountants did that," they say.

My usual response is, "This accountant does."

Many get over their initial apprehension and decide to take a chance on me, either because they're intrigued by the concept of Therapeutic Accounting® or because they know my reputation for helping clients make money—or both. Once they take the plunge, they quickly see I bring added value to the table by extending the traditional accounting role to serve the whole client. Essentially, I'm a combination of accountant, confidant, financial gatekeeper, and life coach, and clients quickly come to realize that this expanded role enables me to do more for their bottom lines.

Sometimes I play good cop and sometimes I play bad cop, because I always want my clients to deal with reality as it is. As I said in that second article on Therapeutic Accounting*, "I recently had to encourage one of my clients to seriously consider putting her husband into an assisted-living facility because he was rapidly taking her health down. I had to advise another one of my clients to cut off all family aid to one of their children because it was ruining my client's own ability to financially and mentally survive, and, more importantly, encouraging that child to believe he was unable to survive on his own. I have had to help a couple of my clients buy their cemetery plots, as they made it clear they did not want to leave that burden to their children but could not get motivated to do so on their own."

Those are a few of the many kinds of issues I've dealt with in expanding the definition of my profession to better serve my clients' needs. Some clients are also my friends, and the boundary between helping a friend and serving a client can get blurry at times. But I have never found the two roles to be in conflict. In fact, more often than not it helps me do more for the client/friend, especially when they need a reality check. I can be perfectly candid when I see someone making what I consider to be a grave error, for example by taking on too much risk. Here is an excerpt from a letter I sent to one such person, edited to protect the family's identity:

Dear _____ :

Sometimes in my profession, I become uncertain as to when I "step over the line" in communicating my concerns regarding my clients' financial condition. In your situation, I find it even more difficult because you and your wife are personal friends.

Several times in the past couple of years, I have expressed my concern over your spending habits. We have discussed the reasons, needs, and enjoyments of spending money, but sometimes we have to step back from a situation to truly and objectively understand why we do what we do.

I just learned today that you are looking to acquire a lot for $4.5 million to build your "dream house." My understanding is that you will spend approximately $2-3 million more to complete the construction of your home.

I know you are a risk-taker, and I commend you for the success you have had in taking this road. However, I would really like you to look at the rationale of needing this type of residence, as well as considering what the monthly costs of maintaining this residence will be.

Even with my concern, I want to assure you that I will support your decisions 100%. I have already started to work with a mortgage broker to get the necessary financing.

You may feel free to take this letter and throw it in the trash (which I would certainly understand). However, I felt obligated as a professional—and, more importantly, as your friend—to share my feelings with you about this home.

To my relief, my clients decided not to go ahead with this risky proposition at that time. They realized their reasons for wanting that dream house were superficial and vain, and the huge, elegant home they already lived in was plenty dreamy by anyone's standards.

My dear friend and longtime client, Michael Rosenfeld, describes our relationship in the following way. It captures quite well my approach to accounting and the way I've been able to work with clients who are also friends:

"I was in my early twenties when I met Harvey socially. It was the mid-eighties, and I had a successful mortgage brokerage business. I was starting to do real estate development, and I needed help structuring my business for tax purposes and liability purposes. So Harvey became my accountant. He took a big administrative burden off me, and he helped me find ways of structuring my companies to be most efficient from a business and tax perspective.

We became friends as a result of that relationship, and a level of trust developed over the years. He was a teacher and advisor, and he even helped me find people to work in my organization. I could always bounce ideas off him. I trusted that he always had my best interests at heart, personally and professionally. This relationship was a nice thing to have as a young guy coming up in business, and it went above and beyond the call of duty for most accountants. I could go to Harvey for anything, whether it was business-related or something I was going through in my life.

"We became brothers, almost, in that we could both share what was going on in our lives, with confidence that the other person was looking out for you and not judging you. We found we had common experiences that really bonded us, and our friendship kind of went from there.

"My first child was born in 1990, my second in '93, and my third in '94. Harvey became the trustee for all three. He was the person with whom I felt most confident in leaving the care and well-being of my children to in case something should happen to me and my then-wife. I think that speaks volumes.

"One of the things Harvey does is get people to examine what they want out of life, not just out of their business decisions, but 'What do you really want?' 'What's going to make you happy?' 'What are you going to do to feel good about yourself?' Without overlaying his own judgment on them, he helps people find their own paths. I think his attitude kind of throws people sometimes, but it is refreshing. The answer may be, 'You know what? My kids are louses and they don't care about anybody but themselves. They just can't wait for me to die and get the money, and that makes me unhappy.' Or someone else might say, 'I'm estranged from my children and it really breaks my heart.' Harvey will understand. He'll say, 'Okay, what do you want to do? What's going to make you feel right?' I think it's beautiful that he helps people not only realize their financial objectives, but also helps them realize their personal objectives. I think that is unusual. He has touched many people's lives in a beautiful way."

I have taken for granted my skills as an accountant ever since I was a kid. That people also respect my talent for doing business and making savvy investment decisions has been extra gratifying. Even my ex-wife Kathy, who hated me with a passion during our divorce proceedings, now trusts me to invest her money and manage our children's trusts and investments.

Having that kind of professional respect and *also* being appreciated for my nontraditional contributions as a *therapeutic* accountant—that comes as a greater blessing than anything I could have imagined in the first part of my life.

How RBZ Changed

The changes in my life and work carried over into RBZ's company culture. When I turned over the reins as Managing Partner to Tom Schulte, he and I took the lead in making policy changes. We had always been a decent company to work for. We were known as hard-working and competent. People wanted to work for us, and our turnover rate was low. Now we set out to make RBZ an even better place to work. Since I had elevated family to the top of my personal priority list, I wanted RBZ to be family-friendly for everyone who worked there. Tom was 100 percent in sync with that. "I wanted us to be the best firm in the niches we chose to work in," he recalls, "and I wanted work to be an enjoyable experience for everybody. I wanted this to be a company people don't mind going home from on Fridays but love coming back to on Mondays."

As the current and former managing partners, Tom and I knew a shift in that direction was not only the humane thing to do, but was also a smart business decision. Scouting, hiring, and training new people only to have them leave and make us go through the whole process again was expensive and time consuming. If we treated people exceptionally well and let them know their personal lives were also important to us, we'd be ahead of the game. As Tom puts it, we asked a lot of our employees, so we should start asking ourselves, "What can we give back to make their lives easier?"

This seems like common sense, but it was far from common practice back then. In the ensuing years, we found that some of the innovations we came up with have been copied by other firms. One of the first was what we call the concierge concept. During the busy season, from January 15 to April 15, when everyone works so hard that aspects of their personal lives invariably fall through the cracks, we hire people to help them pick up the slack: drop off the dry cleaning; clean their homes; wait for the plumber or the cable TV guy to show up; drive them to work when their cars are being serviced; take their dogs to the vet; and so forth. Over time, we added all sorts of amenities, like massages, pedicures, and manicures at the office, free car washes, and good hot food for supper four nights a week for those who work late. It's good for them, and it's good for the company, because it allows everyone to keep their full attention on the clients at that crucial time of year.

The changes in RBZ's culture came to define the heart of RBZ. Over the years—essentially ever since the new century began—we kept improving on our commitment to being a company that does great work and is also a great place to work. As I write this, in 2012, the trade publication *Accounting Today* named us the seventh-best medium-size accounting firm in the entire country to work for. The survey, conducted with Best Companies Group, is designed to identify, recognize, and honor the best places of employment in the accounting industry. This was the second year in a row that RBZ ranked in the top ten, and we were the *only* Southern California firm in the top twenty. We have earned this kind of recognition on other occasions as well. I consider it a testament to the environment we created, where, in Tom Schulte's words, "You don't have to give up your personal life in order to have a professional life." That became my own goal, and I'm thrilled we made it easier for everyone at the firm to do the same.

Over time, as I continued to grow as a person and as a therapeutic accountant, I came to define certain principles that guide my approach to work. In the remaining chapters, I will share them with you.

Chapter 14
Do It Your Way

A s I grow older, I find people often ask me when I'm going to retire. They act as if they expect me to be counting down the days to the sweet joys of golf and cruises. I get it. Some people view retirement as some sort of ultimate vacation. This is just not the case for me. I can't imagine retiring. When people ask, "When do you want to stop working?" I say, "When do you want to stop enjoying life?" To me, there is no contradiction between work and enjoying life. I know I might not work forever, because my health may not allow it, so I say, "I'm going to retire when I can no longer work."

One reason I look forward to going to work every morning is that I conduct business in a way that's deeply personal. I believe if a person wants to feel happy at work, they should put themselves in a position to do things their own way as much as possible.

Often, people are so focused on pleasing others that they end up displeased with themselves. They may be so eager to prove themselves to their bosses, their colleagues, their spouses, their parents, their friends, or their mentors that they imitate whatever behavior they think will earn them respect and professional advancement. There is something admirable about looking up to senior people in your field and wanting to emulate their best qualities, but replicating their style or their behavior won't necessarily make you a winner. You become a winner by working hard, presenting yourself well, and being the best you can possibly be—and it's a whole lot easier to do all three of those if you do things *your* way, not someone else's.

You'll find it's nearly impossible to do your best when you're busy trying to fit in. You can end up lost in the crowd, sacrificing your best self in a misguided effort to be respected and accepted. I learned at an early age that I'd rather be genuine and alone than inauthentic in the company of others. That's one of the reasons I was such a loner in school; I wasn't interested in trying to fit in with everyone else around me. I cared more about doing the business-related things I loved. As a result, I not only became great at what I do, I ignited a fire for work in me that still burns brightly. Throughout the years, I followed my inner mandate to do things my own way. I recognize not everyone can do that, but I always tell people: if you can possibly do work that comes naturally to you, and if you can perform that work in a way that's true to your personality, your style, and your skills, you will be far happier— and probably more successful—than if you attempt to be something you're not.

It is said that imitation is the sincerest form of flattery. Maybe so, but I believe imitation can also be the worst form of self-denial. Imitation can lead straight to disillusionment. Some things just can't be mimicked, and certain qualities just can't be reproduced. If you force yourself to do something that doesn't come naturally to you, you'll eventually get worn out or come down with a stress disorder like high blood pressure or depression. On the other hand, if you can do things your own way, you're likely to end each day happy about the choices you've made. Being true to yourself preserves energy and prevents burnout. And this approach isn't just good for you as an individual; it's usually good for business too. People can spot a phony, and no one wants to do business with someone they don't trust.

A Culture of Authenticity

In my company, I not only insisted on doing things my way from day one, I've strongly encouraged others to do the same. As RBZ grew, we were smart enough to let people do their thing, and that authenticity has paid off big-time in our reputation for employee satisfaction, client trust, and profitability. As I said earlier, right from the get-go Ted and I knew we needed each other like a head needs a heart. I needed Ted's stable personality and technical skills, and he needed my go-getter passion. Then we added Dave, and the three of us needed others, and then others, and we needed Sunny and the junior accountants and the support staff—every one of them playing different roles like musicians in an orchestra. Right now, there are fifteen partners at RBZ, and if the other fourteen were all like me we'd have sunk into oblivion a long time ago. Even two Harveys would have been too much. The same is true of everyone else. There's one Harvey, and one Ted, and one Dave and ... well, you get the point. Each person brings his or her uniqueness to the team, and that's a big reason we're successful.

I always understood that concept intuitively, but I didn't fully appreciate it until the time my alma mater, Cal State Northridge, honored me as a distinguished alumnus at the school's fiftieth anniversary celebration. During the gala festivities, they surprised me by playing a video with my RBZ colleagues talking about me and how I've contributed to the company and their lives. It was a combination tribute and roast. On the video, Ted Roth says, "In all the years I've been working with Harvey, he never forced me to be somebody I wasn't. He let me do it the way I needed to do it." I got emotional hearing him say that. His words were concrete recognition of something I had always preached and always tried to practice. But I never knew until that moment how much it meant to Ted.

I was deeply moved to know my original partner was grateful for that aspect of our relationship. The truth is, of course, that I didn't do it as a favor to him. I did it because I wanted the same thing from him: to let me be myself. And in fact he gave it to me, because he knew what I knew: the way to get the most out of people is to let them do things their own way. Why would business partners want to copy each other? It's not only undesirable, it's impossible. Ted couldn't be me any more than I could be him, no matter how hard we tried. If one of us tried to make the other something he was not, the partnership would have ended in our cramped office in Century City.

"Harvey is a very good marketing person, and I am much more of a technical kind of guy," Ted says, when asked about our complementary skill sets. "I'm very conservative and traditional, and I'm not a risk-taker. That's just not my nature. Harvey is a much bigger risk-taker than I am. He's much more outgoing than I am. He likes to talk, and I'm a little more reserved. I have good relationships with my clients, but people come to me for different reasons than they come to Harvey. We attract different people and provide different kinds of services." He adds: "In the early years, I always did the technical work. I did the complicated tax work, and all the financial statement work. Harvey was more the client service partner. He spent more time with clients, while I would do the final reviews and the detailed work. We'd go out on joint solicitations in the early years, and it worked fine. We were a nice balancing act."

The same thing happened with Dave Zaslow and everyone else who has ever joined the firm. To this day, when we take on a new employee, I advise them, "You're going to be working with fifteen partners. We are all very different. Don't copy any of us. Take the best from everyone, get rid of the parts you don't like in each of us, and develop your own style." The best way for someone to learn and develop personalized skills is by osmosis. They need to touch, smell, and feel what being a professional at RBZ is all about. They need to apprentice, just as I did with my father. I think apprentice-style training is the best way to learn most professions. Who are the best carpenters? The people who banged in nails for excellent carpenters. Who are the best physicians? The ones who studied under great doctors as interns and residents. Who are the best musicians? The ones who broke in under the guidance of great performers. Whether you're mentored by a relative, a professor, a boss, a stranger—it makes no difference, as long as you learn by doing. That way, you not only acquire good technique; you also become accustomed to finding your own path within your work. It becomes easier to eventually develop a style and a voice of your own.

Do you see what I mean by "Do it your own way?" It's not just that old hippy motto, "Do your own thing." It's more than that. It has to do with using the skills and methods that come naturally to you. In a company setting, it also has to do with teamwork. At RBZ, those who are good at auditing do auditing, and those who work well with entrepreneurs do that, and those who excel at bringing in new business bring in new business. What makes the firm successful is the uniqueness each of us brings to the team. I'm not just talking about being tolerant of differences; I'm talking about having genuine *respect* for differences and using those differences to build the kind of teamwork that is indispensable for success.

You Can't Always Get What You Want

I have to add some caveats, though. Realistically, you can't always do what comes naturally to you, and you can't always do things your way. Even if you're a lone wolf, an entrepreneur, and your own boss, someone else will be hiring you or buying your product, and they'll have demands. Plus, most professions have an inevitable breaking-in period, when newcomers have to pay their dues and learn the ropes. The first few years of an accountant's career are not always fun by any means, especially in a big firm. Everyone dumps the worst part of the job—all the boring, tedious stuff—on the newbies. As you move up, you start becoming the dumper as well as the dumpee, and when you rise high enough, you not only stop getting dumped on, you also get a voice in your company's policy.

Another caveat: there are times when doing things your own way can be a double-edged sword. When the principle is misused, or taken too far, consequences occur. For one thing, doing it your way doesn't mean imposing your way on others. Try to get everyone to sing "My Way" according to your tune, and you become a tyrant, or maybe never reach a position of leadership in the first place. If you want to do things your way, you must be prepared to let others do the same; ignore their wants and needs and you become alienated from everyone who matters. I'm proud to say the partners at RBZ try to maintain an environment where people have enough autonomy to gravitate to the professional areas that are right for their personalities and skills.

Of course, there will always be times when compromise is not only necessary but wise. We need to recognize those instances and act accordingly. I know there were times in my life when I could have been more yielding, instead of stubbornly insisting on doing things my way and watching it backfire. On one such occasion I took my life in my hands. A handful of people from the firm were planning a skydiving adventure. On an odd whim, I said I wanted to join them. This was a few months before I turned forty, and I guess I thought it would be an interesting way to celebrate that landmark. In all honesty, I was just toying with the idea until my ex-wife, Kathy said I was forbidden to go. Her reasons were sound: "You're a parent. You're a husband. It would be irresponsible to do something that risky." I took her words as an attempt to control me. The more she said "You aren't going," the more I wanted to go. When she said, "You can't do it," I thought "Watch me." Kathy came to the site and yelled at me not do it, while our kids, who were five and nine at the time, cried. That should have altered my decision, but it did the opposite: it made me more adamant about going ahead.

Kathy's argument about why I should not jump out of that plane was compounded by the weather, which was so bad we had to wait four hours for the wind to die down. On top of that, another problem arose. A plane went up before us, and when one of the professional divers jumped out her chute didn't open. We watched her plummet toward the ground to a certain death—until, just before impact, her parachute finally deployed. She survived, but with several broken bones. As it happens, she was our instructor's girlfriend, so he rushed off to be with her at the hospital. This was a serious blow, because he had won our confidence. He'd made us feel we would be in the best possible hands in that plane. Now he was gone, and his replacement didn't exactly win us over. He had a metal leg, having lost the real one ... you guessed it, skydiving. This entire calamity unfolded while my wife screamed at me not to get into the plane and the children cried their eyes out. My nerves were totally shot. But I went up.

In the air, I was terrified. As we got ready to jump, I had to put my hands on the wing and hold on. I was supposed to let go when the instructors said, "Skydive," but after three passes I still couldn't loosen my grip. My knuckles were as white as snow. The instructor threatened, "Either jump or come back in, or I'm going out there with a hammer." Eventually, I decided to let go. But I panicked. I totally abandoned the proper technique, which involved arching your back so you can pull away from the plane and not get caught in the propeller. Despite my frenzy, and despite doing it all wrong, I landed perfectly, right on my feet. I received a score of ten out of a possible ten. That was pure luck.

Although the episode had a happy ending, it was something I should not have done. I was the class nerd, not some ex-jock with a lifelong habit of physical prowess. It was totally reckless of me to put myself and my family in jeopardy, especially when the weather wasn't right and someone else—a professional—had already gotten terribly hurt. I think that part of me wanted to prove something to other people. I basically risked my life to disprove the image others had of me and defy their expectations. I also wanted to defy Kathy, but all I did was exacerbate the tension between us. I probably traumatized my kids in the bargain. It's true that I'm proud of having had the courage to jump, but I know it was idiotic, and I'd certainly never jump again. My motives for doing it were just plain wrong. Sometimes "My Way" is exactly the wrong song.

Do It Your Way the Right Way

Doing things my own way is as important to me as ever. But I've learned over the years that doing it my way is more complex than I thought. I discovered that being true to yourself should also be consistent with being agreeable, flexible, and considerate of others. That goes for both business and personal affairs. I'm very strong-willed by nature (some call it stubbornness), and I can be that way at home as well as at work. But Harriet, who is petite and appears unthreatening, is probably stronger than I am. I love and respect her so much that I'm more willing to give in to her wishes than I've ever been with any other human being. She doesn't always get her way, and I certainly don't always get my way. Instead, we try to listen to each other's perspectives and find mutual ground to stand on together.

Sometimes, paradoxically, I find that doing it my way actually means doing something totally selfless, for the sake of another person. Try it. Making someone happy can bring the best kind of joy, and it gets you through the day feeling good about yourself. My ability to do that now has made my life far happier than before, and I learned how to do it from Harriet and Dr. Jones.

In business too, sometimes compromise and generosity is the best way of doing things your way. This approach can pay off big-time in trust, referrals, future transactions, and a good reputation. Strategic compromise is different than doing things someone else's way out of fear or weakness. It's not the same as acquiescence or appeasement. Caving in, whether to a colleague or a spouse, leads to feelings of inadequacy, shame, and resentment. The point is, doing it your way doesn't always mean *getting* your way. It means you do things in a way that bolsters your self-respect and lets you go to bed at night feeling good about yourself.

For all these reasons I'd like to modify the principle "Do it your way." Let's make it "Do it your way, but do it consciously, conscientiously, and with a conscience." Doing things consciously means being aware of what you're doing and why you're doing it; doing things conscientiously means paying attention to the full range of consequences of your actions; and doing it with a conscience means taking into account other people's needs and wishes.

If you do that, everything falls into place. By contrast, when trying to do things your way leads to lying or cheating or cutting corners, that's when you stop being completely honest with yourself. You lose your energy, you forget who you really are, and you end up feeling ashamed because you did the *wrong* thing your way. The goal of "Do it your way" is making sure you are true to yourself, comfortable with your actions, and proud of the person you've become.

Chapter 15
Do It With Passion

*T*here are two types of workers: those with passion for what they do, and those without it. Success usually favors the former. Most of us spend about a third of our lives working, another third sleeping, and the last third doing other things. Unfortunately, most people either dislike the third spent on their jobs or show up with an attitude of indifference, just to collect their paycheck. I can't imagine living that way. Luckily, I never have. For me, work is a joy. I bring a great passion to it every day. I've been fortunate in feeling that way all my life, and it got even better when I learned how to devote most of my energy to the aspects of my profession I love the most. That's why I can give it a lot *more* than one-third of my life.

People are often astonished that an accountant can love his work as much as I do. They think of accounting as a boring, number-crunching job. And you know what? To a certain extent, they're right. Accounting can be boring. It can be routine. It can be tedious. It can be monotonous. But not for everybody; it must be said that what some people find numbing, others find fascinating. Where I'm concerned, however, the usual image doesn't apply. As I said earlier, if ordinary accounting was my only choice, I'd have gone into a different line of work. I changed the definition of my profession to make it work for me. I keep the fire burning in my belly by turning accounting into something with heart and soul. I was doing that long before I came up with the term Therapeutic Accounting®, but once I got to know myself I got better and better at turning my day-to-day work into a personal art form. As a result, I bring passion to the office and bigger numbers to the bottom line.

When I look at my schedule in the morning, I get excited if it's packed with six or seven appointments, meetings, and other obligations. But you know what makes me even more excited? Blank spaces. Not because they represent downtime. On the contrary, to me, those openings symbolize the unexpected. That's when I'll have to deal with crises, emergencies, unpredictable challenges, and baffling problems no one saw coming. You know, the kinds of issues most people dread. The ones they avoid. The ones that break up their easy routines and ruin their days. I love that stuff. They raise the temperature on the passion I already bring to my work, and I approach them like a confident athlete who wants the ball when the game is on the line—the one who tells the coach, "Call my number," while the other players avert their eyes and pray it won't be them.

I enjoy confronting difficult situations. I love being the problem-solver. I get turned on when things are messy. Circumstances that most of my colleagues see as a nightmare are a dream to me. Most people hate pressure. It keeps them up at night, and upsets their tummies in the morning. They whine to their spouses over breakfast, "There's a pile of trouble on my plate today. I wish I could call in sick." Harriet never has to put up with that. I live for those days.

The Case of Mr. B.

Fortunately, there's plenty of trouble to go around in my line of work, so my passion rarely simmers down. For example, one day I got a call from one of my clients. Let's call him Mr. B. The son of one of the wealthiest people in L.A., he sits on the board of a bank, and a year earlier he took out a multimillion-dollar unsecured line of credit from the same bank. This was perfectly legal, and a smart business decision; he took the loan to purchase a property that offered a nice cash flow. Well, it seems the bank came to him and said the regulators were getting tough on unsecured loans to board members. It would help if he could pay it off, they told him. My client said, "No problem." However, he was going through a divorce at the time, and while he's a rich man, he wasn't very liquid. So he turned to his wealthy friends. One of them promised to lend him the money at eight percent interest for thirty-one months, which was when the first mortgage was due. Problem solved, just like that. Unfortunately, the friend soon called back to say he couldn't lend him the money after all, due to a family dispute that prohibited him from making certain types of investments.

That's when Mr. B called me. He was in a panic. "I made a commitment to the bank," he said, "but I don't have the cash." He said he was willing to pay up to eight percent interest. I asked for a full write-up on the property, and when I worked out the numbers I saw it was a very good value. I told Mr. B. I could solve the problem by bringing in another client of mine who had the necessary cash. Putting clients together is something I do all the time, so I knew exactly whom to call. Let's make him Mr. L., for Lender. Sure enough, Mr. L. went for it. He not only knew a good deal when he saw one, but he'd come to trust my judgment because we've made a lot of money together over the years. He had his own terms though: twelve percent, not eight percent, plus an assignment of the rent, which means the checks would be sent directly from the tenant to my trust account instead of going through Mr. B. I immediately called Mr. B. and told him the terms. I also asked for a personal guarantee, so Mr. L. would be protected if, for any reason, he did not get paid off in a timely manner.

Crisis resolved; case closed. The whole thing took less than twenty-four hours, and everyone was happy. Mr. B. was happy because, even though he'd done nothing illegal or immoral, he'd been vulnerable to the embarrassment of breaking his commitment to a bank whose board he was on, and now he was spared that. Mr. L. was happy because he was getting good interest on his loan, and if he ever had to foreclose he'd be sitting on a nice asset for his money. And I was happy because I got a big, unexpected problem to work on, and I solved it quickly and effectively.

Financially, all I got for my efforts was my normal billing rate— in this case about $500. I could have charged an additional fee for making the deal, or taken a percentage of the lender's profits. But I didn't want to. I got to help two clients I cared about, and the process itself turned me on. I can justify it on bottom-line grounds too, of course, because there's no better marketing campaign than earning the respect and gratitude of satisfied clients. In fact, as I write this Mr. B. is looking for someone to do a certified audit on a new company he's starting. I'm sure, because of all I've done for him, that RBZ will be at the top of his list. As for Mr. L., he was already a partner in thirty or forty of my investments, so this was just one more way to prove my value to him.

What I've just described is not what a typical accountant does. But as a therapeutic accountant, I go above and beyond my ordinary duties to secure what's best for each person. If I have a client in pain, I find a way to help, and I love doing it. I get a rush from clients who are in a panic when I believe I can solve their problem, as in the case of Mr. B. If I worked in a firehouse, I would be counting the minutes until the alarm went off, and when it finally did I'd whoop for joy, while the other guys would be cursing because it had broken up their card game. People think I'm a madman because I love the tension and the pressure. But problem-solving makes me feel like I'm making a real difference. I compare it to people who do charity work to help the less fortunate. That might sound strange, since my clients are usually wealthy people. But in a crisis, they're the unfortunate ones. And some are unfortunate even without a crisis, because they have family problems or they just don't know how to handle their own financial affairs. If I can make their lives a little better, that's a big win for me. And I get paid to do it! It still blows my mind that people pay me to have fun at work.

The Downside of Passion

Of course, as with most things, there is a negative side to being passionate: if you're not careful, that passion can take you over the edge. Passionate people like me experience many ups and downs. My partner, Dave Zaslow, says, "It's like the movie where Steve Martin is working day and night trying to balance family and business, and he's ready to throw in the towel, when someone asks him, 'Do you want to live your life on a merry-go-round or do you want to live your life on a rollercoaster?' And Steve Martin says, 'Rollercoaster.' That's the way Harvey is. He deals with extremes. It's a positive thing, but also something to be watchful for, and I think he knows how to control the negative part."

I also learned the hard way that too much enthusiasm can be dangerous if it clouds good judgment. I once joined the board of a bank that was failing. I wanted to be its savior. I was going to use my Midas touch to fix it. I worked hard as a board member, and after a few months I was asked to be the new chairman. I agreed—not a good decision. My love of problem-solving landed me in an environment where I ended up hating what I was doing. I had to go to the bank periodically and see people I knew who were going to be laid off. The board members surrounding me were always afraid the bank would be taken over and they would lose their money and their reputations. I got constant phone calls from regulators, who wouldn't let me take the necessary steps toward good business policies. It was way more than I bargained for, and the furthest thing from a pleasant experience I can imagine.

At a certain point I had to come to terms with how bad things were. "What the hell am I doing here?" I asked myself. "I don't know enough about the banking system to make this work." Bottom line: my passion for problem-solving led me to become the chairman of the board of a bank that failed. Lesson learned: having passion for what you do is vital, but you'll lose that passion awfully fast if you direct it toward the wrong things. You not only have to be passionate about what you do, you also have to do what you're passionate about. That usually means doing what you're naturally cut out for and are good at.

Passionate Accounting

At RBZ I can feed my passion in a setting that's made to order for me—partly, I admit, because I made it that way. The only times I'm not happy at work is when things get too slow, or too easy. Feeling that way makes me the opposite of most people, but I'm used to that. I get alarmed when I don't have eight hundred messages pouring in. I get agitated when I don't have twenty files on my desk to deal with. I start thinking, "Oh, my God, everyone has abandoned me. I've got no clients left." Without problems popping up, I have to resort to routine, which I equate with boredom.

I often transfer non-challenging clients to one of my partners. That's good for the clients, because I can't serve them well if I lose interest. And my partners usually appreciate it too. Most accountants like routine work, such as doing financial statements. I understand that entirely, but I happen to find that kind of work boring. Who cares what happened last year? I want to know what's happening *next* year. As I said earlier, the primary job of most accountants—the "green eyeshade" accountants—is to report the events of the past. They're historians.

They keep track of what happened. That is obviously necessary. But I care more about the future. What's the goal? How are you going to get there? What's in the way, and how will you fix it? That sort of thing gets my blood flowing. I like thinking ahead. I like averting dangers, and making good things happen instead. That makes me more of an entrepreneur than a typical accountant.

My father used to give me monotonous paperwork to do. Boring! Back then, I understood I was getting paid for learning the fundamentals of my profession. When I started working for Kenneth Leventhal & Company, I had to start at the bottom like everyone else, and I did work I wasn't all that excited about. But I knew what I had to do to move up the ladder, and I climbed it as quickly as I could. I always tried to jump ahead of everyone else—not because I was out to beat them in the usual competitive way, but because I wanted to get away from the kind of work people at the bottom have to do. If that was all accounting could be, there's absolutely no way I could have stayed in the field.

Luckily, I discovered many aspects of accounting I find incredibly exciting. Over time, I converted my profession to what I wanted it to be. I was always passionate about work, but, when I changed the definition of accounting to suit who I am and what I love to do, the passion really took hold.

To me, the term Therapeutic Accounting® means truly working with my heart. My work is like a machine in some ways: it functions smoothly, it runs with precision, it's reliably successful. But it has a heart. I genuinely care about my clients. I worry about them. I feel bad when they have problems. When they're faced with an important decision, I try my best to help them make the right choice. When they don't, I feel I've failed.

Ordinary accountants don't need passion. They just have to be good and know what they're doing, and not make mistakes. Most accountants are not cut out for my style of work. That doesn't mean they aren't good accountants. They may be great auditors, or excellent with taxes, with a rock-solid knowledge of the rules and regulations. Rip-roaring passion for what you do is certainly not a requirement, but it sure makes life more interesting. The more passion you can muster, the more satisfaction you'll get from the one-third—or more—of your life that you spend at work.

Work with Passionate People

Passionate people make the workplace better. Their enthusiasm and verve are contagious. One bored, apathetic, or bitter person can bring down an entire office. I'll give you an example. RBZ used to have a glaring shortcoming: we weren't good at removing bad people. At one point, we had a young accountant who visibly disdained his work. Anyone could recognize it, and his attitude showed up in his results. People encouraged him to do better, but it didn't happen, and no one wanted to fire him. Eventually, I had to tell the guy through an evaluation that he wasn't a good fit for RBZ—and not only that: I thought he should completely get out of accounting. He didn't welcome this news. A couple of months later, we finally let him go. He was upset, but he went back home, reevaluated his life, and ended up getting a law degree. Now he's an attorney and he loves it.

I did that guy a favor. I knew if he stayed in accounting he'd end up regretting it for the rest of his life. He would come to feel that his years as an accountant were a waste of his precious time. I helped him leave a profession he wasn't good at and didn't care about.

That's a great example of how lack of passion can be an indication that a person is ill-suited for the career they've chosen. If you aren't passionate about your work, maybe you should reconsider your profession—or at least the aspect of your profession you've staked out for yourself. Is there another way to do it? Is there a different specialty you can focus on? Is there another place to bring your talents? There are many ways to put yourself in a position where your dormant passion can be ignited.

One of them is not to sit around and complain. Most successful people hate being around whiners and complainers. Complainers are not doers. They don't take proactive steps toward fixing problems. They just dwell in the misery. In fact, I originally had resistance about going to therapy because I thought it was just for whiners. I thought the dialogue in therapy was: "This went wrong in my life, and this didn't go so well, and maybe I should have done that instead."

I'm so grateful I got past that misconception; it kept me from pursuing what I needed for a long time. I was surprised and relieved when I learned therapy is a lot more than whining. I don't go to Dr. Jones to complain, but to discuss issues I need to understand better and then find ways to tackle them.

I like to think of myself as a man of compassion and empathy, but I have a low tolerance for whiners. I just can't give them the sympathy they're seeking. I'm not good at patting their backs and reinforcing their complaints. I usually listen for a while, then tell them to grow up. Except if they're clients. With clients, I'm Mr. Understanding. It's my job to hear their problems, even if they complain and whine, because I'm the guy who's going to pull them out of the quicksand. Besides, when I'm with a client, I'm on the clock for billable hours, so they can whine all they want. Sometimes, I actually tell them, "If you want to use up our time with this, it's your business. You're paying for it. But I think there are more productive ways for you to use my time." They respect me when I tell them that, because they know I'm there for them, whatever they need.

Overall, passion is great for business. Clients respond well to passionate people. I know personally that prospective clients are always impressed when they come to my office. They may be interviewing four other firms, but I'm always 99.99 percent certain they're going to give me their business. Why? Because they rarely come across accountants with my level of enthusiasm. They see that my passion is genuine, not something I put on to impress them. To be honest, I seldom get dismissed when a client is considering which firm to hire. When I *don't* land a client, I believe it's almost always because I'm expensive. When that happens, I have no regrets. I don't want to be the cheap passionate guy; I want to be the high-priced passionate guy. I'm worth it, and people recognize that I'm a good investment. I tell them, "If I don't earn you back five times as much money as you pay me, then you shouldn't be using me." My clients know who I am, and they have confidence in me.

I'm an accountant by training. I'm an accountant by pedigree. I'm a founding partner of an accounting firm. But I don't work like most accountants, and I declare what's different about me right up front. Clients quickly learn that the passion I bring to my work enables me to go the extra mile. I put my heart and soul into it. People who appreciate my passion want to work with me, and that's what's made my career so successful and my life so fulfilling.

Chapter 16
Do It With Integrity

One of the many things that make RBZ a unique accounting firm is the large amount of time the partners dedicate to analyzing the firm's operations. I'm not just referring to issues like marketing, niche selection, hiring practices, staff training, and marketing. We spend only a fraction of our time discussing such matters. When the partners convene, we mainly address issues we consider even more basic. At one partner retreat, for example, we dug into how to ensure continuity of the firm long after we retire. We covered many topics in that context, including how the firm and the industry in general were changing. After a long evaluation, we decided that two words would prove vital in maintaining the longevity of RBZ: "heart" and "integrity."

"Heart" proved the more difficult word to define. After hours of discussion, we had to conclude that it was simply indefinable. We could only cite examples of what heart looks like. My examples tended to involve being personally invested in my work. I mentioned things like having genuine excitement for our clients' success; taking into account a client's problems at home (not just at the office); making solid recommendations even when clients are reluctant to listen; networking with clients and learning about their lives as a whole. Other partners suggested that "heart" meant selflessness, as in making decisions that benefit the firm as a whole, not just specific individuals. We agreed that heart comes from people with good character and is exemplified through their actions.

After we discussed "heart" at length, we tackled "integrity." Most people equate the term with honesty, and they tend to take it for granted. But court cases and revelations in the press regularly show that integrity is no more automatic in accounting than it is in other professions. My partners and I wish it could be taken for granted, as integrity is something every person should regularly implement in their lives and their work. We concluded that "integrity" meant trust. People with integrity are trusted to be respectful and discreet. They are open to new perspectives in pursuit of the best possible outcome. They create an atmosphere in which everyone feels safe discussing their frank opinions. Above all, it means being totally honest in your dealings with the other partners, the clients, the staff, your business associates, your family, and society as a whole.

Putting Integrity to the Test

We at RBZ have had to call ourselves up to high standards of integrity many times over the years when specific issues arose. For instance, in 1998, we invited Dave Roberts to join the firm and add an important niche to our services: law firms. Dave specialized in accounting for law firms, and he had more than a hundred firms as clients at the time. He was tired of running his own firm and wanted to join a larger one like RBZ. He was on the fence, however, about bringing his practice to us. Why? Because we had an unfunded retirement program. I asked him to explain why our current system was inadequate. I listened carefully; if our policy was not in the best interest of everyone affected by it, I genuinely wanted to be aware of it. Dave explained that, in his experience, unfunded retirement programs were a leading cause of law firm breakups. They're basically blue-sky promises to pay a certain amount of money in the future based on today's financial picture. Dave was reluctant to join a company whose deferred compensation plan he considered a ticking time bomb. He basically said, "You have a great firm, but I don't want to be on the hook for everyone's retirement."

We realized that our deferred compensation plan, although it was standard for professional firms, was not in the best interest of RBZ's future if it prevented us from bringing on high-quality people like Dave. We discussed the alternatives, and we made a promise to change the system. Dave was skeptical that an established company would completely overhaul its retirement policy based on a suggestion from some outsider we hardly knew. We were serious, but Dave didn't know us well enough to take our word for it. I asked him to trust that we'd follow through; changes of that magnitude can't be instituted overnight, and he had to make a decision quickly. He was understandably reluctant, but he went with his gut feeling about us. "My gut was telling me to trust them," he later said. "So I closed my eyes and jumped. I brought my practice over to RBZ." It cost the partners a considerable amount of deferred money to change our plan, but it was worth the cost to create a better future. We made Dave a promise, and we kept it. That's integrity.

Integrity Can Be Complicated

Those who know me have heard me discuss the importance of integrity many times. I talk about it at home, at work, in meetings with clients, in speeches, and even during social gatherings. I've heard people say, "Never lie to Harvey. It's better to tell him the truth and take the consequences." They're right. Honesty is so important to me I can accept practically anything but a lie. I expect honesty from my friends, family members, business associates, and employees. I hold other people to the same standards I apply to myself. I've built my reputation around integrity, and I always speak the truth. At the same time, I realize that acting on the basis of integrity is not always cut-and-dried.

RBZ is fortunate enough to have a client whose business is *about* integrity. The company is the Joseph & Edna Josephson Institute of Ethics. The institute is headed by Michael Josephson, a non-practicing attorney, who discovered he had such a passion for ethical philosophy that he gave up law to educate others on the subject. I've learned an awful lot about ethics, honesty, and integrity from Michael. At one point, before I ever met him, Michael agreed to be the guest speaker at our company's State of the Firm meeting. I was ecstatic, because I'd heard good things about him and his work but had not yet heard him speak. Unfortunately, I suffered an accident and needed knee surgery, so I couldn't attend the meeting. I was disappointed, but I sent my two sons in my place. They told me basically what Michael said, but with little enthusiasm. Then, a few days later, one of them told me he couldn't stop thinking about the Josephson presentation. He kept reflecting on how he hadn't been living a completely honest life, and he wanted to change that. Nothing could have impressed me more. I hoped Michael's speech had the same impact on everyone at RBZ, and I believe it did. All our employees, top to bottom, seem to value the importance of integrity.

When I finally met with Michael one-on-one, he confirmed my notions about integrity while introducing me to new concepts. He explained the complexities of ethical behavior, like how telling a white lie is not strictly ethical but is nevertheless not always the wrong thing to do. We discussed how there are situations with clients that make the assessment of honesty more complicated than it appears on the surface. For example, when government auditors review a client's record they sometimes misdirect themselves by asking the wrong questions. I always refrain from steering them back to the right track. Is that ethical? Integrity often means having a strong sense of duty, and there are times when duty and absolute truth-telling might conflict. Michael understood these complications and said he'd faced many similar situations when he was a lawyer.

On many occasions clients have asked me to take deductions on their tax returns that were seriously wrong, and I simply couldn't do it in good conscience. They've gotten mad at me and threatened to find another accountant who would do their bidding. Some actually did. That's fine with me; I slept well those nights. I don't like losing clients, but I won't compromise my integrity by participating in something that is absolutely wrong. That's not to say I don't try every means possible to support their goals. Some clients don't expect their accountant to violate the law, but they do want him or her to feed them exactly what they want to hear. I usually try to transfer such clients to someone who's better than I am at being a yes man. If that's what a client wants, I'm not going to throw them out the door. But I won't participate.

I've always been that way, and it requires a certain amount of vigilance. As a young junior accountant at Kenneth Leventhal & Company, for instance, I refused to sign the work papers on a particular project because I objected to something I felt was ethically questionable. I brought the situation up to the appropriate committee, and the members understood my position. "Okay, don't sign," they said. "We'll have one of the partners sign." Years later, long after I was gone, the firm was sued, and one of the contested issues was the case on which I refused to sign off. When I heard about the lawsuit, I was concerned because

I could have been sued personally as someone who'd been involved at the time. I met with representatives of Leventhal, and they said the firm would not defend me if I was named in the suit because I no longer worked there. "But I shouldn't be named at all," I said, "because I didn't sign the work papers." They informed me the work papers had been lost, and therefore it would be assumed I could be named in the suit. Were the papers really lost? I don't know, and I may never know. But even as a young accountant I knew that having integrity can be used against you, so I made copies of the documents and held onto them. I informed the firm that I had those copies, and somehow I was never named in the lawsuit, even though Kenneth Leventhal & Company was.

Honesty Trumps Duty

When push comes to shove, honesty is more important than duty. A number of years ago, to cite a memorable example, we had a client who wanted us to adjust some records to make his books look more favorable. This was early in the life of RBZ, and I didn't want to lose a major client. I discussed the situation with Ted Roth. He was adamant; he wouldn't have anything to do with it. I pondered the situation for a while and realized that keeping a client simply isn't worth the misery that comes from worrying about being sued or doing something that might be illegal. It would also have established a terrible precedent. If I'm willing to bend the rules for one client, that means I would do it again for another. Losing a big client hurt, but in the long run we were better off. I take my responsibility to clients seriously, but it comes in a distant second to the responsibilities of being a good person. That's sacred.

I learned the hard way to separate myself from people who choose to conduct business dishonestly. I used to be on the board of a public company that manufactured woman's apparel. The three primary owners of this public company, who were also board members, were completely out for themselves. They used their inside information to influence the share price while misleading shareholders and not properly revealing the facts to the public. In addition, they had several other self-dealing issues I had to address with them. I was never involved with any of the misconduct, but felt I needed to report their misdeeds in a more public way. Eventually, the company was sued by shareholders, and even though I had reported the misconduct I was still initially named in the suit because I was a board member. After six months of torture, I was finally dismissed from the case. I had taken on a responsibility to the shareholders, not to those three principal owners. Of course, they were furious. They complained I was costing them another round of financing. "How could you do such a thing to us?" they said. I told them I wasn't doing it to them; they did it to themselves when they started being dishonest. In that situation, my integrity protected me from being manipulated into doing the wrong thing.

Being ethical is not always easy. I've often had to tell clients, some of whom were also friends, things they didn't want to hear. One client, for instance, always felt guilty because he'd made so much more money than his friends. When he asked my opinion about a business venture he was considering with one of those friends, I assessed the deal and said, "The deal makes no economic sense, but if you want to help the guy, just write him a check." My client was sixty years old and wealthy. The deal in question was a start-up company that would take many years to become a profitable venture. That is, if it *ever* did that well. Meanwhile, it would cost my time, his time, his lawyer's time, and a lot of extra work on his tax returns.

I understand that being so candid with clients can be a risky proposition. I try to measure my words carefully and not come across as too frank. But I truly want to help them, and sometimes that means pointing to the elephant in the room. In the end, integrity comes before my comfort or the comfort of the client.

Truth and Consequences

My wife Harriet says I like to "stir the pot." She means I can be provocative and blunt. My intention is to amplify issues so they can be addressed and then resolved. Sometimes I play the devil's advocate, taking an extreme stance I might not even agree with just to offer a different perspective. Disagreeing with someone's assertion, even if it means bringing up an improbable scenario, can often trigger a fruitful discussion. I admit my tactics might come across as mean-spirited to a family member or a business associate, especially when I press an issue they'd rather not talk about, but there are times when uncomfortable facts need to be addressed. People usually feel better for it afterwards.

I play devil's advocate with clients too, so they can see all sides of a financial decision before making a commitment. Many clients get carried away with excitement over a new business venture. They think about how they're going to maximize their earnings without considering what the people on the other end of the deal are trying to do. I get them to look at the possible pitfalls, and I bring up all the little things that can go wrong with an investment. My analysis may deflate them or raise their anxiety level, and I feel bad about that. But it has to be done. My clients know I want them to have the best possible outcome, and I also want them to be well prepared for *every* possible outcome.

Another example of when I might come across as *too* honest is when I offer guidance to people who haven't asked for it. I can't help it; when I see someone has lost his or her way, my conscience compels me to do something about it. More than once, a client has planned to buy a property he or she simply can't afford. They get carried away, like someone whose eyes light up when he sees a scrumptious desert even though his stomach is full. Accountants typically focus on finding a way to finance the cash flow through loans; it's not their job to evaluate the wisdom of the deal itself. But I don't operate that way, and when I have serious concerns I feel I have to voice them. I've told clients why they should not go ahead with the purchase of a property they covet. Some are surprised, because they're asking for my accounting services, not my opinion. I don't separate the two. If you work with me, you can't get one without the other. In the end, my clients are invariably grateful.

As I write this, in fact, I'm planning to give my unsolicited advice to a client I'll soon be meeting with. This guy needs tough love. He's a hugely successful man in the entertainment industry, but he sometimes makes terrible decisions. He keeps throwing good money into bad deals, and it's going to catch up to him very soon. Despite his wealth, he could easily go bankrupt. I'm going to have a heart-to-heart with him. I'll tell him that I will always support him, but he should give up the custodial rights to his finances and focus on what made him such a big success in the first place. His forte is the entertainment business, not managing his finances.

In truth, he was struggling financially even when I met him about nine years ago, and now things are ten times worse. He went through an ugly divorce with his wife of more than thirty years. She was unstable and sometimes violent. Soon after he left her, he got involved with a woman forty years younger, who may be even wilder than his ex-wife. It's hard to watch this downward spiral. On top of everything else, he's being sued by two artists he used to work with. They claim he owes them ten million dollars. Truthfully, I don't believe he actually owes them any money, but because he didn't keep proper records he'd have a hard time winning in court. Disorganization is not a legal argument.

I know he'll resist my advice, and possibly take offense. I am still going to tell him he needs to walk away from economic decisions. In my judgment, he desperately needs someone to stop beating around the bush and tell him bluntly what he needs to do if he doesn't want to lose everything. He's my client, and I will be that person for him. I can't predict what he will do, but I know he will listen carefully to what I have to say and will accept it as sincere concern for his well-being. Like all my long-standing clients, he knows he can trust me because he has seen evidence of my integrity many times. I have earned my reputation as trustworthy. One client has used my services for many years even though his own brother is an accountant. If you were to ask that client why he brings his work to me and not his brother, he will tell you two things: (1) his brother is too conservative about risk-taking, and (2) he trusts me more.

Taking Integrity Too Far

I say all that proudly, but I have to admit there are times when I come off too strong in the name of integrity. Friends of mine have used the word "extreme" to describe the intensity with which I stand up for my principles. One said that if I was on my way to a meeting while the city was on fire, I would brave the smoke and the heat because if I say I'm going to be someplace at a certain time, then I'm going to be there, no matter what. They think I'd expect everyone else to show up on time too. Okay, even I probably wouldn't go that far, but I take their point. I think too many people allow distractions to deter them from keeping their commitments. Me? I don't care if the phone rings or there's a contract on my desk for me to sign; when I promise someone my time, I give it to them.

I have to confess that my commitment to my vision of integrity can come across as stubbornness, and it's sometimes made business and personal relationships messy. Once, I had a meeting scheduled with a business associate who is also a long-time friend. The meeting was about something that would benefit him, yet he was late. I waited and waited, and by the time he finally arrived, about half an hour after the scheduled time, I had already left. He couldn't believe it. I'm sure he had a good excuse, but he hadn't called to tell me he'd be late and I found that intolerable. Later, he told me the incident shocked and embarrassed him, but that in the long run it had been a good thing. It got him to take stock of certain of his bad habits, and to be more accountable for things like showing up on time. This wasn't the only time that expecting more of others caused them to expect more of themselves. I'm grateful the incident had a happy ending, and that our friendship is closer than ever.

But I have gone too far at other times. You'll recall I had only one close friend in my high school years, Bob Karp. Bob and I stayed close after we graduated. We saw each other often when he was at UCLA and I was at Santa Monica City College and CSUN. We had a regular poker game and a favorite pizza place on Wilshire Boulevard where, on Tuesday nights, you could get a whole pizza for a buck and change. During the 1968 presidential primary season, Bob got me to do volunteer work at Senator Eugene McCarthy's campaign office in Westwood. That was my second and last political campaign, the first being my unsuccessful run for class treasurer, which Bob also instigated. One summer after college, he and I traveled cross-country to Boston and back in a VW bus, camping here and there along the way. After college, Bob worked for his father's business, an aerospace precision machine shop, and when I started my accounting firm their company became one of my first clients. Then, sometime in the 1970s, Bob disappointed me.

We had been so close that I shared thoughts and feelings with Bob that I didn't share with anyone else. I thought he did the same. Then, one day I received a letter from him, telling me he was gay. It was terribly upsetting—not that he was gay, but that he hadn't told me sooner. That he kept such an important and intimate part of his life secret from me felt like a betrayal of our friendship. I felt I'd been lied to. It was a lie of omission, and an understandable one, but it still felt like a lie to me, and learning about it in a letter instead of face-to-face made it feel even worse. I remember going to Bob's house for dinner after I received the letter, and telling him how disappointed I was. I think I called him dishonest for hiding something so important from me. I believe that was the last time I saw him until 2011, when Bob called me out of the blue and I flew to Phoenix to visit him.

That reunion was very important to me. I realized over time, thanks in large part to therapy with Dr. Jones, that I had sacrificed a valuable friendship—the only real one I'd had at that point in my life—based on an exaggerated sense of principle. I had not been compassionate when Bob came out to me. I hadn't considered how difficult it was to be gay in the 1970s, when he could never be sure how anyone would react to such information. I failed to appreciate how painful it must have been to hide who he was and sneak in and out of the closet, worrying all the time if his secret would be revealed. It was all about me. How he could be that dishonest with *me*? How he could keep that secret from *me*? Didn't he trust me enough to know it wouldn't have made a difference to our friendship?

I thought I was standing up for integrity, but you can't really be in integrity if you don't have empathy for the people you care about. I know that now, but back then I was too immature to ask myself what Bob was going through. I learned a great deal in the ensuing years, thanks in part to my other gay friends, such as my beloved rabbi, Donald Goor. It's true that my issue with Bob was not his sexual orientation, but rather that I felt deceived. I had to learn that not every deception is the same. I regret turning away from Bob when I could have made it easier for him to come out.

Bob has a different memory of why we stopped talking. As he remembers it, the rift between us was related to my disappointing him and his father in the course of our business relationship. In the context of this book, the point is that integrity and honesty are more nuanced than I once believed. I'm glad Bob is back in my life. Maybe he will serve as a reminder that it's neither fair nor realistic to hold others to the high standards I apply to myself.

My definition of integrity has even cost me money when I've been more pigheaded than principled. In negotiating a deal, for instance, I might come up with a number that represents the lowest amount I'm willing to accept. If the person I'm negotiating with insists on paying even one percent less, I've been known to hold the line. I prefer to lose out on a good deal and not feel I got taken advantage of, rather than compromise on that one percent, which would amount to a hill of beans in the long run. That sort of thing happens rarely, but it happens, and I've been forced to think, "If I wasn't so stubborn I would have done well on that deal."

On one occasion, my high standards almost cost me one of my dearest friends, Michael Rosenfeld. At the time, his company, Woodridge Capital, a real estate development firm, had between fifty and a hundred accounts with RBZ. Each account was a separate company with its own set of books and business strategies. Some of those companies were managed by a third-party investor who was independent from Woodridge Capital. At one point, the investor didn't pay his portion of certain expenses. Michael wasn't going to foot the bill because he didn't want to set a precedent of covering for an outside investor. Well, one of these expenses happened to be the bill for RBZ's accounting services. I told Michael he had made a commitment with us and he needed to honor it, even if the third-party investor was responsible. My relationship was with Michael, and I expected him to honor his obligations, regardless of the circumstances. I spoke to him about it twice, and the problem had still not been resolved. I made the decision to cut off our work for the Woodridge companies.

Michael couldn't believe it. We'd been friends and business associates for seventeen years, and my action put us in a terrible spot. He knew I had high standards, but he didn't think I would be so extreme. He thought that, because of our special relationship, I would be more flexible. But that's how much I value commitment. The issue was deeply personal to me. At the time, I was managing partner of RBZ, and I'd told all the other partners they needed to be tough about collecting what was owed to us by our clients. Michael put me in an awkward situation that challenged my character: how could I demand something from my partners I didn't do myself? The issue wasn't the money, it was the principle.

Michael and I took quite a while to recover from that incident. I'm grateful our love for each other was strong enough to overcome the disturbance. I would have regretted the loss of that friendship terribly. Other relationships have been less resilient, and in fact I may have lost some friends because I was so ferocious in standing up for principle. I believe the relationships that didn't survive were not true friendships to begin with, just as any clients I've lost because of my principles were clients I shouldn't have had anyway.

Still, thanks mainly to those two great women in my life, Harriet and Dr. Jones, I've learned to dial back my stubborn integrity, especially when it comes to my children. I've also learned to be more forgiving when people let me down. I take honesty as seriously as ever. Integrity means as much to me as it ever did. But all virtues have to be applied with discernment.

I truly believe that if you're an honest soul and you consistently do what you think is right, everything else falls into place. When you lie and cheat and you're not completely honest with yourself, that's when you get into messes. Living with deception saps your energy, scrambles your memory, makes you feel ashamed, and eventually leads to even bigger mistakes. Having integrity keeps things simple. Like good preventive medicine, it keeps trouble from arising in the first place.

Chapter 17
Seize Opportunities

I'm an opportunistic guy. Early in life, I learned to keep my eyes peeled for the small window of chance that can open up anywhere at any time. I tell everyone I care about to do the same: keep your radar tuned to opportunity, and when one shows up, jump on it quickly. That applies to more than the usual business propositions, like good investments or the chance to land a new client. It also includes subtle opportunities, like occasions to learn something valuable. I've come to realize that if your mind is open, even unpleasant and difficult events can be learning opportunities. My difficult first marriage taught me how to have a wonderful second one. The frustrations I faced while raising my children have taught me how to be a nurturing grandfather. Struggles can be opportunities in disguise.

I've learned a great deal from my clients over the years, because I'm inquisitive. I like to inquire about their businesses, their careers, their families, and their personal interests. I study their actions and the consequences of those actions. Because I engage so deeply with my clients, I've been able to act on ideas of theirs that other accountants might not even know about. I hear the client's dreams and try to turn them into reality. Paying attention to the people around you can help you spot those rare moments of opportunity.

I always look for ways in which opportunities can work not only for me, but for my clients and RBZ as a whole. Sometimes that means taking less for myself in the short run. One situation occurred when I was putting a new company together. The firm needed several certified audits, which is one of the more profitable types of audits. I had a choice: I could be one of the owners, or I could give up the ownership position and act solely as an accountant. As an owner, I stood to make about fifty times more money, but I chose to give up the extra income to allow RBZ to participate in a significant way as the new company's accountant. I knew this would be a great opportunity for the firm. Sure enough, we gained tremendously from having a great long-term relationship with a terrific client. The new business not only became a profitable account, but helped us grow substantially in other areas.

Fearing Fear Itself

Sometimes, opportunity also creates difficult decisions. In my experience, successful people rise to the challenge. They don't get nervous, they don't get flustered, they don't back down. They act swiftly—but not impulsively or rashly—and make decisions with the right combination of analysis and experience-based intuition. Because even the smallest decisions can have long-lasting effects, the pressure to make the right choice can overwhelm some people. Many opt out of making choices altogether. They just wait, hoping the decision will somehow get made for them, or what's now uncertain will become obvious tomorrow. They fail to realize that not making a decision is in fact making a decision. It's called procrastination, and leads to unwanted consequences. At the very least, it leads to opportunities *not* seized. As Franklin D. Roosevelt said, "There are many ways of going forward, but only one way of standing still." Waiting is standing still. Not deciding is standing still. The cause of the paralysis is usually fear—mainly fear of failure and fear of the unknown. To cite FDR again, when opportunity presents itself, the only thing we have to fear is fear itself. Seizing an opportunity might mean seizing the opportunity to overcome fear.

Some of my proudest moments were times when I chose to stand up to my fears. I remember the tension I felt when my son asked me to speak to his business class at the University of Nevada, Las Vegas. Like many people, I was afraid to stand in front of an audience and speak. But I decided to do it, despite my discomfort. I was nervous for days. In fact, I was so scared I was able to write down only about five minutes of my speech, which was scheduled to go for a full hour. While waiting to step to the microphone, I was a total wreck. My shirt and my jacket were soaked with sweat. When the moment came, I had no choice but to start talking. I took a deep breath, slowed down (just as Harriet had taught me to do), and let my passion speak for itself. I talked about nontraditional accounting and how there was more to the profession than financial statements and tax returns. Before I knew it, an hour had gone by. I was later told I was the class's favorite guest speaker.

The choice I made to fight through my fear of public speaking opened other doors. I was later asked to speak to the graduating class in business and economics at my alma mater, Cal State Northridge. About 1,500 students and 1,300 guests were expected. Again, I was terrified. About a week before the event, a representative of the alumni association came to me and said, "Here's what we want you to say." I was basically given a script. There were to be seven or eight graduation speakers, each one speaking to a separate college at the university, and the planners wanted every speaker to drive home the same message about alumni supporting the school. It would have been less scary to just say what they wanted me to say. But that's not my style. I said, "You may as well just put my picture up and play a recording." They asked CSUN's president if I could add my own words, and she gave me permission with the proviso that I keep it to five or ten minutes.

Maybe my rebellious nature inspired me to overcome my fear of public speaking. Maybe I was energized by the thought, "No one tells me what to say." In any event, I seized that opportunity. In front of the graduates, friends, families, and dignitaries, I read the statement I was given. Then I added, "That's what they wanted me to say. But you know what? There are times when you need to fit in and follow the rules, and there comes a point when you need to say 'Screw it.'" I crumpled up the canned speech and threw it into the audience. "You've got to say what you feel," I said. The students started cheering. They loved my honesty.

I continued from there. I spoke about the true importance of accounting and how it relates to other business disciplines. Then I got personal. I disclosed that I'd been a D student at one time. I said it's great to have a 4.0 grade point average, but to be terribly honest, no one in my long and successful career ever asked me about my GPA. Not only did the students love it, but so did most of the family members, alumni, and school officials. The president later said she'd never seen anyone get such a reception. She'd also never seen anyone speak so candidly and so straight from the heart. No one complained that I took more than ten minutes.

Seizing the opportunity to overcome my fear of public speaking is one of the biggest challenges I've ever overcome. My success led to many speaking invitations and the tremendous satisfaction of knowing my talks have affected people's lives—especially the young business majors at CSUN, to whom I've given many speeches over the years. I have come a long way from the time I stood petrified before my son's class with my shirt soaking wet, and it all stemmed from the decision to push through my fear. Seizing that opportunity opened a whole new world of opportunities.

Strategic Opportunism

I've been an opportunist for so long that I think I now see possibilities that others don't, and I've learned to use my position and my reputation to make things happen. I recall the decision to make Tom Schulte the managing partner at RBZ. He wasn't voted in. I was so adamant about giving him the position that, ever since, the other partners have joked that I anointed him. I knew he was right for the job at the time, and that the firm would benefit from having him replace me. At a partners' meeting, I gave a little speech, saying I'd given my all to the company for twenty-plus years, and now I wanted to devote more time to my family—both my new wife and children and my own kids. Not only that, I said, but the firm needed new blood. We had a new generation of partners, and I thought one of them should take over as managing partner. No one questioned my choice. Tom himself wasn't so sure about it, but I told him, "I see something in you that you may not even see in yourself, and I think this position needs you." I listed all the qualities that made him right for the job, some of which he hadn't recognized in himself. Years later, Tom said, "Harvey's confidence in me is what enabled me to do the job. He's always the guy behind me saying, 'You can do it.'"

The takeaway here is that I've learned not only to seize opportunities, but to help others seize them. When you do that, everyone wins. It's one of the key factors in RBZ's success over the years. That spirit pervades the company culture, and it's a primary reason we've been on "best of" lists, including best workplaces in Los Angeles and best-managed accounting firms in the U.S.

Another measure of how strategic opportunism leads to success is RBZ's steady growth rate over the years. But here's another lesson: Seizing opportunity doesn't mean snatching up every loose marble; it means grabbing the right marbles at the right time. We now have specialty niches in different types of accounting: real estate, nonprofit organizations, middle-market companies, law firms, business management, international tax, and high net worth individuals. We seized the opportunity to get into those specialties, but we did not seize *every* opportunity to expand. We purposely limited ourselves to those seven areas of expertise, and each was carefully analyzed before we leaped in. That isn't to say we would pass if an opportunity arose in a new area, and if it included qualified talent.

A pivotal moment came at an all-day retreat in 2008, during which the partners discussed the firm's vision. One key point was that we wanted to create "a culture of excellence, creativity, and teamwork that is also fun and oriented toward heart, integrity, work-life balance, and social consciousness." That's quite a mouthful, but we agreed the spirit of that statement was important to all of us. In fact, having "heart" later became one of the requirements for becoming a partner. Hard to define for sure, but you know it when you see it.

After the meeting, I began thinking about problems that might hinder our ability to achieve that vision. One problem I saw had to do with the speed of our company's growth. I thought we might be so focused on short-term opportunities that we were losing sight of the long term. Growth brings with it more than the obvious challenges, like securing space, hiring and training staff, purchasing equipment and supplies, and so forth. For a firm like ours, growth represents a challenge to maintaining the high standards we have developed over many years. I questioned whether new employees could learn the RBZ way if we didn't have enough veteran RBZers to train them. How will we provide our clients with the high-quality performance they expect from us if our way of doing things isn't thoroughly taught to newcomers?

I woke up in the night worrying about these issues. I shared my concerns with Dave Roberts and Mark Baumohl, who at that point shared the tasks of managing partner with me. Dave and Mark agreed the three of us needed to make a decision on how to handle future growth.

We met several times and struggled to come up with a definitive plan. We could not use past experience to determine a sure-fire solution, because we were experiencing an unprecedented amount of expansion in a short time. We discussed a variety of issues and pondered many possible solutions. Eventually, we developed a concrete approach to the problem and decided to present our ideas at the next partner meeting.

We had reason for concern. Not only would our proposal require several adjustments to the way we did things, it also appeared disadvantageous to some of the partners because their compensation was partially based on continuing to bring in new clients. At the meeting, new concerns were introduced and new solutions proposed. In the end, to my great pleasure, everyone agreed we were more interested in the long-term success of RBZ than the short-term growth, and that measures had to be taken to uphold the firm's integrity.

We went on to consider all the ramifications of putting a brake on unlimited growth. For example: Who determines when we need to stop bringing in new clients? On what basis would that decision be made? When can we go back to our "normal" process of developing new relationships? If we're all booked up, so to speak, should we move away from weaker clients and build a better client base? What exactly would a "better client base" look like? How should we let the staff, referral sources, clients, and others know about our new policies? Throughout, we kept our eye on the main purpose of the discussion: making sure our clients continued to get the high-quality service they'd come to expect from us. The end result was a new company policy regarding growth and development, designed to generate the best possible future.

I take two important lessons from that experience. First, sometimes seizing an opportunity translates into carefully and strategically *limiting* the opportunities you seize. Second, sometimes seizing an opportunity means seeing potential problems before they arise and solving them before they become unmanageable. I realized that too much expansion could threaten the company's integrity and the quality of our performance. I could have dismissed those concerns and waited to see if the problems actually arose. But my gut told me to seize the opportunity to take preemptive action before there was real damage.

Not Every Opportunity Should Be Seized

When it comes to making correct decisions, short-term opportunities have to be weighed against long-term goals. When people focus only on the immediate benefits, they can be blinded by immediate gratification. I believe that was one of the chief causes of the real estate bubble that burst in 2008. Five years earlier, in 2003, I actually wrote an article expressing my concerns about the soaring real estate market. I noticed back then that unsophisticated investors had started jumping in headfirst. Some were novices who had done so poorly in stocks that their investments were starting to lose principal. Some were "savers" who had their money in cash or bonds and were feeling left behind by the low rates they were earning. Many people saw real estate as their big chance, and they dove into the pool even though they had no experience swimming in it. Unsophisticated investors saw real estate prices rising, plus the lowest interest rates in forty years, and they didn't know enough to take into account all the moving parts involved in real estate projects. Overall, the combination of extremely low interest rates and huge demand for property meant that prices did not truly reflect a property's long-term value. As a result of these and other factors, the market went kaboom.

The point is, not every apparent opportunity is a viable opportunity. Another point is, no opportunity is guaranteed in the long-term just because it offers short-term benefits. Some choices need to be re-evaluated constantly, and to do that well you must know where to turn for good advice and reliable information. During the real estate bubble, many investors were following the pack down a dangerous path. It's easy to get caught up in other people's opinions, especially if they mean well and they're passionate, but you have to listen to the right people. Sometimes, the best voice is your own gut feeling.

I recall a memorable situation with a famous entertainer. For the sake of privacy, I will keep him anonymous. Mr. X has a reputation as a nasty, demanding pain in the butt. He was looking for a new accountant, having burned through five of them in the preceding six years, just as he had burned through producers, directors, assistants, and other people who worked for him. My partners told me not to take the meeting. They didn't want RBZ to be the latest firm to go through his revolving door, and they didn't think I, of all people, could tolerate a prima donna client who screamed when he didn't get his way. They were right about that. But they were wrong to think they could tell me what do.

They were also wrong to think I couldn't make the relationship work. I chose to view Mr. X from the perspective of opportunity. My strategy was to talk to him directly and honestly. We sat down together in his huge mansion, and I told him, "You don't need me, and I don't need you. You have a reputation for screaming at people. If you want to scream at me, that's fine. I'm on the clock, so you can scream at me eight hours a day, for all I care. But you can't scream at my staff." He was surprised by my candor, to say the least. I didn't stop there. "Here's how we're going to work," I said. "I'm going to meet with you every month. I'm going to come with an agenda. I'm also going to prepare minutes of our meetings so we have a record of everything we discuss."

I thought he would boot me out. That was the *good* scenario. The bad one had him screaming and throwing things and threatening to destroy my reputation. Instead, he laughed. Then he agreed to my terms 100 percent.

My partners couldn't believe it. They placed bets on how long he would last as a client. That was 2002. He's still with us, and he hasn't screamed at me once. Nor does he disrespect my staff. I'm glad I didn't listen to the naysayers. So are my partners, who were only too happy to eat that particular crow.

Things don't always work out that well, so there's a flip side to saying yes when a good business opportunity comes along. Sometimes you have to seize the opportunity to *not* seize an opportunity. One time, my friend Dan Rosenson was considering buying a new business, and he asked me to run the numbers and advise him. The proposal looked attractive on the surface. At a key meeting with the seller's accountant, Dan did his usual dog-and-pony show about who he was and what he did, while I sat there quietly and went over the company's books. Something leaped out at me. I stopped Dan right in the middle of his spiel and asked the accountant how certain numbers tied into the company's actual inventory. It looked to me as though the numbers were inflated, so the potential profit on paper was about five times more than the real inventory could yield. The accountant admitted they had essentially picked a number out of the air.

Dan turned to me and said, "I don't buy businesses with plugged inventory numbers." We walked out. As we were leaving the building, Dan asked me how I knew the numbers were fake. I told him it's a gift, like musicians with perfect pitch or editors who spot typos in everything they read. It actually drives my office nuts because I can spot everyone's little errors. But it pays off. You may not have my talent for numbers, so find someone who does before you sign off on a deal. Conduct your due diligence and be prepared to walk away, no matter how big the potential rewards might seem. Sometimes an "opportunity" is nothing but a mirage.

Bottom line: stand ready to seize every opportunity that feels right to you, but do it wisely, sensibly, and rationally, and always do your homework before you sign on the dotted line.

Chapter 18
Do Right By Others

I like earning money. I derive enormous satisfaction from my work. But what really makes me happy is helping to make other people happy. I've found that wanting the best for others, really caring for their well-being, is one of the most important qualities to have as a person. And it's just as important in business as in the personal realm. One of my main objectives is to look out for the people I do business with, whether they're RBZ colleagues, my partners in various investments, or my accounting clients.

I love seeing my clients do well. Many of them are far wealthier than I'll ever be, and I like it that way. I often come across accountants who think the opposite; they're jealous of their clients' success. They think they're smarter and more capable, and therefore they should be making more money. In my view, they are looking at their profession from the wrong perspective. I like helping rich clients get richer. Even more, I like helping ordinary people achieve a level of financial security that changes their lives. I've had the great satisfaction of seeing numerous people go from struggling to comfortable because of my advice and help. I pat myself on the back when I do something that makes money for someone else. It means I accomplished what I set out to do.

I believe, in many ways, that my work is charitable. Charity means doing something for other people, and I go the extra mile to ensure my clients' wishes, needs, and desires are fulfilled. That attitude is a key element of Therapeutic Accounting®. When I make deals, I do my best to not let my ego get in the way of doing right by everyone involved. If that sounds goody-two-shoes, I assure you it works to my benefit. That attitude is the main reason I get so many referrals. Sometimes, prospective clients complain to the person who recommended me. They say I'm too expensive. Their friends usually tell them I'm well worth the price, because I look out for my clients day and night and the return on their investment in me will far exceed the cost.

My feelings about doing right by others have been reinforced over the years by seeing others operate under the same principle. One example of selflessness I encountered really stood out. I was structuring a trust and will for a client. He wanted to leave sixty percent of his wealth to his son and forty percent to his daughter. The son lived nearby and always went out of his way to take care of his dad. Favoring him in his will was my client's way of saying "Thank you." But when the son learned about the intended inequity between his and his sister's bequest, he objected. He thought it was unfair to his sister, and he knew the disparity could damage their relationship for the rest of their lives. He was adamant about making sure that never happened. His concern for his sister's happiness and the harmonious state of his family meant more to him than money, or even his father's wishes.

I respected that immensely. The son's selflessness inspired me to use all my persuasive powers to convince my client to change the document. I'm glad he did. When he passed away, the two siblings split everything equally. To this day, the daughter doesn't know she would have gotten the short end of the stick. As for the son, what he came away with is far more important than extra money in the bank: a loving relationship with his sister and the joy of having done the right thing.

The Downside of Doing Right

Of course, there are times when going the extra mile for others can lead to unanticipated problems. I recall one situation in which it actually created a conflict with a client. I'll call her Mrs. W. I promised Mrs. W's husband before he died that I would help take care of his wife for the rest of her life. They named me trustee of their estate. I took my commitment to him seriously, and I did well by his widow after his death. But it wasn't long before Mrs. W said she did not want my assistance. Unfortunately, she needed it desperately. She had married a man who was thirty-five years younger than she was, and he was clearly after her money. So were her children. I quickly realized how prescient her late husband had been; he knew his wife would need protection.

As Mrs. W's trustee, I found myself constantly intervening in order to keep the vultures at bay. She complained that I was interfering in her life. But I could see I was all that stood between her and disaster. I wasn't going to walk away from the promise I'd made to her husband. She threatened to sue me. I told her, "If the court removes me as your trustee, I will adhere to that decision. But I will not go away voluntarily." She actually took me to court. I pressed to have her prove she was completely capable of managing her own finances. She even underwent tests. Some people felt I was overstepping my boundaries. They said I had gone too far. They advised me to just let it go. I persisted because I absolutely knew it was the right thing to do.

The court had me removed as trustee. The judge ruled that Mrs. W was indeed incompetent, but nevertheless she had the right to do foolish things with her money. Six years later, I was asked by the judge (a new one) if I would agree to come back and serve as trustee. It had become clear that her new husband was trying to steal her money. Now the family agreed I was the only one who could control Mrs. W, and the only time she was at all stable was when I was trustee.

There are times when I care far too much. When I see someone else fail, I take it to heart as if I were the one who did not succeed. When one of my own clients suffers a setback, I invariably feel I could have done more to prevent it, even if the circumstances were out of my control and had no connection to my responsibilities. If I can't figure out a solution to someone's problem, I feel like I'm failing. I know that's unreasonable, but I can't help it. In the end, I'd rather have the problem of caring too much and expecting too much of myself, than to care too little and not expect enough.

Looking Out for Colleagues

My clients are not the only people I look out for; I believe in taking care of my co-workers as well. At RBZ, we look out for all our partners. One way we do that is with a unique compensation system I created around 1990. We wanted a system where our partners think of RBZ as their firm and of their clients as clients of RBZ. So I developed a formula in which financial reward is based in part on how well you do with the clients you work with: if you work hard and bring in business, you make more money. What you get out reflects what you put in. But it's also a profit-sharing arrangement. We're not like other firms, where every partner is essentially an individual owner. Here, if I do very well and you do poorly in any given period, I'm going to make less than I otherwise would, and you're going to make *more*, because we're all in it together. There's no compensation committee; no time is spent trying to figure out who should get what; no one has to plead their case for a higher salary; there are no jealous people feeling "I should get more because I did this and so-and-so didn't." All that is gone. Everything is done by computer. No cliques. No groveling. No political calculations. No "You vote for me and I'll vote for you" deals. And guess what: in over twenty years, we've never once had an argument over compensation.

One feature of the system is that seniority and fancy titles do not automatically mean you make more money. Technically, a new partner can come in and make as much as someone that has been with RBZ for years. The odds of that happening are highly unlikely; the newcomer would have to work a vast number of hours, generate a huge amount of business, and supervise an enormous quantity of work to reach the same level as someone who has been with us a long time. The point is, we don't pay extra for seniority, or even for being a founding partner. Individual motivation counts, and individual achievement separates one person's compensation from another, but the person who does specific work with a specific client does not get 100 percent of the income that's derived. He or she may get a significant portion of it, but the amount is adjusted according to the formula. The percentage of profit is not important if the firm doesn't make any profit. Twenty percent of a lot is much better than eighty percent of nothing.

This makes for a more collaborative atmosphere. Some people are excellent technicians, for example, but they don't know how to market, and they don't bring much business through the door. Others, like me, are the opposite: we're terrific "rainmakers" who bring in business, but we're not necessarily great technicians. The formula rewards the technicians as much as the rainmakers. I bring in a ton of business, but I don't do financial statements, even though many of my clients require them. I refer them to a technical partner, and he or she gets a piece of the action. I would not want a firm full of rainmakers any more than I'd want a firm full of technicians. Everyone here can do what they do best and not be forced to do something they don't want to do because there's more money in it. At most firms, because everyone is basically an individual operator, if one accountant doesn't collect receivables from a client, the others don't really care. If that happens at RBZ, everyone is hit—although the partner responsible for the client takes the biggest hit—so everyone cares.

This arrangement also means that power is less concentrated at the top. In most firms, the big earners have the preponderance of power. They can threaten others into submission because they bring in the most money. At RBZ, the compensation system creates a dispersion of salary, which creates a dispersion of power. The partners prefer it that way. Theoretically, I could try to toss my weight around because I'm a founder and I bring in so much business. So could Ted and Dave. We could make a lot more money with the typical system, but we would not be as happy and the company culture would be very different. Instead, we choose to take a smaller piece of the pie in return for a better life and, frankly, a bigger pie. That's one way that looking out for others pays off.

I'm proud that under our compensation system, the incomes of RBZ employees and partners went up steadily during the post-2008 recession, while many other firms in our area saw forty-to-fifty percent drops. I also consider loyalty to be truly priceless, and the RBZ culture encourages loyal employees. At firms made up of individual operators, people tend to safeguard their best clients the way young men guard their dates at a frat party. They not only don't want to lose clients to their colleagues, they want to carry their clients away when it's time to leave the company. As a result, partners are reluctant to assign clients to junior-level employees. You see situations where the older partners don't work as hard as the younger ones, but still make most of the money. So the younger guys, who think they're not being adequately rewarded, feel justified in running off with clients.

RBZ's compensation system creates a different kind of culture. I don't have clients; I'm a partner in a *firm* that has clients. I may have worked hard to bring in Client A; I may do almost all the work for Client A; but I don't think of Client A as mine. I don't place a protective shield around him. One great result of that attitude is an exceptional degree of loyalty.

We extend our concern to the personal lives of everyone who works at RBZ. They're not mere employees; they're individuals we care about. When Dave Roberts joined the firm, for instance, he was married with two daughters aged five and seven. Then, in a nanosecond, his life was turned upside down by a sudden divorce. Dave was stunned. Suddenly, he became engrossed in conflict and drama, with attorneys, accountants, and psychiatrists. The situation was bizarre and tragic. Without warning, he turned into a single parent. He found himself in the impossible position of being a full-time dad and a full-time partner in a new firm. Naturally, it affected his work. He was sure one of the senior partners would come into his office at any moment and tell him we couldn't carry his weight anymore.

I did go into his office, but with a different message. When I shut the door behind me, I could tell by the look on Dave's face that he thought I was going to fire him. I sat down next to him and said, "Three things. Number one: you're going to lose some clients, but don't worry about it. Number two: we'll take care of your clients' needs while you're out. Number three: get out of here and go take care of your kids. Tell me what kind of support and help you need, and we'll take care of it. We do not expect to see you here."

Then I got up and walked out the door. Dave was utterly shocked. At most firms he would have been given a choice: take care of your work life or take care of your family life. We forfeited our position and told him to put his family first. Because of our system of compensation, no one else would have to completely carry his full workload. He would lose income, but we were not going to punish the man because he had found himself in a tough situation that was not of his choosing. We earned Dave's loyalty from the start, and we've kept it ever since, to our lasting benefit.

Doing Right by Dolls and Giraffes

My company is successful because the leaders know the importance of looking out for others. I do the same in my personal life. When the people I love are passionate about something, I love to help them pursue it. My first wife Kathy wrote books about antique dolls, and was a renowned collector who probably knew more about certain dolls than anyone else in the United States. As for me, I always thought dolls were a waste of money. I couldn't believe people would spend five or six thousand dollars on something that would have cost ten bucks thirty years earlier. But my wife loved dolls, so I helped her collect them. I didn't complain when she lined the walls with dolls. We probably had over three hundred on display. My kids hated it; they thought our home felt like a museum. They could never touch anything. We even had a designated doll room. I went along with all of it because I loved the fact that it made my wife happy. As a husband, I took pleasure in seeing my wife feel good.

When I fell in love with Harriet, I discovered she, too, liked to collect things: giraffes. When we got married, she had about twenty giraffe items. Not long after that, I bought her a giraffe pin. I couldn't believe how much pleasure she got from that. I loved making her happy, so I became Mr. Giraffe. As I write this, we've been married more than fifteen years, and we have over 1,200 giraffes in the house. We have an actual stuffed giraffe made by a taxidermist in 1922. We have a hand-blown glass giraffe that's six feet tall. We have a metal giraffe that's eighteen feet tall. We have about a hundred giraffe paintings. We have giraffes made out of all kinds of things, like puzzle pieces, watches, and recycled musical instruments, with clarinets for legs, a trombone for a body, and a neck made out of a trombone slide. I doubt anyone could find a more extraordinary giraffe collection. We even bought a real giraffe and donated it to the L.A. Zoo. She was later transferred to the San Diego Zoo, but she kept her original name: Harriet. I go giraffe shopping for one reason only: I get joy from Harriet's joy. I love seeing the glow on her face when she sees a new item. She says I turned her from giraffe lover to a giraffe-aholic.

I never cared much for "things" myself. But I love watching other people enjoy things—like when I saw how much my daughter Roni loved pigs. I told Harriet I wanted to buy a real one for her to have as a pet. That was early in our relationship, so Harriet didn't know I was serious. She thought it was just a whim that would pass. But I put my assistant on the case, and we eventually located a baby pot-bellied pig farm thirty miles from where we lived. We got the pig in time for Roni's twenty-fourth birthday. I'll never forget the look on her face when she saw the pig (whom she named Peggy Sue) walk down the stairs with a bow on her head. Roni thought it was hers only for the day, like a loan. It blew her mind when she realized Peggy Sue was hers to keep.

Having a pig in the house wasn't easy. She was well trained: she walked on a leash, and she learned to use a litter box. The problem was, Peggy Sue just kept growing. We were told she wouldn't be more than twenty pounds. Well, she grew to *sixty* pounds. Slowly but surely, she started destroying things. In the middle of the night she would crawl under the kitchen chairs and get stuck. We would hear loud rattling sounds at two in the morning, and then a bang! That meant another broken chair. She would uproot every blade of grass in the backyard. But none of that mattered to me. What mattered was seeing my daughter happy.

I don't know where it came from, but I'm grateful that I learned that what makes me happiest is looking out for the happiness of people I care about. Giving to others is one of the main reasons I have such a wonderful life—and, incidentally, it's also a prime reason for my successful life in business. I believe anyone reading this will find the same satisfaction and success in doing right by others. It's the best way to do right by yourself.

Chapter 19
Treat Everyone With Respect

From the second we are born we need others to help us. Our parents and guardians feed, protect, love, and teach us throughout our childhood and adolescence, and well into adulthood; as adults we need each other; as elders we need the young. No matter what, relationships will always be central to our lives. And no matter how much two people have in common, relationships bring together two separate minds, two sets of beliefs and values, two collections of needs and wants, and two different personalities. Obviously, that leaves room for conflict. For a relationship to work well, the two parties must learn to adapt to one another. That goes for business as well as every other relationship in life.

All that may sound obvious to you, but I didn't completely understand it during the first part of my life. During my first marriage, I had my own way of approaching things. I thought my approach worked well for me, and I took it for granted that it suited my wife too. I was in for a rude awakening. Whenever I had problems, I would slink into my cave and deal with them on my own. I didn't share my challenges with my wife because I didn't want to burden her. I thought I was doing her a favor. If certain issues made me miserable, why would I want to make her miserable too? To me, that was like sneezing on someone when you have a cold. I had no idea I was hurting the relationship. Kathy would see me upset or moody, and because she didn't know why, she assumed I was mad at her when I was not. She also thought I didn't trust her enough to share my concerns, which was not the case.

The truth is, I didn't always want to listen to *her* concerns either. I thought that's what her female friends were for—to hear her stories, let her vent, and provide comfort. My job was to solve her problems. That was how I dealt with the world: see a problem, figure out how to fix it, and get right to work. When Kathy would spell out in detail what was on her mind, I rushed her to get to the bottom line so I could roll up my sleeves and take care of things. From my point of view, I was being manly. I was the problem solver. She didn't appreciate being rushed and not being heard, and I couldn't understand why. I felt she misunderstood me. That may have been true, but I definitely misunderstood her. This greatly damaged the relationship.

I eventually learned that what I just described was classic male-female stuff. John Gray's famous book, *Men Are from Mars, Women Are from Venus,* was a big help. His book showed me how vastly different the male and female psyches are. I came to realize that, for marital relationships to work, each partner has to appreciate that the other has a different way of interpreting the world. Now, with Harriet, I've learned how to listen. I admit it wasn't easy, and I still don't do it perfectly. For a guy like me, who was locked into a certain way of dealing with the world, it can still be an exhausting task. But I happily work at it.

I've learned that having a healthy relationship often means readjusting yourself to accommodate the other. I've already mentioned how much joy I get from helping others get what they want and need. Well, people don't just need financial help, or a shopping companion. They also need to be heard, and to be treated with respect. Meeting those emotional needs is not as much fun as shopping for antique dolls or buying giraffe art, and it's not as creative as springing a big surprise or buying someone a special gift. But it's far more important. So important that I've worked at it steadily over the years, and I can confidently say I've come a long way, baby.

Respect in the Workplace

Understanding and respecting another person's perspective is not only crucial for marriages; it's a good business practice as well. The partners at RBZ are similar in many ways: we are all driven, we all enjoy our work, we all want the firm and our clients to succeed, and we all value our families and our private lives. But we also have very different viewpoints. I believe I bring a visionary perspective to the team, for example. I'm a big-picture guy. I dream up new ideas and go after new business. When it comes to style, I like to get right to the point. I tend to be direct and outspoken—some would say *too* outspoken. Dave Zaslow, on the other hand, likes to focus on the process. He's methodical. He likes digging into details and working with the complexities and structures of the work. He's great at that kind of thing. I'm not. Maybe I could be if I had to, but frankly I'd rather not be bothered. That's why Dave and I are good partners: we respect each other's way of doing things.

Some people are not cut out for partnering at all. They don't like dealing with the disagreements and conflicts that inevitably crop up. They work alone, and when they need assistance, they hire subordinates and yes men. I couldn't stand being surrounded by yes men. My partners balance me out—and balance the business too. If I get upset or angry, I know I can count on Ted Roth to keep me from going off the deep end. He's the voice of calm. He stays right in the middle, never too elated and never too upset. That's why they call him the glue of RBZ. I'd need a lobotomy to be that steady. To Ted it comes naturally, and it's great for our company.

I've also discovered that part of showing respect for those you work with is to let them have their way as much as possible, even if you don't completely agree. I argue, I debate, I try to persuade, but I've learned to let go and not insist on having my way all the time. Of course, I'd never compromise on important values, and I'd never acquiesce to something that would damage the firm or a client's business. It's just that I know I'm not always right, and when something could go either way it's sometimes better, for the sake of the ongoing relationships, to yield to someone else's judgment. With my track record, and my powers of persuasion, I could easily have the biggest say at RBZ. But I try to let my voice be one of fifteen. If the partners decide against my ideas—and sometimes they do—I lock arms with them and support whatever decision they've made. In the long run, cooperation brings a lot more success than power trips.

Respect for Diversity

A successful business needs multiple visions, with support from multiple people. My advice has always been to respect people for their uniqueness and to appreciate what sets them apart. That's one reason RBZ has conscientiously created a diverse workplace. In 1989, for example, we became one of the first local firms in the Los Angeles area to have a Filipino partner. We were also one of the first to have a female partner. That took place in 1984, and it should have happened sooner.

One would think that in this day and age there would be more equality in the workplace, but the truth is we still have a way to go. At the same time, things are far better than they were when I started my career and the accounting profession was almost exclusively male and white. Today, fifty-five to sixty percent of accountants are women. There's also been a significant increase in accountants of Asian descent. I think the increased diversity is great for everyone. I've always rooted for the underdog. I've always stood on the side of minorities and the underprivileged. Even in sports, which I don't pay much attention to, I feel good when the team that's not favored by the odds makers wins. For whatever reason, I've always been that way, and I'm proud that Americans have come so far in overcoming our legacy of inequality and bigotry. I admire the people who fought their way through it and struggled to change history.

RBZ is a far more interesting place to work because of the diversity of our team. Each person brings a different dimension to the company culture. We're also a much more agile business, because those differences add value to what we can do for our clients. The proliferation of women has not only helped us better serve our female clients, it has given us greater insight into how to take care of our own employees. We have instituted flex time, for example, to accommodate people who have children to take care of. This helped not only the mothers in the firm, but also the fathers, since men now play a more significant role in raising their kids.

It saddens me that some of the old attitudes persist in the business world, even in a diverse and sophisticated city like L.A. For reasons I could never fathom, I've known accountants who did not want to work with women or ethnic minorities. This was especially true in the past, of course, and at one time such people could get away with that attitude because there were so few successful women who needed accountants.

Happily, that's no longer the case. But I still run into stereotyping and subtle prejudice. For instance, I hear men addressing women they don't know as "Honey" or "Dear." You won't hear those terms at RBZ, but unfortunately I have had to deal with male clients who do that and worse. Some treat women in an unbelievably demeaning way. I try to nip it in the bud, and there have been times when I've come down hard on men who disrespected my female employees.

I've actually had women come to me in tears over something a client has said or done. I usually give the offender a chance to redeem himself. "You can treat your own staff however you want to," I tell them, "but you do not have the liberty to act that way with mine." If the woman he upset is an accountant assigned to the client's account, I tell him he has three choices: "One, we keep her on and you start treating her better. Two, we fire you as a client. Three, we switch you to another accountant, and if you fail again you're out."

Maybe I can afford to risk those confrontations because RBZ is successful enough to pick and choose our clients. But I'd like to think I'd stand up to sexism even if we were lean and hungry and couldn't afford to take the risk.

Reshuffling Relationships

Sometimes, relationships need to be reevaluated. One benefit of getting older has been learning from experience which relationships to add and which ones to drop. I'm constantly reexamining my business relationships, and I'm learning to evaluate them rationally instead of determining their fate impulsively. In my real estate investing, I've been successful in developing new relationships as well as maintaining old ones. Some have gone bad, but that's inevitable. For the most part, I have developed great working relationships and, in some instances, lasting friendships. My decisions would not have been half as profitable if I hadn't invested a great deal of time thinking through what each potential relationship would be like. Listening to the people who want to do business with me, and trying to understand their perspectives, makes it infinitely easier to get a new relationship off on the right foot—and stay there.

The truth is, as I've said before, I can be hard on people. I demand a lot from myself, and I demand a lot from others. My standards are high, and when people don't meet those standards I can be tough—

sometimes too tough—but I'm getting better at setting the bar at a reasonable height. One upside to having high standards, in addition to getting the best effort from the people I work with, is that it weeds out people I don't need in my life. I use my high standards as a yardstick: those who can handle them tend to be really fine people, and my standards actually strengthen our relationships. Many have told me they appreciate my form of "tough love." The people who can't take it do not need to be around me. Some relationships are just not worth keeping.

Where troublesome clients are concerned, I feel I owe it to them and my company to give them a chance to reform. In some cases, it's a matter of teaching them to treat me and my colleagues with the respect we deserve. One of my clients, for example, is about as nasty as can be. He's a prima donna lawyer who gets away with being mean. I get the feeling he enjoys making people upset. Originally, he was another partner's client, but that partner got to the point where he couldn't tolerate the attitude. He wanted to toss him out as a client. I suggested I give it a try before we dismissed him completely. I figured we didn't have anything to lose; if I saw it wasn't going to work I would pull the trigger on the guy in a flash. It turned out not to be necessary. I was able to teach the client how to treat me respectfully. More important, I got him to act appropriately with the staff members who work on his account. He's been with us now for over three years, and we have gotten a lot of work from him. This is a good example of how reeducating people can pay off on the bottom line.

Of course, some attitudes and behaviors are simply intolerable. Once, a female RBZ partner informed me about a client who deserves to be called a sleaze ball. She was working late at the office one night, which is commonplace at the company. This guy came up to her, having obviously downed too many drinks, and started hitting on her in a crude and disrespectful way. I saw him the day after I learned what happened, and I said, "You're fired. Goodbye. Have your new accountant call us." No excuses, no explanations. I owe a lot more allegiance to my staff and my partners than I do to any client. Clients can be replaced, but productive, effective, loyal, goodhearted colleagues are more precious than gold.

A Matter of Trust

For the relationships that are worth holding on to, I give my all. People who recognize that about me respond with trust. With clients, their trust often puts me in a role that carries with it an awesome responsibility. People share all their financial information with me. As a therapeutic accountant, I come to know the details of their accounts, investments, trusts, wills, and other matters, including their intentions, fears, wishes, and hopes. Once I digest all the information and interpret it through the lens of my expertise, I end up knowing more about their financial affairs than they do—and a lot more than their spouses, children, business associates, brokers, or bankers do. My job is to give them my honest perspective and recommendations, even if they won't like everything I have to say.

With that trust comes the grave responsibility of maintaining confidentiality. Clients have to know that if they say "This is between you and me," it really is *only* between them and me. Not between us and my partners, or my staff, or my wife, or anyone else on the planet. This is terribly important, and I advise every accountant to see confidentiality the way I do: as a sacred duty. There is no Hippocratic Oath for accountants. There is no professional monitoring organization like the American Medical Association or the Bar Association. In the absence of formal protection, clients have to rely on the safety of deeply felt personal trust. I'm proud that my clients have that with me.

Of course, new clients haven't yet learned enough to give me that level of trust, even when they've been referred by their closest friends and colleagues. That's perfectly understandable. When they hesitate to confide in me, I tell them, "If you're afraid you'll be embarrassed about what you say, or judged by what you say, or think I'm going to share what you tell me with anyone else, let me assure you none of that will happen. Whatever you tell me in private stays that way." Sometimes they're reluctant to share facts with me because they have good business instincts: they know their competition would seize upon the information if they could, and they know I might have other clients in the same business. They could even be negotiating a deal with one of my clients. "How do I know you won't tell the other side?" I've been asked. I have to assure them I won't share their trade secrets with anyone—and I won't share the other side's information with them either.

Of course, the proof is always in the pudding, so trust tends to grow gradually, one step at a time. One advantage of having a stellar reputation for integrity is that it doesn't take long—and in many cases the trust is fully present before I walk in the door.

Most people who work with me end up trusting me, and frankly they should. I might set high standards for other people, but I set even higher standards for myself, and being trustworthy is at the top of my list. Trust is an indispensable element in any relationship, personal or professional, and nothing is more important than having good relationships. I learned that early on, and as I grew in self-understanding I learned more and more about how to uphold my end of the bargain. Trust is as important in accounting as it is anywhere else in life, and for a therapeutic accountant it's more important than the stuff you memorize to pass the CPA exam.

Chapter 20
Take Smart Risks

*I*n business and in life, you must be prepared to take risks if you want to reach beyond the ordinary and grab something more rewarding and fulfilling. But taking risks is ... well, risky. The key is knowing how to take *smart* risks. For most of my life, I've been good at assessing risk and deciding which risks I should take. I even did quite well in my one venture with a notoriously risky business I knew nothing about: independent filmmaking. The film was called *Frozen Assets*, and it starred Shelley Long and Corbin Bernson. One of my long-time clients was a Hollywood agent who dreamed of writing and producing a movie of his own. He put up his own money, raised still more, and lined up the talent, only to realize he was a million dollars short of the budget he needed to shoot the film in Canada. I got him the money, using my own funds and calling upon five or six investors.

This would ordinarily have been a very big risk because few independent movies turn a profit. But I attached conditions to my investment that not only reduced the risk but guaranteed a good return. The conditions were: guaranteed twenty-five percent annual return per year for two years, plus the return of the initial one million dollars to be paid to my investors *before* anyone else—other investors, talent, producers, etc.—received any of the proceeds. The movie was uniformly despised by critics (either Gene Siskel or Roger Ebert called it the worst film of the year; the other called it the worst of all time), but two years later my partners and I walked away with a half million dollar profit from sales of the video. That happened because Siskel and Ebert told viewers to buy the video. Why? Because it established a new baseline for bad movies!

I haven't always been so smart. After the meltdown of the stock market following the 2008 financial crisis, I looked at my portfolio and was happy to see I hadn't lost a cent. However, I didn't make a nickel in the bull market before the crisis either. How is this possible? The answer is deceptively simple: I hadn't owned any stocks or bonds for several years. So, while I avoided financial disaster during the downturn, I also missed out on the biggest rise in the market since its inception.

After some self-reflection, I realized I'd fallen into the common trap of not following my own advice. The doctor lectures his patients about the need to eat properly, then sits down to a meal of prime rib and baked potatoes swimming in butter and sour cream. The attorney carefully draws up wills for his clients while leaving his own assets unprotected in the event of his death. I always tell my clients it's important to diversify their assets. I've told many of them they should at least diversify the real estate portion of their portfolios. If, for instance, someone is a Class A apartment house specialist, I recommend he take a portion of his assets and invest in office, self-storage, industrial, or even Class C apartments. I also suggest geographical diversity. Why invest only in your own backyard when you can diversify into other regions of the country, or the world, by working with experts in those areas?

In other words, I have urged clients to move beyond their comfort zones. Yet I found myself reluctant to enter the stock market when it was booming. I was simply scared of it. I am a very logical thinker, and I find the stock market rarely acts in a logical manner. I've never been able to understand how the market can rise when there is overall bad news in the economy, or why it sometimes dives during strong economic times. Likewise, it never made sense to me that a stock would drop while its earnings are beating best expectations—and vice versa. So I made the mistake of investing too conservatively. In years that the market was rising, I invested in CDs and other "safe" instruments. Although I didn't lose when the market plummeted, I also didn't win on the upside. As a result, I found myself behind where I would have been if I'd taken my own advice and diversified more.

That experience taught me an important lesson: I lost out because I was operating out of fear. Not a good idea. When it comes to investments and other business transactions, fear is not a bad thing in and of itself. It can be a useful brake on overzealousness. Fear can prevent you from getting carried away by the dream of a big payoff. But some fears are warranted and some are not, and giving in to the unwarranted kind can severely limit your success. The question is: can you confidently seize opportunities when circumstances are unpredictable and you don't have a complete grasp of the facts?

What You Don't Know Can Hurt You

I have found the first step in combating fears is to identify and understand them. Only then can you address the reality behind the fears and put them to rest. My investment fears stemmed from the fact that I didn't understand the nuances of the stock market. Once I recognized that, I took steps to counteract my fear. Instead of letting my lack of knowledge hinder me, my solution was to partner with someone who had expertise I lacked. In other words, one key to overcoming fear is to hire a trustworthy advisor.

Most people who know me are aware that I've always had a strong inclination to invest in real estate. For most people that is an extremely challenging form of investment, because the market is incredibly complex. That's why the average investor has stayed out of real estate, for the most part. But even with something as complex as real estate, a smart investor can do well if he or she teams up with an expert. I believe having the right manager, whether a general partner or a managing member, can make all the difference.

I feel perfectly competent to handle my own real estate ventures (although not the day-to-day operations) and to lend my expertise to partners who know less than I do. But I'm glad to leave the management of my other assets in the hands of professionals in those areas. That way, I benefit from having a well-diversified portfolio without suffering from anxiety over a market that I just don't get. Because my investments are in the hands of trusted professionals, I don't have to think about how to respond to all the ups and downs.

Finding experts to work with is an important step in managing risk. But sometimes it is not enough. There are some variables the greatest experts just cannot anticipate. I guarantee you that, prior to September

11, 2001, no one contemplating an investment in New York real estate would have considered the possibility of terrorists flying planes into buildings. Much less horrific events can take the best-informed, best-prepared investors by surprise too. I've personally been stunned when the unexpected left me in a serious predicament. Here are some examples:

1. I owned a property in another state with two general partners who also lived in California. They died together in a helicopter crash. How do you quickly find new general partners to deal with out-of-state property?

2. I found out the general partner in one of my investments was receiving kickbacks on the sale of some properties. How do you confront the general partner when you have other investments with him?

3. After I did extensive due diligence and acquired a property, serious mold was discovered in the building. How do you determine what, if anything, went wrong and fix it?

4. After agreeing to fund a large project, the two managing members got into a feud. Should I take one side in the matter or back out altogether?

5. I co-invested in a significant project. The deposit "went hard," meaning I wouldn't have the right to get the funds back if I did not go forward with the transaction. The deposit was released to the seller. Then my co-investor backed out before the closing. Do I find a new co-investor? Put up all of the funds myself? Walk away from the project?

6. I was offered a great opportunity by the managing member of an investment. Based on a handshake agreement with him, I rounded up all the investors for the project. After funds were raised and placed into an escrow account, the managing member brought in other investors and did not use our funds. He did this because the other investors asked for a lot less profit from the transaction. Should I sue the managing member? Compromise? Walk away?

7. A lender failed to deliver loan proceeds three days before the required closing. Do I sue the lender, or maybe the managing member? Or do I pay the seller heavily for an extension?

8. A managing member wanted to buy out his partners in a project at what appeared to be the fair market price. Shortly after the partners agreed to the sale, it was determined that the property was worth far more than the amount agreed to. Should I confront the managing member and attempt to renegotiate the deal, or go ahead with the sale at the original price agreed on by all the members?

Those are just some of the unpredictable situations I've encountered. I've heard many similar stories from clients and others. The unpredictable can't be avoided. But can it be managed and controlled? To some extent, yes. As I mentioned earlier, partnering with experts can help a lot, but that introduces a new kind of problem: can you trust the expert with your money?

Who Do You Trust?

There are good people out there who have both the skills to competently manage your money and the integrity to keep your best interests at heart when they make decisions on your behalf. You can find them, but you have to do your homework and exercise careful discernment and good judgment.

Doing research on someone you're thinking of doing business with is always a good idea, especially when it comes to promoters. These are the steps I recommend when dealing with promoters:

1. Ascertain exactly who the promoter is. This includes doing a background check of the person's history, both from a financial and a personal standpoint.

2. Make sure you understand the promoter's financial goals and expectations, and determine whether they are in sync with your needs.

3. Make sure the deal calls for you to get your capital and preference returns back before the promoter shares in the cash flow.

4. Make sure the promoter has a financial investment in the project in addition to sweat equity. This should be in addition to any fees he or she stands to make upon the formation of the investment.

5. Try to ascertain if the promoter has another project that may be causing "heartburn." The promoter's bad project could put your own investment at risk.

6. Make sure the financing is in place at the closing.

7. Have an attorney look at the deal from the investor's perspective.

Once the investment is in place, I always talk to someone who's in a position of oversight. I want to know how the promoter performs as compared to the initial projections. Many times, when a project runs into difficulty the promoter chooses not to share that information. I want to be aware of problems as soon as possible, so I can try to fix the situation before it gets worse.

These are all ways to minimize potential risks. Keeping your eyes wide open about the people you're involved with helps limit the unexpected upheavals that can come with investing. When I get involved in a real estate investment, I have to remain vigilant, no matter how much I know, no matter how much due diligence I perform, no matter how much I trust the people involved. I have to continually review the project's performance and keep tabs on the people in charge.

Law and Order

Lawyers are another group of experts most of us need on our team. They too need to be investigated thoroughly before taking them on. In my thirty-eight years at RBZ, I have dealt with hundreds of attorneys. Their range of disciplines is virtually endless: estate planning, transactional, divorce, litigation, bankruptcy, healthcare, personal injury, intellectual property, and on and on. Their personalities range from shark to guppy, and they also vary widely in their level of ability. I've learned that certain guidelines make a big difference between finding the right attorney and the wrong attorney—and between making a legal transaction effortless and making it a nightmare. In my experience, there are some basic rules to follow.

One is to determine the lawyer's level of expertise. Initially, I choose a person or firm with the necessary skills and background to handle my particular needs. I do not simply choose an attorney out of convenience, friendship, or reputation, or because they did a good job for someone else in an unrelated matter. Once I get a good referral—preferably the same one from several sources—I check with the local bar association to make sure the lawyer is in good standing. Then I interview the candidate. It's important to interview attorneys as thoroughly as they interview you. Remember, they're providing a service to you and not the other way around!

If you're involved in a legal conflict, another important aspect to consider is location. Every court has its own personality. You want an attorney who's familiar with the legal environment in that specific locale. It's obviously an advantage to have a lawyer who knows the personality and preferences of the judge hearing your case. But there are more subtle reasons too. For example, having a lawyer who's on a first-name basis with the bailiff or court clerk can make a gigantic difference in how efficiently your case is handled. That's why attorneys commonly hire local counsel when trying a case away from their own turf. It's like a sports team having home field advantage.

Another rule is to determine the fees. The essential question is: what are you getting for the price you pay? If the attorney charges a relatively low hourly rate but doesn't have the specific expertise you need and runs up your bill doing basic research, what have you saved? An efficient case can be mounted by using lower-fee paraprofessionals to supplement the higher-priced associates. This limits the use of high-priced attorneys, who should be used only for developing strategy and supervising the matter. Always inquire as to whether hiring experts might be required. While often effective at making or breaking a case, they usually carry a high price tag.

I recommend you work with the lawyer to determine a budget. If you don't agree on a range of fee for services in advance, you can seriously jeopardize your relationship. If you later come to feel that you're paying too much, it will only cause friction. Which brings me to the next important rule for working with lawyers: seek a person or firm you can relate to. You're going to be in a room with this person and reveal intimate details of your business and/or your life. You must feel comfortable with him or her, and trust they will represent your interests well. A good attorney doesn't dismiss clients' suggestions out-of-hand, but rather listens and considers them. Also, make sure the attorney has the time to take care of your needs. Even if you find the best available person, what have you gained if he or she is too busy to pay attention to you? You do not want a lawyer who will shuffle you off to someone else in the firm because your case isn't big enough.

I had to learn these lessons the hard way. I once hired a highly regarded attorney in a firm with a superlative reputation, only to end up firing him. When I first met with him, he was all business. By contrast, as anyone who's known me for more than five minutes knows, I am a people person. I like to schmooze. I like getting to know the people I do business with. It makes me feel comfortable. The attorney was schmoozeless. That should have been a big clue. But I succumbed to the notion that I needed *the best*. After a slow, painful learning process I accepted I'd made a mistake, and we parted ways. The lawyer might have been perfect for the people who referred him to me. But for me, he was clearly an inappropriate choice. With all my years of experience, you'd think I would have avoided wasting time and money on the wrong attorney. But it can happen to anyone. What's important is to learn from such mistakes, and one thing I came away with is this: when you choose an attorney, you're selecting an ally who is going to serve as your advocate. That attorney-client relationship is both professional and personal. If you approach it from that perspective, you have the best chance of finding the right attorney for you.

Personal Risks

Doing research and carefully selecting experts to work with are vital risk-reducing tactics, but they apply mostly to business. When it comes to personal matters, there are risks that no amount of research can prevent. I learned this when I separated from my first wife, Kathy. As I said earlier, my initial intention was to separate for a short time and figure out how to get the marriage back on track. When I realized there was no way I could go back home, the uncertainty of the future felt overwhelming. How could I live without being with my kids all the time? Would they turn on me? Would I end up broke after going through the divorce process? Would I lose the respect of my family, clients, friends, partners, co-workers, etc.? Would any woman ever want to date me, let alone share the rest of her life with me?

In my mind, divorce was a risky proposition. Financially speaking, I found my initial fears were well founded. A highly contested divorce is prohibitively expensive. That's why, as I said earlier, I usually recommend using mediation. I lost many hours of sleep during the two-plus-year process. As I mentioned earlier, I was so afraid of ending up penniless that my dear friends, Dan and Linda Rosenson, offered to lend me a substantial amount of money. I was grateful beyond words, but my fear actually *increased* because I was terrified that if I borrowed money I would never be able to pay it back, and that was unthinkable. I should have known I'd never have to borrow, but fear has a way of making us lose touch with reason. I forgot that, no matter what I lost in the divorce, I would not have to give up my experience, my knowledge, or my brain. The risk of actually becoming destitute was about as low as that of a snowstorm in L.A., but at the time it seemed as if a blizzard was coming. All of which is to say, when you assess the risks in any particular situation, make sure you do it on the basis of facts and rational analysis.

Sometimes research is not an option and facts are hard to come by. In these days of rapid change, uncertainty is a constant. And when it comes to human beings with unique personalities and emotions, uncertainty is usually greater than it is with quantifiable business factors. Even so, sometimes a risk must be taken. I don't just mean financial risks, but emotional and interpersonal risks as well. I remember one such time vividly. I was consulting with two female clients. They were partners in an import distribution business, and we were meeting for the first time. We sat on opposite sides of my desk and began talking about their business. But the conversation kept getting sidetracked by their bickering. One would say, "It happened eight months ago," and the other would say, "No, no, it was seven months ago." Or, one would say "The goods came in two days late," and the other would respond with "No way, they were *four* days late." The details they argued about had zero relevance to the work I had to do for them. They were fighting because each of them had to be right. It was personal. In fact, they were bickering the same way husbands and wives often do.

The thought came to me: maybe they *are* like husband and wife. This was long before homosexuality was even discussed, and gay marriage was totally off the radar. You just didn't ask someone if he or she was gay. So I paused, thinking about how I was going to deal with the situation. I didn't want to insult or offend them, but their interaction was making it impossible to do my job. I decided I had to risk it, come what may, for the sake of my clients. "Do you mind if I ask you a personal question?" I said. They told me to go ahead. "Are you two lovers?"

They were shocked, to say the least. They looked at each other, wondering what to say. Then they turned to me and admitted they used to be lovers. That was an awkward moment, but it was a terribly important, and the risk paid off. "Now let's talk about how we can separate the business issues from your past relationship," I said.

The revelation freed us to deal with the business at hand. We needed to focus our concerns, and their baggage was getting in the way. We would have wasted a lot of time, and a great deal of the clients' money, if we hadn't cleared the air of old feelings that still clouded their business relationship. Knowing what was going on with them equipped me to serve them better. They were much more comfortable around me than if they'd continued concealing their secret. They also became far more willing to disclose information I needed to know.

Sometimes, business is business. It's numbers. The main factors are business logic and business history. But sometimes we need to include relationship logic and relationship history, and those factors add to the uncertainty and the risk.

With the former lovers, it was important for me to understand the nuances of their relationship. Businesswise, one handled sales and the other distribution. I asked them, "If one of you died tomorrow, how would the surviving partner do the work? Neither of you knows the other's part of the business." They both said they'd have to find someone else to take the place of the deceased. Clearly, they added value to each other, and the business couldn't survive without someone in each position. In that context, their personal history was extremely important. It was the key to realizing their "business problem" wasn't really a business problem. They delayed making decisions; they procrastinated; they neglected important aspects of the business; and they blamed each other for all the inefficiencies and mishaps. All of that dysfunction stemmed from their personal baggage. I could never have solved their problems if we'd kept things on a strictly business level.

Realizing this, I boldly took another risk. "You're bickering and arguing so much that you can't move forward," I said. "It's all due to your past history. Now, one easy way to solve it is for each of you to start your own business. Go off and find new partners and do your own things. You'll probably both succeed. But if you want to succeed together, as a unit, you've got to resolve some of these past issues."

From that point on, they talked to me in a different tone. Instead of pretending to be just business partners, they became two vulnerable human beings. They started sharing with me the mistakes they'd each made, and offering up ideas about how they could improve things. The personal and the professional were no longer separate in their minds. This was an eye-opener for them, and it changed the way they did business together. As a result, they turned their faltering business around. I don't know what happened in the long run; they were clients only for a few years. I do know that my hunch about them, and my decision to risk asking a deeply personal question, was a key to their future success. The risk of offending them outweighed the risk of their business failing. I'll always be glad I took that risk.

Chapter 21
Be Prepared

Throughout my life, I have seen the dangers of not being properly prepared. My type of accounting—Therapeutic Accounting®— calls for me to work closely with my clients. Therefore, one of my primary responsibilities is to make sure my clients have a broad and comprehensive perspective, not only on their finances, but on all the life circumstances that impact their finances and are impacted *by* their finances.

Some people don't understand how critically important it is to anticipate the curve balls life can throw. I often come across clients who believe that they don't need to do estate planning, for instance. They like to believe they're years away from old age and death, and can therefore procrastinate on dealing with important matters such as wills and trusts. I tell those clients, "If a bus hits you, it won't matter if you're a hundred years old or fifty—you ain't walking away from that alive."

I stress the issue even more for clients who are parents. People like to think their children will be entirely self-sufficient by the time they reach adulthood. That belief doesn't leave room for their children losing well-paid jobs in an economic downturn, or getting divorced and needing a place to live, or suffering a serious illness, or falling into debt, or even needing to be bailed out. I often have to remind parents their duties did not end when they stopped changing diapers, or even when they made that last tuition payment. Not even when they walked their youngest child down the aisle. Parents are parents for the rest of their lives. Actually, for the rest of *their children's* lives: even after parents die, they have a responsibility to help their kids. The main duty of a parent is to do what is right by their offspring, even when it's difficult, inconvenient, or uncomfortable—and that includes preparing for the end of life. That means getting over the discomfort of thinking about the eventuality of death and taking steps to transfer assets to their children.

Get Ready for Rainy Days Ahead

Sometimes we get slammed by events totally out of the blue. You can't plan for those, but you can still be prepared for crises and emergencies in general. I have had the sad task of helping clients rearrange their finances and their lives because they suddenly found themselves in the position of raising their grandchildren. This isn't something many people anticipate, but according to AARP the incidence of grandparent-headed households increased by 76 percent between 1970 and 2002. Far more common, of course, is something unexpected happening to a spouse. The fact is, as we inch closer to old age, the likelihood of our spouse being afflicted by a major disease increases dramatically. With medical costs soaring out of control and the future of Medicare in question, this is no small matter. Already, older consumers spend far more out-of-pocket for medical expenses than ever before. These are harsh realities that no one likes to think about, but denial is a recipe for disaster, and anticipating such needs can prevent financial ruin. Doing nothing is not an option. In fact, it's a decision to leave everything up to chance—and, incidentally, to make matters worse because deniers invariably end up paying far more in taxes.

Anticipating future problems used to be easy. In the old days, when I planned for my clients' retirement, I simply had to calculate their long-term assets to get them comfortably to the average ripe old age of eighty. Nowadays, it isn't uncommon for people to live well into their nineties and even surpass 100. According to the U.S. Bureau of the Census, 40.3 million Americans were sixty-five and older on April 1, 2010. That's a 15.1 percent increase since 2000; the overall population grew only 9.7 percent by comparison. Also, the older population itself is getting older. Now we often see middle-aged people planning for retirement while also providing for both their children and their parents. More than 20 million households have someone who's caring for a disabled or elderly family member, and about a quarter of these caregivers are in their fifties and sixties themselves. In fact, I have seventy-five-year-old clients supporting ninety-five-year-old parents who used up their net worth when they hit eighty.

All of these factors make planning for retirement far more challenging and far more complicated than ever before. That's especially true when the economy is in the doldrums, as it has been since 2008. Interest rates for savings accounts, which used to be a stable, predictable way to earn decent returns, are as close to zero as I've ever seen. More and more people have to ask themselves questions like, "Will I be able to maintain my standard of living in old age?" and "How can I earn a decent return on my savings and also protect the fruits of my labor?" People work hard their entire lives; it should not be wasted because of a mistake in investment strategy.

In the old days, people also knew they would receive a fixed amount of pension income. And they could calculate their expenses because they too were more or less fixed. In today's complex world, so many things are in motion at all times that it's important to stay flexible. As personal circumstances and economic conditions change, we need to continuously reevaluate and frequently make adjustments, no matter how old we are. You may not be able to retire as early as you thought, or you may not be able to take a full retirement. If you're already retired, you may need to reduce your travel plans or eat out less often. And those are minor compromises. More drastic action may be needed, such as selling your home and moving into a rental unit, or getting a part-time job to supplement your income.

The Importance of Documentation

All in all, planning for the future now involves a longer string of issues. If you want your retirement dreams to come true, you need to consider cash flow, investment strategy, estate planning, Social Security, Medicare, housing options (including home safety), special mortgages (such as reverse mortgages), ways to lower your tax bill, inflation predictions, part-time work, transportation needs, personal care and meal preparation, specialized legal representation, and life, disability, and long-term care insurance. Each of these matters has to be looked at separately and at different times. But it should never be forgotten that they all fit together. And all of those nuts-and-bolts issues have to be seen in the light of personal values, family responsibilities, and all the emotional factors that arise in close relationships.

The task may seem daunting, but failure to plan for the future means certain trouble. One key factor in being prepared is maintaining accurate and complete documentation. Throughout my professional life, I have helped many families cope with the financial aftermath of life's triumphs and tragedies, from the birth of a child to the death of a loved one, and nearly everything else in between. When such milestones occur, people tend to neglect critical paperwork. In the face of rejoicing or grieving, documentation is easy to forget, and even when we remember, who wants to be bothered? So they often put off dealing with it indefinitely. But the consequences of ignoring the essential documentation can be disastrous.

In most cases, the amount of effort required to document life changes as they occur is quite minimal. I advise all of my clients to make sure the necessary paperwork is completed immediately in the event of a marriage, a birth, a sudden change in financial conditions, a divorce or separation, an inheritance, or a death. My most frequent advice is to plan ahead. Of course it's one thing for a professional like me to suggest that, but it's quite another for clients to follow through. Take prenuptial agreements, for example. No one wants to broach the possibility of a future trauma when they're in the throes of romance and planning a wedding. Nevertheless, the possibility of a prenuptial agreement should be discussed early if you don't want to be haunted by the lack of one in the future. Perhaps your fiancé will suspect you are not truly committed to the marriage if you suggest such an agreement, or will assume you don't trust him or her. Whatever your qualms, the discussion should not be avoided. I've seen more than one client delay the topic for months, and then finally bring it up days before the wedding. Bad idea: that only looks like you're getting cold feet, or else listening to the wrong family members. Plus, it probably won't even hold up in court. In the long run, grabbing the proverbial bull by the horns and launching into the discussion early on will be less painful than procrastination.

By the way, the same argument applies to unmarried couples who are planning to move in together. Their equivalent of a prenuptial agreement is called a palimony agreement, and it follows the same type of format.

As Time Goes By

Being prepared means redirecting what we are focused on, as the economic climate and personal circumstances change. Sometimes, for instance, it's better to focus on cash flow than on tax savings. Something I have preached for years is having little or no mortgage on your personal residence, if you can afford it. Even though this might not be a good tax strategy, it can give you much less to worry about during financial downturns when cash flow is a high priority. In my case, it means a lot to me to know that, upon my demise, Harriet will be able to live in the home she loves by paying only property taxes, insurance, and maintenance. Being free of mortgage payments would not only ensure she can live where she wants to, but would also be cheaper than renting an apartment with comparable amenities in a good location.

In the past, many of my real estate clients have felt the need to find a tax-free exchange when selling an investment property in order to avoid paying taxes. Some of them discovered that wasn't the best strategy after all, when they couldn't find a good qualified exchange property at the time. They lost more on the new investment than the taxes they would have paid on the gain if they hadn't done the exchange.

How about all those deferred compensation plans people use to avoid paying taxes on a current basis, only to discover that the company they worked for (which created such a "helpful" plan) filed for bankruptcy and the deferred compensation turned into *no* compensation? How about holding onto stock with a large unrealized gain for over one year so you can get the long-term capital gain rate, only to find there is no reason to worry about the taxes after all, because the stock's value dropped and the gains were eliminated before you could realize them?

It is human nature to avoid the things that bother us the most, and paying taxes is certainly one of those things. Usually we look only at the short-term effects of our decisions. Taxes are always considered bad in the short term because we need to spend money now to pay the government what we owe. But there can be a benefit in going through that short-term pain, just as the pain of a minor medical procedure is worthwhile if it means avoiding the bigger pain of major surgery.

The Issue of Aging

A question I constantly hear from clients in their mid-sixties is, "Should I collect on Social Security now, at a smaller monthly payment, or wait three years and get the full amount?" Even if Social Security were completely solvent, which I fear it is not, you would have to wait in excess of twelve years (150 monthly checks) to break even by waiting for the non-discounted amount to take effect. This does not even include the fact that much, if not all, of your Social Security income will evaporate when you die. Nor does it take inflation into account.

Another common question involves making gifts to children while the parent is still alive rather than having them wait until death to inherit the money. That's an area where Therapeutic Accounting® becomes part of the process. Gifting during life can be very beneficial financially. But the psychological effect should be taken into account as well. Would large gifts signal heirs they can stop working, or exert less effort on their own? Would it make someone with an inflated sense of entitlement even more spoiled? Would it create jealousy or conflict among siblings, or with a stepfamily?

Harriet and I love to see our children get a few extra benefits from our success while we're still alive. We've helped them with some of their financial challenges, for example, and have covered their education and medical costs. We take the whole family on an annual vacation so they can see places they might not get to visit on their own. Even when we give them more than the maximum tax-free gift amount, which triggers gift taxes we have to pay currently, it can still help our overall estate and the needs of our heirs in the long run. The point is, there are many ways to make life easier for your heirs in the future. One is to invest in long-term care insurance or second-to-die life insurance. Harriet and I have done both, for two reasons: to make sure we do not become a financial burden to our heirs, and to minimize the inheritance tax for them.

Be Realistic

All of this is just the tip of the iceberg when it comes to being prepared. On any given day we might encounter issues that need to be examined both from a short-term and a long-term perspective. In doing so, be careful not to let your judgment be blinded by optimism. Optimism is good, but not at the expense of realism. For example, preparing for the possibility of a divorce or separation can be vitally important. One of the most common problems arises when clients neglect to change their wills. If they have a living trust, for example, upon their death some of their assets may automatically go to their ex-spouse. This might not be what the deceased wanted. People are often incredulous. They say, "But an ex-spouse can't be regarded as a beneficiary." Yes, they can: if the ex-spouse is included in the will as a beneficiary by name, he or she will benefit at the cost of what you may have really wanted.

The same is true for many types of insurance policies, including health, automobile, and even homeowner's policies. An ex-spouse may also be named in important documents such as safe deposit boxes, home security systems, and whom to call in an emergency. They may also sign on checking accounts and investment accounts, or have title to various items such as the family car. You may decide to leave your ex-spouse's name on some of these documents. However, that should be done on purpose rather than by accident.

Not only traumas and tragedies necessitate updating various documents, or filling out new ones; happy occasions can have the same effect. The birth of a child is one of the most glorious events in a person's life, and may kick-start the *busiest* time of life. Still, it's important to take time out from midnight feedings and trips to the pediatrician to update your medical insurance and other forms. A financial windfall is another happy occasion that leads to paperwork. Whether you get promoted or become TV's newest game show millionaire, an upswing in your financial situation requires the same thoughtful analysis as a downturn. If your net worth increases dramatically, it's time to update your estate plan, or maybe begin making gifts to family members, friends, or business associates. You might need to consult with attorneys, bankers, and accountants, or hire a financial professional to manage your portfolio.

Till Death Do You Part

The most traumatic event that can change your financial status, of course, is death. Even the most on-the-ball clients become foggy about practical matters when they lose a loved one. The emotional trauma is so severe they can no longer think logically. I have often seen a look that combines shock and fear in my clients' faces when I describe what can happen if they don't attend to the details. For instance, if the death precipitates a sizeable inheritance, there are many important financial and legal issues to consider. This might mean creating an estate plan for the first time, or changing an existing one. It might require rethinking the amount you plan to give to your own beneficiaries, or changing the trustee or executor if the current one does not have the necessary financial acumen to handle a large estate.

Many people spend the time and money to establish a solid estate plan with the help of a professional. Once the plan is created, however, some people neglect to follow through with the correct asset transfers. For example, if you created a living trust to avoid probate at the time of your death, you still need to have each one of your assets properly transferred to the trust, including your home. If you don't, all your diligence in setting up the trust will be for naught. This can be a tedious process, but a terribly important one.

One of the most important items to deal with upon the death of a spouse is to change the title on the assets of the deceased (unless they are in a trust) to minimize problems on future transfers. This is true whether you own the asset directly, in a joint tenancy, or in a partnership. You'll find it costly and time-consuming to make these changes if you let too much time pass. Hopefully, once a client understands the importance of documentation at all major life changes, they will take the necessary measures to get the job done. If it feels overwhelming, they should try to accomplish one step at a time rather than putting off the task entirely. In any case, proper paperwork at the outset can prevent costly blunders in the future.

Individual Differences

Getting people to think about such heavy subjects is difficult. But to me, as a therapeutic accountant, it is necessary. At the same time, I recognize individual clients may not share my point of view on these matters, and I've learned to separate my perspective from their wishes and their emotional state.

Similarly, one of my most important tasks is to fully recognize that different people want different things from their investments. As a therapeutic accountant I go beyond the numbers and inquire deeply into my clients' dreams, hopes, risk tolerance, and aspirations. Some only want cash flow, others want a tax shelter, some want equity build-up, others want to buy real estate for estate planning, and so forth. Some investors want a combination of these priorities. In all cases, however, the key elements of preparation are the same. One basic factor, of course, is to consider the risks along with the potential rewards.

In my experience, the first step in planning investments is to know the background, experience, and track record of the person making the key decisions. In real estate, that would be the project manager. Having firm knowledge about the manager is so important that I recommend talking to previous investors who've worked with him, and also to hire private investigators to check the records for financial, criminal, and other critical information. The deal should be structured so the manager co-invests or guarantees the investment. In return, the manager should be able to earn a handsome amount of money, but only after the investors get their money back with a reasonable initial return. There are many ways to determine what the return should be (cash flow, internal rate of return, debt coverage ratio, etc.). The bottom line, as John Long, a successful manager, once said, is: "Just make sure the project makes a profit."

Being prepared doesn't stop there. Another vital step is to protect the investment from loss. One way to do that is to diversify. In real estate, that could mean making investments in various geographical areas, with a variety of property types and managers. Another important factor is oversight. Maintaining a good investment means obtaining periodic reports that indicate how the project is fairing compared to the initial projection. I also recommend acquiring an experienced real estate attorney to exclusively represent the investors. This is in addition to the attorney who represents the manager and the project itself.

I always tell my clients that, before committing to an investment, they should determine the period they intend to be in it, and to also have an exit strategy. People should prepare for the possibility that the initial plan will not work out.

Don't Go Over the Top with Enthusiasm

You'd be surprised how many people get excited by an attractive investment and don't want to hear about the possible downside. In their minds they turn an optimistic scenario into something like a guarantee, convincing themselves they're going to double their investment in a short time. As a result, they approach their investments with way too much enthusiasm. It usually falls on me to tell them enthusiasm is good, but they need to ask themselves some serious questions, like, "Where is the capital going to come from?" I've told many a client, "You've given me a plan for where you're going to end up, but not the plan for how you're going to get there." They might reply by saying the money will come from, say, advertising. Then I'm forced to ask, "Okay, who's paying for the advertising? Right now you're making X dollars. How are you going to take that X and convert it so you have enough advertising to earn double X?" Or, I might ask, "How are you going to do it with the same staff you have now? You're already filled to the brim. How are you going to take on new staff without obtaining more space? And how will you pay for that space?"

I not only get them to think about such practical matters, I also encourage them to think more deeply about their goals. People need to not only set explicit goals, but also understand the price they'll have to pay to achieve them. If they don't, they can easily fall short of meeting their goals. I've seen too many unprepared people jump into enterprises undercapitalized. I make sure my clients do a reality check, so they can face what is truly happening. I'm not being negative. My intention is not to dissuade them or to put them down. I'm on their side. If clients want to think of me negatively, I prefer they think of me as greedy. I greedily want my clients to be successful. Their success is my success. I don't make money if they go out of business. I make more money when their businesses double their revenues. Sometimes I tell people "I hope next year you pay $20 million in taxes." Some people get upset when they hear that. I explain, "Well, you have to make $40 million to pay $20 million in taxes." It shocks me when people are upset by comments that seem so obvious to me.

Sometimes people simply have to adjust their point of view, and I don't mind being the one to broaden their perspective. I try to bring in reality without lowering their goals and aspirations. It's just that some people think they will go from A to Z in record speed. They want to immediately go from the lowest to the highest level. I like to have them focus on the fact that progress comes one step at a time. They also need to know if their goals are set too high. If the goals are always just out of reach, or if it takes many long years to achieve them, the client can get exhausted and become so off balance and distracted that he or she goes off on a tangent that's doomed to failure. My job is to make sure this doesn't happen.

Some accountants allow clients to get carried away with unrealistic goals. They don't want to burst the bubble because they're afraid of losing them as clients. They think their clients don't want to hear anything negative from advisers. I believe an attitude like that sets the client up for failure. Someone has to be the reality check, and I take on that role as a therapeutic accountant. For example, suppose a client is so excited by the opportunity to merge with another company that he doesn't pay attention to what's going on around him. I'm the one who says, "Okay, if you sell your business and you're on an earn-out, you'll get a piece of the profit over a period of time. Have you considered whether or not the company will start loading itself with their corporate overhead, which means there will be no profit?" At that point the client usually goes through a phase of disillusionment. They might initially disregard my warning, but most of them come to their senses and make a more realistic agreement.

Of course, there have been times when I forced clients to weigh all the potential consequences of a deal, and as a result they end up killing it altogether. I like to believe if a deal is cancelled in the planning stages it's better that it was never made. Success doesn't always mean accomplishing a goal; sometimes it means knowing when to hold back and *not* pursue the goal.

I feel bad sometimes, because I don't like to see people in anguish and pain, which is what can happen when I bring up areas of discomfort. I just believe in being prepared, and in the long run it's healthy to face reality early on. For example, I had to make one client see that if he bought a particular house, he would eventually lose because he wouldn't be able keep up the mortgage payments. He would have had a short period of glory, a few years of bliss, and then suffered tremendously. I advised him against it, and fortunately he listened.

Another client was in a similar position and *didn't* listen. I begged him not to purchase what he called his dream house. He bought it anyway. He purchased the land for $5 million and invested an additional $23 million in improvements. He ended up with a mortgage payment of about $180,000 a month, plus property taxes of $25,000 a month, plus insurance premiums. In addition, he was having temporary cash flow problems. It was a difficult time, but he could have managed it easily if he hadn't taken on the obligation of financing the dream house.

As it happened, I had a chance to sell the lot for him right after he bought it, to someone who offered me a significant profit. But at that time my client was flying high. He couldn't wait to move into that dream home. The thought that his balloon could burst never entered his mind. The balloon was leaking air right from the start, but he wouldn't hear about it. He remained a wealthy man, and he's still living in the house. His cash flow has improved considerably, so this is no longer a major problem. But it could have gone the other way if his cash flow *hadn't* improved.

A similar situation happened with a client who wanted to start a yogurt chain. This was in the 1990s when frozen yogurt was at the peak of its popularity. I was half-successful in preventing him from losing all his money. He originally wanted to set up sixty locations, with half of them in K-marts and Walmarts and the other half as free-standing shops. He let me convince him to only do the easy ones—the ones in the big chain stores, where he didn't have to pay rent or lease space. The companies just took a percentage of his revenue. The business failed after about eight months. When all was said and done, he thanked me for recommending that he not open the other thirty locations. That would have been far more costly, since leases typically require payments for five years, whether the business is successful or not. I was disappointed that I didn't completely protect him from failure, but at least I got him to readjust his expectations to a more realistic level.

I have a few clients who were highly successful in the United States and then tried taking their businesses overseas. They thought they could easily duplicate their success. I tried to explain that the tax structure and union situation are very different in France. They didn't want to hear about it. They went forward, and less than two years later they had lost a few million dollars. I did prepare them enough so they didn't put all their eggs in one basket, and therefore didn't lose their company. Still, a large part of me considered that a failure. I could not get them to see the holes in their plan.

Financial Literacy

As you can see, I am passionate about getting people to prepare. Good preparation means looking realistically at both the upside and the downside. It also means recognizing that if key pieces of a transaction are missing, you have to walk away. That's why I stress that people should become financially literate, so they can tell not only when to say yes to a deal but also when to say no.

I think it's critical to train young people in how to handle money. One of the best ways to do that is through a course called 360 Degrees of Financial Literacy, developed by the AICPA (American Institute of Certified Public Accountants). The AICPA has even gone so far as to furnish thousands of elementary schools with educational material and newsletters.

People who know me know I've been discussing this issue for years as a therapeutic accountant. My clients know I'm apprehensive about giving their children too much too soon, and about not giving them enough guidance for what may come their way in the future. Parents need to prepare their children for the responsibility of handling substantial amounts of money. I have helped several families by sitting in on their "family board of directors" meetings. These meetings are generally held quarterly with the parents and children (no in-laws), to discuss the family assets, charitable giving, key outsourced professionals, and other matters. Families have found this to be a useful tool. I believe every family should do this, whether or not they're wealthy.

The AICPA has also applied financial literacy to eleven phases of life, from birth to retirement; thus the name 360 Degrees of Financial Literacy. They have developed a website: www.360financialliteracy.org that I believe you may find useful no matter what period of life you are in. I'm happy to see that CPAs are becoming more than just "bean counters."

Chapter 22
Persevere

Several years ago, when I was at an international accounting meeting in New Zealand, I saw a poster that stuck with me. It said:

He failed in business in '31.

He was defeated for State Legislator in '32.

He tried another business in '33. It failed.

His fiancée died in '35.

He had a nervous breakdown in '36.

In '43 he ran for Congress and was defeated.

He tried again in '48 and was defeated again.

He tried running for the Senate in '55 and lost.

The next year he ran for Vice President and lost.

In '59 he ran for the Senate again and was defeated.

In 1860, the man who signed his name "A. Lincoln" was elected as the 16th President of the United States.

The difference between history's boldest accomplishments and its most staggering failures is often, simply, the diligent will to persevere.

Abraham Lincoln's story should inspire anyone who is tempted to give up in the face of adversity and setbacks. Even I have been inspired by it at times, and I was born with tenacity. I've always had a knack for persevering in pursuit of my goals, especially when they truly matter to me. I work hard at everything, partly because I have a strong will for mastery. When I want something meaningful, I pursue it like a bulldog. I don't let anything distract me from my goals. Setbacks, dead ends, low moments, losses—I don't let any of those issues take my eyes off the prize. That's why I didn't stop trying after I failed the CPA exam the first time—or the five times after that. I don't like setbacks. I can't stand failures. But I know a certain number of them are inevitable on the road to success, and I always end up grateful for them in the long run because I learned vital lessons from every hard knock I endured.

Setbacks also allow me to have greater appreciation when things go well. There's always something good to be found in something bad, if you look for it, and the good will make itself known if you refuse to get dissuaded during the low periods and the dark times. Everybody gets knocked down once in a while—and I mean *everybody,* even the superstars for whom things appear to come easy. But as they say, it's not whether you get knocked down that matters; it's whether you get back up. The ones who know how to bounce back onto their feet, who quickly put the knockdown behind them without losing an ounce of confidence or self-respect, who learn the right lessons and keep on fighting—they're the ones who win the day. That's why a key element in the ability to persevere is to believe in your heart that every downturn contains the potential for the next rise, just as the frozen winter soil contains the seeds of spring.

I believe the ability to persevere will always guide a person to success. It may take a while, but that never-give-up attitude will pay off in the end, as long as the desire is strong and the goal is worth pursuing.

What We Need to Persevere

By its very nature, perseverance is more than just trying. It's more than merely dreaming. And it's more than just wishful thinking. Perseverance means making a firm commitment to attaining your goals and then refusing to quit or to settle for less. I don't care if your goal is to make a ton of money, build a philanthropic nonprofit, win an Olympic gold medal, make a hit record, earn a Ph.D., get elected to public office, or raise the best possible children—whatever you aspire to, all of your talent, training, opportunities, and connections will not be enough to get you there if you aren't prepared to persevere.

Persevering is essential in business, of course, but personal matters demand it too. When I started therapy, I brought to my sessions with Dr. Jones the same willful intensity I bring to my business. I then used that same tenacity to apply everything I learned in therapy to real life. My will to succeed was the reason I was able to reconstruct and reorient my personal life at a time when it seemed to be falling apart. I remain dedicated to self-understanding to this day, and will stop at nothing to gain more of it. Unlike other goals, such as obtaining a college degree, starting a business, or reaching a certain level of income, there is no defined end to this process. My perseverance in this private realm is driven by the satisfaction of learning more and more, and using that knowledge to create a better life for me and my loved ones.

I admire people who refuse to be deterred from reaching their goals—and that means everyone who perseveres, not just the Abraham Lincolns and Warren Buffets and Michael Jordans of the world. I also admire people who help others persevere. You know that old saying about the woman behind every successful man? It's quite often true, and it's also true that successful women often have supportive men behind them, and successful people in general usually have parents, friends, mentors, and others behind them. The point is, it's hard to persevere without others to help us get back up when things go bad, and to lift our spirits when they sag. For example, I admire my son-in-law Jeff, who took almost ten years to graduate from college. A big reason Jeff was able to persevere was that he had a hugely supportive girlfriend who eventually became his wife: my stepdaughter Roni. She constantly reminded him of the importance of getting that degree, and her own perseverance helped to fuel his.

That's why it's important to have supportive people around you. The strong will of one person can help reinforce another's will, especially if one begins to falter. I'm certain my own tenacity, and my history of persevering in the face of setbacks, helped instill those qualities in my children and others. When people I care about dream of goals that some would consider out of reach, I encourage them. I tell them they should never give up dreaming and never stop striving for lofty goals, because success comes from going beyond what would normally be expected, as long as those goals are also realistic. And you can't do that if you don't persevere.

Which brings me to an important lesson I've learned about parenting: If you want your kids to persevere, you have to let them set their own goals as opposed to coercing them into pursuing the goals *you* have for them. It can be difficult, but parents need to let go of their own expectations for their children and let them find their own way. How can our children persevere if the dreams they're striving for are not authentically their own? Each person is different. We're passionate about different things; we aspire to different things; we want different things. And we each proceed at our own pace. All we can do is encourage our children to find out who they really are and help them persevere in becoming the best "them" they can be.

As a therapeutic accountant, I had to learn that lesson about my clients as well as my children. My clients' wants are different from my wants. Their goals are different from mine. Their priorities, their dreams, and their values are not the same as mine. I had to make sure the service I provided fit what the clients thought was best for themselves, not what I thought was best for them, or what I would want if I were in their shoes. I've also had to act this way when serving as the trustee of clients' estates after their deaths. This isn't always as easy as you might think.

Some of my clients—especially the highly competitive ones—talk only about money. They often stop short of examining why they want the money in the first place, or why they aspire to success. They don't realize that, in their pursuit of wealth or power, they might be sacrificing important aspects of their lives, and way too often they fail to see they missed the boat on what's truly important until they're too old to make up for lost time. When I see that, all I can do is encourage them to think beyond money. I can't make them do so, and I can't allow my work for them to reflect my own values instead of theirs.

Persevere on Your Own Terms

We all measure our lives by particular standards, whether they are moral standards, financial standards, or others. We acquire these standards through our own experiences and observations, and from our environments—our parents, siblings, friends, religions, schools, etc. As we grow and develop, our goals continue to evolve. Our dreams for the future change. Our expectations shift. We start out thinking about finishing school, then about getting our first job, and before long we're thinking grown-up thoughts, about financial security, marriage, whether to have children, owning a home, progressing in a career, and so forth. Later, new and unexpected goals may arise: for adventure or for learning new things or contributing significantly to society.

Every step of the way we measure where we are according to our expectations and standards. We use many methods to determine how we're doing, including the common practice of looking around to see how we stack up against our peers, siblings, and parents. That's when jealousy and envy and feelings of inadequacy often raise their ugly heads. If we don't measure up to our standards and models we feel bad about ourselves, and perhaps start making up excuses. We might also find rationalizations for other people's success, just to make ourselves feel better: *"They're just lucky; they're hiding the real facts; they 'bought' their way in."* A wise person once said the surest way to make yourself miserable is to compare yourself to others. I'll add to that: the surest way to cure yourself of envy is to find out what's really going on in the lives of people you envy. Unfortunately, we usually compare ourselves to those who achieved more than we have. But while they may be more successful in one aspect of life, you may be more fortunate in other ways without even knowing it. They might secretly envy you.

Eyes on the Prizes

Our lives are multifaceted and complex, and happiness, contentment, and fulfillment seldom correlate with visible signs of success. No one has a completely ideal life; there is always something more to seek. We need to skillfully adapt to whatever curveballs life may throw at us, so we can persevere in pursuit of our important goals, whether material, emotional or spiritual.

Keeping your gaze fixed on meaningful long-term goals is also important, even as circumstances force you to make significant adjustments in the short term. During the economic crisis of 2008, Harriet and I had to adjust to the fiscal changes that engulfed us. We were certainly better prepared than most people. As we built our net worth, we made sure a healthy portion of it stayed liquid for times like those. We had set aside plenty of money for rainy days, and back then it was pouring. But although we were well-cushioned for the financial blow, adapting in the short-term to preserve our long-term goals was still a challenge. We changed our budget to spend half as much on vacation expenses as we normally would. We decided to wait an extra few years before replacing our cars with new ones. We ate in less expensive restaurants. We reduced our trips to the mall so as not to be tempted to buy things on impulse, as we often did. At the time, my daughter Michelle was getting married, and we looked for ways to have a great reception that would be less expensive than the hotel ballroom we'd intended to use. We ended up having a fantastic time on a boat in Long Beach Harbor.

In other words, we wanted to persevere toward our long-term goals and make sure our most important needs would continue to be met. That covers a wide spectrum, including our medical needs as we age, educational pursuits for our children and grandchildren, family vacations, charitable contributions, and the well-being of our family as a whole. All in all, the challenging period brought on by the economic crisis confirmed something I've always believed: individuals, families, communities, and entire countries can benefit from tough times in the long run, if they learn the right lessons along the way. One of those lessons is that perseverance demands flexibility. You have to adapt to unexpected changes without being distracted from your long-term goals, quickly designing alternative plans when adjustments become necessary. If you do that well, you will always prevail, even if sudden upheavals create temporary discomfort or even pain. The old saying "When the going gets tough, the tough get going" is a great adage to follow. Winners always persevere.

Chapter 23
Attend To What Really Matters

*F*ar too often I hear people define *success* as making more money. They might mean making more than certain other people, making more than they did the previous year, or just *more* in general. With my clients, I like to challenge that definition of success. I've learned that true success has to be measured independent of money, and we need to pause in our hectic lives to see whether we're investing our time in ways that are true to our deepest values. We have to ask ourselves, "Am I attending to what truly matters?"

Thomas Moore, author of *Care of the Soul*, once remarked, "If you have learned only how to be a success, your life has probably been wasted." If he were writing for the average businessperson today, he could not be more right. Most of them seem to think making more money is the most important goal in life. If they don't think that way, they act as if they do, based on how they spend their time and energy. There was a time when I was one of them. But after all I've been through, all I've learned, and all I've achieved, I know for certain money is only a minor part of true success.

If you can't afford to feed your children or obtain medical care when you need it, then money is certainly a huge factor in determining your happiness and well-being. If you get more of it, you will be a lot happier. But for people who already live well and have established a reasonable level of financial security, getting more money doesn't necessarily add to their happiness beyond the temporary satisfaction of another victory or the fleeting pleasure of a shiny new car or even a bigger house. Scientific research has recently verified the common observation that having lots of money simply does not guarantee happiness. All over the world, people living with a lot less than the average American are often happier. And I've personally known many wealthy people who are miserable. When I press them and ask if are they are truly happy, they become very quiet.

True Success

I tell my clients that if they want to be truly successful, they need to achieve success not only in business, but in life as a whole. That doesn't mean giving up your material possessions, nor does it mean suppressing the drive to accomplish your business goals or focusing only on charity and good deeds. True success means *also* attending to what really matters deep down in your heart of hearts. As we discussed earlier in this book, one important factor is making sure you enjoy the work you do. If you sincerely love what you spend the bulk of your days doing, everything else has a way of falling into place.

Even beyond the actual work you do, the people you do it with are part of your success. Look around at the associates, co-workers, and clients you deal with every day, and ask yourself if you like being with them. Do you have truly good relationships with them? Life is too short to spend your time with people you don't care about or want to be with. If you don't like the work or the people, it's time to look for a different way to earn a living or a different place to do so. If you cannot change your job, perhaps you can get better at learning to like what you do. Sometimes it's more a matter of adjusting your attitude than your outer circumstances.

Many people, especially business people, allow themselves to get wrapped up in their day-to-day lives. Some of them create a series of unending crises to fix, so they can avoid focusing on what's going on in their personal lives. My advice is: face the reality square on. Look at the fear, the anxiety, and the discontent, and deal with it. Use the same skills you call upon to solve your problems at work. Incorporate your business plan into your grander life plan. Develop your own criteria for success instead of measuring yourself by the usual standards.

Gauging the consequences of how you spend your time and where you invest your energy is vitally important. If your business grows by twenty percent but you only see your children two nights a week, are you truly successful in your life? Don't just think short-term; take a long-range view and consider how you'll feel about that down the road, when your children are grown and you close in on retirement. How will you feel if your family members seem like complete strangers to you? Will you be one of those people who regrets all the time you spent at work? Will you wish you could turn back the clock and spend more time with your family? I believe reasonable limits have to be set, and every business plan has to take into account your life outside of work. Maybe it's better to grow the business by ten percent instead of twenty percent, if that means you can go on a trip with your loved ones, or pursue a passion that has nothing to do with the workplace.

I understand that for some people redirecting their focus and shifting their priorities can be difficult. I literally needed an earthshaking event to make me understand the importance of attending to what truly matters. I was so determined to have stereotypical "success" that I was blind to how my family was impacted by my working all day and most of the night and getting home around eleven o'clock. If my kids wanted to see me, they had to stay up late or wait until Sunday—family day, which my kids will tell you was not always a fun time. In fact, we spent most Sundays bickering with one another.

Now I make sure my loved ones are part of my everyday life. I have dinner with Harriet every night, no matter how busy I am, and every year I take a vacation with the whole family. I have improved tremendously in finding true balance in life, and yet I still find there are ways I can do it even better—not just for my own satisfaction, but for the happiness of everyone around me. I learned from Dr. Jones that people usually cannot see how they're blocking their own happiness. They complain about others: "My wife needs to improve in this way," or "I want my husband to get better at such and such." They seldom ask, "How can I improve? How can I be a better parent? How can I be a better spouse?" I learned to ask those questions early in the therapeutic process, and ever since I constantly assess how I can be a better person. I approach that task with the same tenacity and perseverance I bring to growing my company, putting together a business deal, or solving a problem for one of my clients.

To be sure, I'm still driven. I still get up before the sun, and I still leave the office late. But I don't skip dinner with my wife unless I'm out of town, and I build in plenty of time for the rest of my family and our friends. I have come to terms with what matters most in my life, and those things now drive me more than anything else. In the past, my partners, business associates, and friends would frequently challenge me to reduce my work hours. I remember Dan Rosenson telling me, "Harvey, you're coming to an age where you need to slow down and smell the roses." At the time, I barely knew what roses were, let alone stopping to sniff them. Dan is now happy with my shift toward more balanced goals.

Too Much of a Good Thing

Actually, at times I'm *too* devoted, and I care *too much* about the family issues I used to neglect. For instance, when my stepdaughter Roni announced she was pregnant, I was ecstatic. My first grandchild! I would talk about it to anyone who had an ear. Unfortunately, Roni had a miscarriage. I took it so hard I went into a deeper slump than she did. I can only imagine the pain she went through; being so excited about the life growing in her body only to lose it must have had a profound impact. I should have been helping her get through that difficult time, but instead the ordeal took such a huge toll on me I couldn't be there for her as a father. Roni chose not to tell me when she got pregnant the second time. She shared it with Harriet, of course, but not with me, because she didn't want me to be disappointed again. At the time, I didn't realize how often miscarriages occur. I thought they were one out of a billion, but it turns out twenty-five percent of pregnancies end that way.

I suppose being *too* devoted and *too* concerned is a lot better than being indifferent. And I have to add that I am now a terrific Gramps!

A similar situation occurred with my son Joel and my stepson Jeff. I helped them with a business opportunity they were excited about, but it eventually fell through. I moaned and groaned to Harriet how terrible I felt about the setback. But I did the opposite of what I did with Roni: I never told my sons how truly disappointed I was, and how badly I felt for them. I think they took my silence as indifference. They thought I wrote it off as just another business deal gone awry—something I'm used to after all these years, but they were experiencing for the first time. The truth is, I had taken it to heart and I felt awful about it, but I didn't express those feelings to them. When I realized what was going on, I asked Harriet if she thought it was too late to share my true feelings with my sons. Wisely, she assured me it's never too late to open up, so I took Jeff and Joel to dinner and apologized. I told them: "You weren't around to know how bad I felt about the failed business venture. Maybe the reason I didn't go to you directly is because I felt like I had failed, and I've always run away from failure. I've never been great at apologizing." It quickly became obvious they needed to hear that from me.

The point of telling these stories is to make this point: even though I pay more attention to family than ever, and even though I have a great therapist and a great wife, and even though I've learned a tremendous amount about myself and others, I'm still learning about life all the time. I constantly find I'm not finished learning how to be a parent, and I probably never will be, since I'll be a dad for the rest of my life.

Once a Parent, Always a Parent

Here's an important insight for everyone who has children: Once you're a parent, you will always be a parent. The job begins even before the birth of your first child—at the instant you learn about the pregnancy. That's obvious for the mother, but true for the father as well. I remember when I first realized my job as a father had already begun: when I saw I had to make sure my wife stayed healthy for the unborn child, as well as for herself. Then I faced things like getting the nursery ready, and making sure luggage was ready at the front door for the trip to the hospital, and buying supplies, and many other tasks in those pre-birth months. With the birth, of course, came new duties, and when my babies became toddlers I had to help them learn words and sentences. Then it was helping them get involved in social activities, and learning how to share, and adopting proper manners, and on and on. As Harriet always says, "Small children, small problems; big children, big problems."

Sometimes we fall prey to a false sense of security. We think that as our kids get older the issues we face as parents will get easier. I learned this isn't true at all. Getting kids excited about going to school and teaching them to understand responsibility were constant challenges for me. Getting them to stay focused and helping them learn to behave with integrity—to always be honest, for example, no matter what the consequences—were even bigger challenges, not to mention making sure they socialized with the right kids, and got good grades, and kept up their appearances, and developed good values, and thought clearly about their future occupations, and on and on.

Pretty soon they were grown and out of the house, and my responsibilities changed. But my duties didn't become any less important. Even now, as my grown-up kids pursue their chosen paths, I have to keep a watchful eye on them. This may sound obvious to those of you who raised children and are now watching your grandchildren go through the same growth process. But if you are not yet a parent, or you're just starting on that journey, please take what I've said to heart: you're a parent for life. And if you're a grandparent, remember this good advice that Harriet and I were lucky to have received: you're *not* the child's parent. Many grandparents want to make up for the mistakes they made as parents, so they try to apply the childrearing lessons they learned the hard way when they're with their grandkids. But it's not a good idea to discipline your grandchildren, or spoil them, or contradict their actual parents (your kids) who are the first line of responsibility.

Parental Finance

Parents who are fortunate enough to accumulate wealth have an additional responsibility. They need to be thoughtful and careful about estate planning. I've frequently seen how the way an inheritance is given—not just the amount of money, but the conditions surrounding it—can have a big impact. In some cases, a child's motivation to succeed on his or her own is diminished. This can seriously damage their self-esteem, as they may lack a sense of achievement in life or feel inadequate because they can never accomplish as much financially as their parents or peers. Many of them don't even try.

Wealthy parents need to teach their children how to handle money every bit as much as middle-class and working-class parents do. I'm often asked for advice along those lines: How much financial support should I give my kids? When they go to college, should I pick up the whole cost, or make them earn enough to cover their living expenses? Should I buy their first home for them outright, or assist only with the down payment? Should I buy my grandchild's first crib? After all these years of assessing what works and what doesn't work when it comes to teaching children the value of money, I've come to one conclusion: there are no easy answers. I've observed how people raise their children for more than three decades now, and I just don't see a clear correlation between parental policies and how kids handle money. This is simply not a one-size-fits-all issue. I do know this: parents have an important duty to teach their kids as much as possible about the subject, and every parent has to do his or her best job, according to their circumstances, their values, their children's personalities and inclinations, and the lessons they wish to impart. And at every step they should keep in mind what I said before: parenting is not a temp job, it's a permanent position.

My own parents believed it was my responsibility to pay for my college education. Even though they could well afford to pay for it themselves, they felt I would appreciate the education more if I worked or used my savings to obtain my degree. They also believed I would have a stronger feeling of accomplishment if I fulfilled the responsibility of paying for it as well as doing the necessary schoolwork.

My parents' strategy helped me develop skills that have served me extremely well. As I described earlier in this book, my father gave me the opportunity to see the business side of life up close and personal, to an extent few young people do. I developed so much self-esteem and confidence in my financial competence that I never had a moment's doubt about my ability to be independent or support a family. These are all essential skills and attitudes for a successful life. In fact, when I think back to my high school years and the class that became famous with the Medved and Wallachinsky book, I note with pride that most of the nerds like me have lived quite well, even as many of the more popular students ended up financial failures.

So my parents' decision worked out just fine for me, thanks to my work ethic. But I chose to do the opposite with my children. I did not make Marc and Michelle work to earn their allowance. They were given what they wanted and needed; I considered it my gift to them as a parent. At one point, however, I realized my policy might have gone a bit awry. I might have been generous to a fault, because they didn't seem ready to take responsibility for themselves and didn't have a sense of reality about money. Thankfully, they have since learned those lessons.

I've seen many affluent parents fall into a similar trap. They give their children more money than they really need, and never ask them to earn any of it. I think it's because they—the parents—feel guilty about working so hard and not spending as much time at home as they'd like to. They often learn too late that you can't buy your way to parenthood. I sure took a long time to learn that lesson, and when I did it was hard to reverse my policy—and difficult for my kids to adjust to it.

Family Meetings

As I've said, there seems to be little consistency when it comes to parental policies about money and children. One of my clients is worth tens of millions and is leaving only two percent of his estate to each of his two children. The balance is going to charity. Conversely, another client of mine is leaving 100 percent of his estate to his children, to be paid over several periods. The final, and most significant distribution is scheduled for when his heirs reach the ripe old age of seventy-five!

Because my clients frequently need help making estate decisions, I often preside over family meetings. Many have children with little interest in business or finance. Their passion may be for the greater good, such as helping the world go green, improving the lot of the impoverished, assisting with animal rescue, saving the rain forest, and so forth. Others are gung-ho about carving out a career in the arts or another field where finances tend to take a back seat to the work itself. Still others are more self-absorbed, focused on their own pleasure and adventures. As parents, we need to allow them to take their own journeys and determine their own successes and failures. However, we should not leave them in the dark about the basics of finance, and family meetings can be a vital form of education.

The meetings generally last from two to four hours, with the parents basically having tape over their mouths. This isn't the time for them to lecture their kids; rather, it's a time to inform and educate. I always act as an independent mediator. While respecting the parents' confidentiality, I help educate the children on the basics of estate planning and explain the rationale behind their parents' financial decisions. I often invite a guest speaker to attend, such as a banker, a financial advisor, or an executive from the family business.

One thing I consistently recommend is to set up an estate plan with provisions for a child's inheritance to be paid over the course of several years. I also recommend a plan that connects the amount given out with the amount the child earns. Typically, for every dollar a child earns, the trust distributes another dollar. This gives the children an opportunity to enter a profession that strongly appeals to them, even if it doesn't pay the biggest salary, and still maintain a high standard of living. Conversely, if they do not take on remunerative work, there is no distribution from the trust and they have to deal with the consequences of that.

I also recommend dividing inheritances into at least three different distributions. One advantage to this is that if a kid makes a mistake with the first sum he or she has the opportunity to correct the situation. By contrast, if the same mistake were to be made with the entire sum of the inheritance it would be an uncorrectable disaster. It's always a good idea to give your kids a chance to learn from their errors.

One situation many parents face is having children who are completely different from one another. This raises questions such as, "Do I have to treat each child the same financially? Do I have to give to them equally, even if one is careless in money matters?" I believe parents should assess each case on an individual basis. I also believe each child's personality should be taken into account. In some instances, for example, one child might receive a portion of the inheritance outright, while the other receives half in a trust managed by a third party.

The most important rule of thumb in family decisions about finances is good communication. Explaining the decisions you make to your children before they go into effect is important, especially in situations that might create confusion, anger, or emotional pain. That's true even in the case of estate decisions that can shock them after your death. You don't want their lasting memory of you to be one of anguish and disappointment. Everyone should have a basic understanding of what will transpire upon the death of a parent. This not only protects the relationship between parents and children, it can also safeguard relationships among the children themselves. As a parent, you want to feel confident that your kids will get along with each other after you're gone, and the love among siblings won't be ruined by disputes over inheritance. Harriet and I have already had two family meetings with our children. This was the agenda for the first meeting:

1. Purpose of meeting
2. Definition of wills vs. living trust
3. Key positions in wills and trusts

4. Description of life insurance trust (second to die) (two trusts)
5. Description of Bookstein Properties and Bookstein Children Irrevocable Trust
6. Description of Bookstein Foundation
7. Funding of Bookstein Foundation during life and after death
8. Asset dispositions
9. Bookstein records
10. Definition of living will

Our second meeting expanded on the first. The agenda included:

1. Purpose of meeting
2. Distributing copies of living will
3. Change in estate law
4. Declaring executors and trustees (any additional suggestions)
5. Future operation of Bookstein Foundation
6. The shifting of assets (management)
7. Ages at which the children may get distributions
8. Cash required for estate taxes
9. Funeral planning

One of the rules was that only our children could come, and not their significant others. Harriet and I felt it was up to our children to decide what they would share with their loved ones, and they were free to communicate whatever they wanted to afterward. Overall, every member of the family—and the family as a whole—benefited tremendously from the two meetings. I have to admit that, even though I had presided over family meetings for a number of clients, I was amazed by the questions my children asked and the answers my wife and I gave them.

Helping Clients with Family Issues

As I said earlier, I try never to impose my own views or personal values on my clients. There are so many options, and families are so different from one another, that only the principles themselves can determine the right choices. Still, I feel strongly about certain things, based on my experiences over the years. One of them is this: if you have multiple children, never ever make one of them the executor or trustee of your estate. If you do, you're asking for trouble. No matter how mature your children seem, there are always insecurities and rivalries buried under the surface, dating back to their childhood years. Jealousy, envy, bitterness, regret, hurt, anger—all of those and other emotions are virtually inevitable if one child is given the role of executor or trustee. The others will start speculating about your motives. They'll think thoughts such as, "Mom loved me less than my siblings," or, "My brother and sister conspired against me," or, "They must have discussed all this behind my back," or, "My sister must have manipulated them to gain advantage." The situation will always seem unfair, and relationships can get so overheated as to cause disastrous rifts.

Unfortunately, people often name the wrong person to be their executor or trustee. They mistakenly believe that having an emotional attachment to the person will ensure the proper decisions will be made, so they choose someone they're close to, and whom they trust. But if that person has no knowledge of finance, you're asking for trouble. Incredibly, very few people name their accountant as executor or trustee. I find that odd because, if you trust an accountant with your money while you're alive, why wouldn't you trust the same accountant after you're gone?

As I've said before, being a therapeutic accountant often means telling clients what they do not want to hear so they can deal with what truly matters. As a result, I've had to tell a number of them that their kids should not be their executor or trustee. Most accountants would not risk telling the truth about such matters, but I care too much about my clients to hold back. In fact, estate planning in general makes a lot of people uncomfortable. I have to push many clients to do it. I tell them that lack of proper preparation virtually assures there will be unintended consequences. I try to take the uneasiness out of it by speaking methodically about the subject. I keep it simple and matter-of-fact as I go through everything step by step. After they've made decisions and drawn up the necessary documents, I follow up with them. I pressure them to constantly reevaluate their decisions and modify the documents accordingly, because many things can change with time.

One of my tasks as a therapeutic accountant is to prevent tensions and conflicts from disrupting families as they deal with financial issues. One aging client, for instance, was threatened by impoverishment because her two children were draining her assets. She simply didn't know how to say no to them. Her husband had died more than ten years earlier, and the children appeared to be going after all her money. I persuaded the client to grant me power of attorney. Then I changed her checking account so she was not allowed to sign checks. I had to sign every check she wanted to write—with her permission, of course. This enabled me to serve as a buffer between her and her children, so I could intervene when necessary.

I've seen many affluent parents cave in repeatedly to their children's requests, to the point where their estates were threatened. I try not to let ungrateful children threaten my client's ability to survive. Once again, this is the difference between Therapeutic Accounting® and ordinary accounting. Most accountants are afraid to be that honest with their clients. But I don't hesitate to tell mine their wills and trusts are wrong for their circumstances and values. It could be argued that isn't the role I should play, but I don't know how *not* to do it. With someone like the client I just described, whose security was jeopardized by her daughters, I was able to strengthen her by being the bad guy. When she was harassed by her daughters for not giving them what they wanted, she was able to blame me. "I can't write you the check," she would say. "Only Harvey can do that." This forced them to explain their situation to me, and try to convince me to write the check. They couldn't exploit my guilt feelings the way they did with their mother, because I could say no with zero guilt.

Another client of mine was in a similar situation. She was worth about $600 million, and she knew her children were after it. Her kids were not just selfish, they seemed virtually emotionless and lacking in proper values. My client didn't want to reward their self-centered attitude, so she decided to leave all her money to charity. When we worked up her will, she left zero to her children—not a penny. The children were well provided for, since their late father had set up a trust for them, and my client felt that was enough. This was a tough decision for a mother to make. She risked spending her remaining years being resented by her children. But she felt it was not only the right thing to do, but the best thing for the children themselves, and I was in complete support.

I don't always agree with my clients' decisions. My duty is to support their decisions once they're made, and also to let them know if I think they're making a mistake. One husband and wife, for example, were in their late seventies when we worked on their estate plan. They had four biological sons and two adopted daughters. They wanted to leave each boy twenty percent and the girls ten percent each. I told them if they really wanted their trust to reflect those wishes, we'll go ahead and draw up the documents. But, I added, "whichever one of you dies first will be the lucky one." I explained that the spouse who outlived the other would have to deal with a lot of drama caused by the inequality in the will. He or she would be faced with questions like, "Did we get less because we were adopted?" "Is it because we're female?" "Do you not love us?" I told them those questions would hound the surviving spouse for years. My clients were persuaded; they changed the terms of their trust so all their children had equal shares of the estate.

Some people would argue that such situations are none of an accountant's business. Some clients might get angry, and even fire an outspoken accountant for overstepping the usual boundaries. As a therapeutic accountant, I'm willing to take that risk.

Part of my job description is to keep my clients focused on what truly matters, because I've seen what happens when they don't. It never ceases to amaze me that extremely successful people who were incredibly savvy about business and conscientious about their financial affairs their entire lives will still avoid attending to what matters on a personal level—like estate planning. I'll never forget the father of one of my clients. He was worth over $2 billion when he died, and the government took about half of it in taxes. That left a billion for his three kids to share. That's a hell of a lot of money, so I don't feel sorry for those heirs. But I'm sure it isn't what the deceased father wanted. He probably made a thousand business deals in his lifetime, most of which were so advantageous that he ended up a billionaire. He could easily have arranged for that money to be used for purposes he cared about. But he never took the time to do the necessary planning. I've seen others do the same thing with a lot less money and even worse consequences for their family members. Don't make that same mistake, and if you're an accountant like me, don't let your clients make them.

Chapter 24
Always Give Back

*L*ife is a web of interdependent relationships. We came into this world needing other people and we will continue needing other people until the day we die. The shoe is also on the other foot, of course; each of us is needed by other people. Giving something back is a way of saying "Thank you" to the people and places that have positively affected us. That's why most caring and reasonable people look for ways to give of their money and/or their time to those who are less fortunate, whether it's family members, a worthy organization, the homeless, or a cause for which they have passion.

This is not 100 percent true among people of means, of course. Some choose *not* to give back. They may believe it's the government's responsibility to help the unfortunate. Some are cynical enough to assume that charitable organizations will only waste their money on excessive compensation for executives or on inefficiencies. I've also heard people say, "I am my own charity. I need to take care of myself and my family." I've never found those reasons for not giving convincing.

Obviously, each of us has to decide the best ways to give back, according to our values, our means, and our life circumstances. Many people say they'd like to directly help a particular charity accomplish its goals, but they just don't have the time, so they write a check. Others have time but not money. And, of course, some have the ability to give both their efforts and their financial support. The important thing is for each person to make the most of his or her desire to contribute.

The What, How, and When of Giving

When it comes to the question of how much money to give, the amount should be determined by your financial capacity, the strength of your commitment to helping society as a whole, and your passion for a specific cause. I've known many people who made bigger commitments than they could afford. In some cases, they feel so strongly about creating a legacy of generosity that they put their own financial security at risk by making excessive contributions. Others want to continue giving at the same level they did in the past when they had more wealth or a larger income. And some give more than they can afford because they feel pressure to keep up with philanthropic people they know, or because they're hooked on the pleasure of being recognized for their generosity. Whatever the motivation, whether it's a purely selfless commitment or a raging ego trip, it's important to make decisions about giving with an awareness of how your contribution might affect your own well-being and that of your family.

The *how* of giving back can be as important as the *what*. There are many ways to think about how to make a contribution. Most people think about writing a check, packing up some old clothes, or giving away the old clunker to a worthy cause. Individuals of means who give more thought to the process might choose to make contributions in stages. They may first give a large sum to their own private foundation, then subsequently distribute those funds to the charities and causes of their choice. Making a gift to your own private foundation offers tax savings as well, as you can bunch up deductions in years when it's most beneficial to you. Another procedure is to make pledges and fulfill them over time. A great, and sometimes overlooked, option is to give assets that appreciate reliably over the long-term, such as stocks or real estate. This not only gives you the satisfaction of helping a favorite cause, but it also provides a tax deduction for the fair market value of the asset you donate without picking up any capital gain on the difference of your basis and the fair market value.

Then there's the issue of *when* to give, which can be as important as the *how* and the *what*. If you ask any charity when the right time to give is, the response will probably be "Now." However, you, the contributor, may prefer timing that enables you to receive the best possible tax break. I always encourage people to take advantage of the allowable deductions for charitable contributions. Depending on your circumstances, there can be a substantial difference between making a contribution on December 31 and doing it one day later, on January 1 of the following year.

Some of my clients have chosen not to give away any of their assets while they're alive; instead, they've made provisions to distribute them after death. In fact, donating certain types of assets at death can save the heirs a big tax bite on the asset that would have been left to them. The heirs can also receive financial compensation by allowing the estate to transfer to a private foundation after death, in which case the trustee (your family) can make the charitable gift and be recognized socially for doing so. There is even the option of tying a contribution to an event, such as breaking ground on a new building, a specific fundraiser, or a celebration in honor of a prominent person.

Charity Is a Personal Choice

While it is important for people—not just wealthy ones, but everyone—to give back in ways that are appropriate for them, it's also important that charities not take advantage of donors. One of my principles of giving is, Don't let anyone tell you what your charities should be. That means *you* get to decide what you give, where you give it, how you give it, and when you give it. Much as I like giving to worthy causes, I tend to say no to most solicitations. Not because I do not believe in the organization, but because I am discerning when it comes to giving my time and money. Only I decide how I will give back; I don't need anyone else to tell me.

That attitude is shared by my partners at RBZ. Unlike many firms, we do not require or pressure employees to give money to specific charities or volunteer their time to specific causes. We made that decision because we feel every person should have the freedom to do what he or she wants. Why should I force my views and my sense of charity down anyone else's throat? We do encourage employees to give back, and to engage in volunteer work, because we believe such actions change people's attitude about life in a positive way. But we consider it a suggestion, not a requirement, and we don't dictate the specifics.

Ted Roth, Dave Zaslow, and I saw the wisdom of that policy because of something that happened when we worked for Kenneth Leventhal & Company. The partners there were required to donate a significant amount of money to the United Jewish Fund each year. Most of the partners were Jewish and didn't object, but one of the Catholic partners thought it was unfair that he couldn't give his share to a charity of his choice. His request was denied. When we started our own firm we knew we wouldn't have such a policy. As I said, we encourage everyone to give, but we don't make donations on behalf of the firm as a whole. We have the same policy when it comes to politics. As a firm, we don't endorse candidates or propositions, or take an official position on any issues of public policy.

I was in my twenties when I came to realize it's neither wise nor fair to pick charities for anyone but ourselves. At the time, the United Jewish Federation asked me for a donation. I agreed to give them $2,000. They said the amount I gave would be in their annual donation book, so I should consider giving a less embarrassing sum, like $3,500. "You're right," I said. "I don't want to be embarrassed. So I'm giving zero. Now I won't be embarrassed, because my name won't be in the book. Problem solved." At the time, I had been a consistent donor, but I was so infuriated by the reaction to my offer that I stopped giving money to Jewish charities for thirty-five years. That's how wrong I think it is for other people to tell you how you should give your money away. From that point on, I've always told people "Don't let others tell you who your charities should be."

Your Business Is Not a Charity

I have another way of interpreting that saying: make sure your business does not become a form of a charity. By that I mean, don't let people get away with not paying what they owe you. I consider myself a generous person, but I can be extremely tough when it comes to collecting what's coming to me in business. If your company has receivables you aren't actively trying to collect, you have essentially become a charity. That's why I tell my partners and our staff, "Don't do work for free unless you *want* to do work for free."

I am in charge of all receivables at RBZ, and I have the right, on behalf of all fifteen partners, to do what is called a cut-off. When a client is badly in arrears, I am empowered to step in and tell our accountants they cannot do any more work for that client without my approval. If they *do* choose to do additional work for that client, they are responsible for the fees. Some accountants believe they should not have to deal with annoyances like collecting on receivables. They think they're above it. I don't. I say we are not just an accounting firm, we're a business that provides accounting services. And businesses are not charities. There are much better ways to give back.

My Way of Giving Back

I am now fortunate enough to have a foundation that enables me and my family to give back to society in ways that make a difference. My preference is to support causes I'm passionate about, and where I can contribute by being involved, not just by writing a check. I've felt that way since I was eighteen years old, when I was moved to do volunteer work for United Cerebral Palsy. I had no prior affiliation with the charity, and no one I knew had cerebral palsy. But I was asked to help out, so I started doing some minor work for the local organization. I got hooked by the feeling of doing good. I got more and more involved over the years, and eventually became the president and chairman of the board. Ever since then, giving back has been an important part of my life.

In recent years, I've been most proud of two instances where I gave back in a significant way to institutions that made a big difference in my life. One is my alma mater, California State University, Northridge. Everything I've accomplished, from the day I was hired for my first job as an accountant to the present moment, I owe in large part to the education I received at that fine institution. So, with a tremendous sense of gratitude, in 2005, I established the Harvey and Harriet Bookstein Chair in Taxation, as well as the Bookstein Institute for Higher Education in Taxation. The million dollar gift was the largest donation the business school has ever received from an alumnus, and the endowed chair was the first in the College of Business and Economics. By giving something back to the school that helped me in such an immeasurable way, I am helping CSUN do even more for students in the future.

Like many major donations, this one had incalculable benefits beyond the value of the gift itself. In the past, the business school at CSUN had never received a lot of money in donations. They might get someone to sponsor a conference, and that person would be rewarded with something like his or her name on the door. The big accounting firms would hire CSUN graduates, but they would rarely contribute anything significant to the institution that trained those employees so well. After I made that million dollar donation, I received tons of calls from other CSUN accounting alums who said my gift had inspired them to give back as well. All of a sudden, people far wealthier than I am saw little old me getting accolades, and they decided maybe they should start contributing, too. Opening the floodgates for others to donate probably did more good than the dollar amount I wrote on my check. CSUN is now talking to Harriet and me about possibly funding a masters degree program in real estate.

Temple Judea and Rabbi Goor

Finally, I want to mention a recent act of giving back that means the world to me, and also says a lot about my personal journey.

As I said earlier, I've never been particularly religious and I count myself as much of an agnostic now as when I was a teenager. I joined a local synagogue, Temple Judea, because my first wife, Kathy, believed, correctly, that it would be good for our children. I was not very involved with the temple in those days; I basically went through the motions, showing up on the important holidays and doing what Jewish fathers do when their children get bar and bat mitzvahed.

After I married Harriet, I became increasingly active, following her lead. She had been a loyal member of a different synagogue for twenty years, but after her divorce she could no longer afford her annual dues and the synagogue said, "Too bad, you can no longer be a member." She couldn't even buy tickets for High Holy Day services. So when we got married she was only too happy to join Temple Judea, where she was welcomed with warm, open arms, especially by Rabbi Donald Goor, who was then an associate rabbi.

I had known Rabbi Goor since I first joined the temple. He presided over Michelle's bat mitzvah and Marc's bar mitzvah; he counseled me at difficult times, like my divorce, the painful estrangement from my children, and the torturous decision to pull the plug on my father's medical treatment; he officiated at my father's, my stepmother's, and Harriet's father's funeral services; he officiated at my marriage to

Harriet and at our children's weddings, the brises of our grandsons, and the baby naming of our granddaughters. He is a good, kind, and caring man, but around the time of my wedding to Harriet I realized how special he was. It didn't hurt that he handled the alarm going off during the ceremony with great aplomb, and that he enjoyed a good laugh when, during my vows, I bragged about how good sex with Harriet was. He was a *mensch* in every sense of the word.

From that time on we became increasingly close, as Harriet's initiative brought me deeper into the life of the synagogue and Jewish customs in general. She has always been more observant than I, and she is extremely conscientious about doing things like hosting Shabbat dinner for the family. This was actually our daughter Roni's idea. Harriet decided to host the dinners at our house and do all the cooking. Once a month for more than four years now, anywhere from fifteen to twenty people celebrate Shabbat with us: our four children, with their spouses and kids and one mother-in-law, plus Harriet's first husband, Michael (the father of Roni and Joel), with his wife and stepdaughter, as well as other invited guests. Those dinners mean so much to us that we tore down walls in our house and relocated the kitchen to make the dining room big enough to accommodate everyone.

Over time, Rabbi Goor became more than a religious leader to us. Then, in the late 1990s, when he was a candidate to become the senior rabbi who would lead the congregation, my respect for him soared. He chose that time to inform the community that he was gay. I thought coming out was an act of great integrity; he did not want to hide such an important fact about himself from the people who would be placing their sacred trust in their new senior rabbi. His act must have taken tremendous courage, and I was thrilled when he received the job.

In time, Rabbi Goor and his life partner Cantor Evan Kent, the cantor at a different shul, became closer to Harriet and me. Rabbi Goor has been an integral part of my life for more than twenty years now, and it's no exaggeration to say he probably knows me better than anyone other than Harriet and Dr. Jones.

Mainly because of our love and respect for Rabbi Goor, we became intimately involved with the synagogue's legacy project, which involved raising a substantial amount of money to replace our aging building with a campus that would serve the community for generations to come. The centerpiece of the $26 million project was to be a spacious, modern sanctuary. That was my baby. Harriet and I, with the approval of our children, made a sizable donation to the project, earmarked for the new sanctuary. Everyone outside of our family assumed it would be named the Harriet and Harvey Bookstein Sanctuary. We had a better idea: to name it after Rabbi Goor. As we later told the local newspaper, *The Encino-Tarzana Patch*, "We wanted to pay tribute to our rabbi in a permanent and enduring way so that his legacy would be forever honored at Temple Judea."

Only we didn't tell him. We kept it a secret until the last possible minute. In fact, we made it a stipulation of our donation: no one must know until the name of the sanctuary was installed on the entrance, and that would be done at the last possible moment. Why? For one thing, we felt Rabbi Goor was so humble that he might try to talk us out of honoring him in that way, or would at least find it embarrassing during the long period of construction. The other reason was that I love surprising people. As I mentioned earlier, I take great delight in concocting plots and fabricating situations that end with someone I care about looking happily stunned, maybe even deeply moved. In Rabbi Goor's case, we got all of that and more: the surprise also resulted in tears.

We kept the naming a secret from everyone except our coconspirator, the temple's executive director, Ellen Franklin. She had to know because she ordered the lettering for the sanctuary's name. To prevent a leak, Ellen scrambled the letters on the sign company's order form. When the construction was completed, she had to think on her feet and come up with excuses because Rabbi Goor wanted to know why the Booksteins' names were not yet on the sanctuary wall.

A few nights before the opening, Harriet and I took Rabbi Don and Cantor Evan to dinner at Mastro's in Thousand Oaks. Over dessert, we took out two bags filled with extra-large wooden Scrabble letters. We told them that we had a tradition of playing a Scrabble-like game after dinner on special occasions. They actually believed us. We told them the object was for them to figure out what the letters in each bag spelled out. They fiddled around with the first batch of fifteen letters, trying different combinations, before Cantor Kent hit upon the answer. The letters spelled RABBI DONALD GOOR. The rabbi said he would hang the lovely letters on the wall of his office. We then challenged them to work out the letters in the second bag. There were only nine, but it took them longer to arrive at the correct word, and when they did they were shocked. The word was SANCTUARY. They stared at the big Scrabble tiles on the table for what seemed like forever, until they realized what the game was all about. "It made me feel completely *ferklempt*," Rabbi Goor told the newspaper. "I just couldn't believe such generosity, that they would want to honor me with my name on our sanctuary. It was emotional, exciting, and I was in tears. I felt tremendously humbled, slightly uncomfortable, and a huge sense of gratitude."

Harriet and I too felt a huge sense of gratitude—for all that Rabbi Goor and the community he created have meant to us, and for the great privilege of being able to honor that fine man in a lasting way. We feel grateful every time we go to services and see RABBI DONALD GOOR SANCTUARY on the entrance.

Me? ... Religious?

"I'd actually say that he's a deeply religious guy," Rabbi Goor says of me. I can't believe it. I'm not only unsure about the existence of God, I'm pretty cynical about organized religion. But he explains what he means, and I think it says as much about what a great rabbi he is as it does about me.

"It would be pretty boring if everybody was pious," he says. His response to my outspoken doubts about God is, "It's a good Jewish thing to say. We love to question. There are a variety of ways that we can connect to God, and we just keep searching our lives until we find the right one. And by the way, the right one may only work that week and you may have to search again, because you change."

He goes on: "Harvey very much sees the world through a Jewish lens. The questioning, and the doubting, and the love of community and family—values rather than belief. I think he's deeply religious because values are so central to him, and our values are central to Judaism." He cites as evidence my increased involvement with Jewish customs. But it's not just that I put the time into things like going to holiday services—even the ones that few people attend, like the second day of Rosh Hashanah, which draws about one-tenth the number of people who show up on the first night—and our lively, jam-packed Shabbat dinners. The wise rabbi knows that many people go along with things like that to appease their spouses, and he knows the changes in my level of engagement can be traced directly to Harriet's enthusiasm. He emphasized that I don't just go through the motions; I enjoy it, I relish it, and I gain tremendous sustenance from it.

"Harvey doesn't just go through motions with anything," he says. "That's who he is. The truth is, he does it with passion and joy. There's a bounce to his step when he's in the synagogue. I think it's a connection to a larger community." He thinks something similar is at play at Sabbath dinner. "Shabbat is not just a day of holiness. It's a day of connection. And I think that value is really alive in the Booksteins' lives. Family is a value he holds probably higher than any other, and to see him at Shabbat dinner with all the kids and grandkids there—he just beams. He radiates joy. It's almost as if this is what he's on earth for. There's an informality and honesty about Harvey and his family. Everything is out there. It's a no-holds-barred kind of interaction. High energy—'laughter and arguments and everything else, and it's going a hundred miles an hour."

Rabbi Goor has known me long enough and well enough to know I wasn't always like that. He's right that the passion and joy he speaks of were not present in my life before the long process of transformation that began with the Northridge earthquake. "It's very Jewish to see your faults and improve on them," he says. "You grow from your mistakes, and you become a better person. Harvey is happy to be himself, about being on his own path. I don't think that he was before. I think he was going through the motions in his last marriage—just going through the motions of making a living and having a family. Now I see him acting on the key elements of who he is. He's really passionate about everything he does. He is experiencing life in a much deeper way than he ever did. His Judaism is part of that. He thinks of it in a deeper way than he ever did. At the bar and bat mitzvahs in his previous marriage, it was just very routine. It was like every other family in the synagogue. You know, they show up for their meetings, they do what they do, just going through the motions, and it's nice, but it's not passionate. Now, at the brisses and weddings and namings and other things I've done with his family, he's always so passionate and emotional. I think that's part of the breakthrough in values."

I still don't think I qualify as a religious person, but Rabbi Goor comes close to convincing me when he speaks about values and ethics. Which brings us back to the importance of giving back. "In Judaism, action is very much what defines us," he says. "You can't just say you're